SPEAKING FROM MEMORY

a guide to autobiographical acts
and practices

Harold Rosen

Trentham Books

First published in 1998 by Trentham Books Limited

Trentham Books Limited
Westview House
734 London Road
Oakhill
Stoke on Trent
Staffordshire
England ST4 5NP

British Cataloguing in Publication Data
A catalogue record for this book is available from the British Library
ISBN 1 85856 082 9
hb ISBN 1 85856 119 1

Designed and typeset by Trentham Print Design Ltd., Chester and
printed in Great Britain by The Cromwell Press Ltd., Wiltshire

Contents

Nothing is more fully agreed than the certainty that memory fails. Memory fails, leaving blanks, and fails by filling blanks mistakenly... But memory also succeeds. It succeeds enormously and profoundly; for it is fundamental to human life, not to say synonymous with it. Karen Fields (1989)

Foreword and Acknowledgements

Every book has its autobiographical story. The story of this one began as some pages of notes I had made for a Nordic linguistic seminar in Kristiansand, Norway, 1993. I thought later it might make an interesting paper, though I wasn't quite sure where or for whom. As I set about it I was lured more and more into reading mostly in recent work which was new to me. Very exciting! The handful of notes became piles which looked suspiciously like draft chapters and then a draft book which is now this book. The process sent me back to school to study memory (now Chapter 5) and the contribution of feminists (Chapter 6).

What kept me going was that it had dawned on me that teachers, especially teachers of English and of cultural studies of various kinds at every level, were scarcely aware of a rapidly proliferating literature. And these were teachers who were sophisticated in literary, linguistic and cultural theory and who had pioneered the introduction into their classes and seminars all kinds of autobiographies and had encouraged their students to produce their own.

So then I hope this book, as well as having its intrinsic interest, will be seen as a kind of users' manual, transforming readers' notions of what constitutes doing autobiography and making them aware of what a huge discursive space it occupies.

***

I have my debts to pay, of course, but none so great as that to my wife, Betty Rosen. She toiled away at her sworn enemy, the PC, for so many tedious hours that had I logged them I'd be ashamed to set down the record. If some feminists are outraged, I can only say I can explain. Honestly. Every single word was processed by her in defiance of the frequent recalcitrance of the PC – its mutiny over pagination, its mischief with indentation and other unpredictable waywardnesses. I was the beneficiary of the fact that everything came under Betty's stern surveillance. The text incorporates her rephrasings and emendations. She has an unforgiving eye for non-sequiturs. Above all, she kept me going when I flagged. My son Michael has acted as a bibliographic scout. Books arrived by post and by hand. Tactful theoretical suggestions were made. He even read through the text and made squiggles in the margins. There was a lot of chatter, too. All of that is as much as anyone has the right to ask of filial piety. Jane Miller has mastered the art, often oblique, of nudging texts into existence, this one included. She even ensured that a chunk of it saw the light of day under her editorship in the journal *Changing English*. I mentioned Esther Salaman's book *A Collection of Moments*. It turned out that Esther was a relative of hers and Jane gave me her own precious copy of the book. In a book of this kind, there can be heard a multitude of voices of colleagues, friends and others who enter the text. I hear some of them; others enter surreptitiously. I thank them all. I am grateful for the generosity of Jane Ray for permission to put the detail from her painting on the cover and likewise her publisher, Roger La Borde. I thank Gillian Klein, my publisher, for her ready acceptance of the book and extraordinary patience with my dilatory periods. It was the late Josie Levine, a treasured friend and colleague, who suggested Gillian. Posthumous thanks.

January, 1998

CHAPTER ONE

INTRODUCTION

A ll human beings are incorrigibly autobiographical. I do not mean, of course, that they have all made attempts to write their life-stories nor that they have deep, unfulfilled yearnings to do so but rather, as soon as their words can point to their own pasts, they set off down the long road to telling in one way or another, their past experiences, the events of their lives. As Lejeune (1989) puts it,

> ...every person has within himself a rough draft, perpetually reshaped, of the story of his life. (p.xxi)

The story of a life, an idea which sounds straightforward enough, turns out to be very complicated, as anyone who has made the attempt to write one or speak one will tell you. Those who write *about* these enterprises agonise again and again about the problems they unearth, as we shall see. My central intention in this work is to go beyond the 'rough draft within' while accepting it readily as a good place to start. I want to propose that everyone does in fact make the attempt, however brief, unremarked and apparently unportentous, to turn the rough draft into speech through the act of speaking about the past. We all offer each other moments from our lives which may perhaps be brief memories of our childhoods or narratives of other kinds of personal experience, significant in some way. It may take the form of a rounded and shaped story or maybe no more than a very short utterance. The 'story of a life' is a much more ambitious, even daunting, project which, if it is realised in writing, belongs with what most people usually think of as autobiography,

1

that is, all those highly respected works which are referred to in the critical literature again and again, and which are halo-ed by that attention. There is indeed a kind of autobiographical canon – St Augustine, Rousseau, Goethe and dozens of others accorded more or less respect.

The focus on written autobiographies has distracted attention from the universe of autobiographical *acts* taking many different forms, many of which have attracted very little attention and have certainly not been seen as manifestations of the same impulses and faculties, constituting collectively as vital a part of humanness as language itself. Autobiography then is not, as I see it, the achievement and invention of a few outstanding authors. It takes nothing from their achievement to say that they are practising a common art which had long preceded them and is to be found everywhere.

I should explain that this work is really a piece of personal intellectual history. It has been asking to be written for a couple of years. If you're lucky there comes a moment when, amongst the books and journals you've been reading, you detect in fields which seem miles apart, a common pre-occupation. Quite often the scholars involved do not seem to know of each other's existence. You can, for example, find volume after volume on auto-biography, not one of which even mentions oral history, a huge auto-biographical enterprise. If you could paste onto a vast sheet the biblio-graphies at the end of all the major critical works, you might be puzzled at what does not figure in them. It is as though excited thinkers and investi-gators have entered the autobiographical arena through different doors and have not noticed each other's entries. A pity, because autobiography has lurking beneath its modest surface the great themes of memory, identity, the making of meaning, and the social construction of reality. There is a collaboration waiting to happen. As yet there is no promising sign that it is about to do so. No one, as far as I know, has attempted to bring together in a single synoptic view what I have termed autobiographical discourse. In fact there have been attempts to do exactly the opposite. Roy Pascal (1960) for example, in his book *Design and Truth in Autobiography* was determined to create a special category, a distinct literary genre, and to banish to outer darkness all miserable intruders like memoirs, diaries and letters. Lejeune (*op.cit.*) writes of his own seduction by Pascal's approach

> I followed the lead of Roy Pascal...identifying autobiography with a particular type of autobiography, that in which the individual focuses on the genesis of his personality. Once having settled on the choice of model, I built the 'corpus' through a system of exclusions. We will judge either as failures or as aberrant

cases, or as elements outside the corpus, everything that is inconsistent with the model. The genre becomes a sort of 'club' of which the critic makes himself the guardian, selecting with the help of exclusions a relatively pure 'race'. If the criteria are too precise we run the risk of schematising the 'horizons of expectation', of being blind to related phenomena and to historical evolution. (p. 149/50)

All attempts to establish a cast-iron genre and a canon by 'keep-out' signs abandon any effort to understand and, yes, to savour fully the truly immense legacy of practices which are exiled, dismissed with derision or quite simply ignored by virtue of being beneath notice. It is, not to mince words, a patrician proscription.

So then, I hope the usefulness of what I am embarking upon lies partly in inviting round the table, so to speak, guests who should talk to one another but have not yet managed to do so.

This book is autobiographical in another kind of way. Over the last ten years I became increasingly aware that, side by side with a proliferation of new autobiographies, there was a relatively sudden, symbiotic, growth in scholarly attention to autobiography. Publications of some weight were tumbling out. All kinds of scholars were writing books, editing collections of essays, publishing papers. Learned journals were publishing special issues devoted to autobiography. Academic conferences had been organised around the theme. Laura Marcus's book *Autobiographical Discourses* (1994) which is devoted in the main to critical discourses *about* autobiography, contains nineteen and a half closely printed pages of bibliography. Literary theorists, psychologists, cultural and social historians, anthropologists, sociolinguists, feminists and others have jostled to enter this new arena in much the same way as a preoccupation with narrative bewitched scholars of all sorts a short time ago. As a retired academic I hear the loud buzzing in the hive from further away than I would like but I must assume that what until quite recently I thought of as a purely personal interest was in fact part of a much more general social-intellectual process. There, as cast-iron evidence, are two shelves of recently purchased books for which I have to make room. It was like discovering that I had joined a movement with its own sacred texts and lexicon. And all this around what had, for a long time, been marginalised as a mongrel foraging around the edge of literature. 'Hybrid' was the polite word often used.

That said, I persist in feeling that, like autobiography itself, my own interest is a conjuncture of a personal history as well as a response to the cultural forces of which it is a part. All the ferment I've outlined was for a time in

3

my peripheral vision and, if it has moved into sharp focus, it is mostly because my preoccupations over many years had strong affinities with autobiographical acts of different kinds. The first of these was narrative itself which I discussed in *Stories and Meanings* (Rosen, 1982) and which gave prominence to oral autobiographical acts. At one point I gave an account of the black trunk which my mother had bought for the sea journey from America to England. It was, after that, used as a storage unit for all the family photographs, documents and mementoes. Sometimes my mother, my sister and I would sit on the floor and, in front of the opened trunk, work our way through every item:

> Every photo, every document, every object was inspected and for each one there was a proper story. There were relatives in Durban and Johannesburg, in Rochester and Philadelphia, in Strasbourg and in Warsaw and Vienna. How did uncles, aunts, come to be scattered over the face of the earth? Why were some men in uniform wearing the uniform of the wrong side? Who was alive and who was dead? Why was the ostrich feather fan so precious to her? The miniature replica of a miner's lamp, what did that signify? Who was Eugene Debs whose bronze bust was wrapped in tissue paper...? Who married whom? Whose children were they? Who died young and how? Who lived in that house? What happened, what happened, what happened? A story for every item. We knew when she would cry and when she would laugh. We sat for hours and discovered who we were, the way of our world, motives, values, beginnings, endings, a kind of cohesion, sufficient stability in our terrifyingly unstable world. (p.8)

I tried to show how in my own life, like everyone else's, spoken auto-biographical tales were indistinguishable from the way we lived, that, unlike written works, they showed the autobiographical impulse to be a consequence of social being, of having a memory, of an unquenchable thirst for meaning. I was just beginning to do for autobiography what I had tried to do for narrative in general, wrench the word away from its bonding with written texts. I have tried to elaborate that in this book.

Most of the work on autobiography emerges from well established departments in universities, predominantly concerned with literature. But my provenance is education, schools and what happens in them and, more particularly, the role of language in education. A group of us over many years tried to establish a place throughout the school curriculum for what we always called 'talk' rather than 'the spoken language' or 'oracy'. By that particular everyday word we wanted to stress the need for a continuation within classrooms of the interchanges which all communities establish as a means of making sense of their shared experiences. We argued that the events of the school students' lives were an essential base for their studies and that a communicative system needed to be established in classrooms which made it possible for students to talk to each other. There is no need to recapitulate the full story of that endeavour. I cite it because one of the repeated observations we made was that in their offerings students were contributing portions of their life stories which were often powerfully moving and which the regime of hands-up-answer-the-question could never yield.

In the late Sixties and early Seventies it became one of the orthodoxies of educational studies that the language of working-class children was impaired in a quite profound way: they spoke 'restricted code' rather than 'elaborated code' which they inherited from their parents and which limited their capacity to respond to formal education. I did not subscribe to these ideas and wrote a pamphlet (originally a paper to a History Workshop conference) attacking them as vigorously as I knew how (*Language and Class: a critical look at the theories of Basil Bernstein*, Rosen,1972) What I noticed among other things was that nowhere were they supported by serious documentation of working-class speakers. When a group of us came to record and study working-class speakers we found that they had a strong tendency to use graphic narratives when developing their ideas and that these were nearly always incidents from their own lives. As Labov (1972) had shown in America such stories were constructed with great skill within a very specific tradition among working-class black adolescents. Nothing could, at first glance, be further away from written book-length auto-biography than these spontaneous conversational events. Indeed, those who write about autobiography rarely if at all recognise the family resemblance. To see autobiography from the vantage point of common talk, a universal possession, is to see it quite differently, and to become preoccupied with different issues and emphases. Therefore this book is not a search for the roots of written autobiography but a consideration of the range of practices which can reveal to us what kind of phenomena they are.

These components of my past do, I think, make clear why my point of entry into autobiography was through its oral manifestations as much as written ones. However, my own original training was a literary one and I could scarcely have failed to encounter and enjoy some of the great auto-biographies, journals and letters and count myself lucky to have made what were for me a few discoveries, Herzen's *Memoirs* (1861-6 trans., 1968), for example, and to have read in recent years Christian Watt's posthumous writings (*The Christian Watt Papers* ed. David Frazer 2nd edit.1988); Von

Rezzori's *Memoirs of an Anti-Semite* (1983) and his *The Snows of Yesteryear: Portraits for an Autobiography* (1991); Tony Harrison's *Selected Poems* (1984) – and much else besides. What exerted the strongest push towards this book was probably my writing a sequence of autobiographical stories all drawn from childhood and adolescence, published as *Troublesome Boy* (Rosen, 1993), a book which also included two papers 'The Auto-biographical Impulse' and 'Talk as Autobiography' in which I first sketched out many of the ideas developed more fully in this book.

I immersed myself in the literature, stimulated to some deeper under-standings and new perceptions. Yet I was baffled. No one had worked over the whole field, had looked at all forms of autobiographical discourse. Each scholar writes from his or her own patch. Literary scholars, who have dominated the field for so long, find a niche for autobiography in their own world i.e. the world of literature and their appraisals are based on the criteria and analytical apparatus which they use to judge novels. Anthropologists work within the tradition of the ethnography of speaking and the concept of 'performance'. Psychologists work within a constructivist model or Freudian psychoanalysis. And so each to his/her own. That was perhaps inevitable given the history of disciplines and the management of knowledge. It is nevertheless something of a shock to find in major works a total deafness to highly relevant studies. Perhaps this deafness is a mani-festation of a general lack of interest in speakers rather than writers. Take, as one recent instance, John Sturrock's *The Language of Autobiography: Studies in the First Person Singular* (1993). This is a totally literary study, in many ways very impressive, but the speaking voice, using the First Person Singular in so many different ways to articulate a past, is scarcely glanced at throughout the book which says that autobiography is 'a dangerously elaborate form'. And yet at the very moment of closure, in the last two pages, Sturrock refers appreciatively to the work of Jerome Bruner, which I shall discuss fully in the next chapter, and his insistence on 'the place which narrative has in our everyday lives' (p.290).

> Bruner is interested not in the élite product of literary autobiography but in 'autobiography' in its plainest, usually oral form, of the partial accounts that people give of their lives to others, whether anecdotal, as in a conversational exchange or more formal, as when interviewed by a sociologist or oral historian. His theory, much simplified, is that narrative is a prime means of cultural bonding which we use to integrate ourselves with our culture and also to make sense of what is going on around us. (p.292)

In this final paragraph of his book, John Sturrock benevolently applauds Bruner for reminding us that autobiography is 'an art rooted in daily life...a mode of discourse we all of us continually enter'. Yet if this is the case why does Sturrock not look more closely at this connection and how it might shed light on his own earnest preoccupations? The answer lies in his comment,

> As a psychological phenomenon, literary autobiography is no different in kind from these mundane spontaneous and formally crude resorts to the mode of the autobiographical. (*op.cit.*)

Nothing could be plainer than this contemptuous description. In spite of the shared psychological base from which all autobiographical acts spring, he does not find it necessary to explore this commonality, let alone acknowledge that the oral and everyday forms may not be in the least crude and mundane. Needless to say, there is not a hint of this condescension in Bruner's work, and it is quite clear that Sturrock has not made the least attempt to study these poor relatives of the blue-blooded authors he has chosen to analyse admiringly. A study of that kind should be a requirement for all those who propose to address us in print on the subject of 'the first person singular', a grammatical resource available to all.

It has recently become the practice to use the term 'auto/biography' rather than or alongside the term autobiography. It has been institutionally established by a British Sociological Association Study Group of that name and by the Group's journal *Auto/biography*. Greater currency will no doubt be accorded to it by two very recent and important books – Liz Stanley's *The Auto/biographical I* (1992) and Laura Marcus's *Auto/biographical Discourses* (1994). I do not intend to use the neologism myself even though I readily acknowledge the motivation for its use.

The kinds of written discourse which we encounter in our society and, for that matter, which have long histories behind them are often presented to us with generic enthusiasm and misplaced passion for drawing sacrosanct boundaries, the crossing of which by a writer is treated as a matter for censure by the border police. Every day we come across writers and speakers who drift across these boundaries effortlessly and sometimes defiantly. A good thing too. Autobiography becomes a classic instance of this kind of transgression, which is just one reason why the efforts to define it as a distinct genre beyond all challenge have proved so difficult. Its Protean nature ensures that it both invades and is invaded by other kinds of texts.

Stanley, speaking of 'biography, diaries and letters', writes,

> ...largely the same epistemological, theoretical and technical issues arise, in relation to the ontological claims of these apparently distinct genres as do for autobiography. (p.3)

Why has biography slipped in here amongst the others? As I attempt to show later, diaries and letters share a crucial similarity with other autobiographical texts, namely the relationship of the writer to the moment of composing the text and the experience it is attempting to recall. Their substance is the writer's life and his/her reflections on it, however transformed, distorted, censored or reconstructed. This sharply differentiates them from biography. That the study of autobiography shares certain theoretical preoccupations with the study of biography does not conflate the two, for it also shares them with other kinds of discourse, the field notes of a geologist, philosophical speculation and, as Stanley notes (see below), with certain kinds of fiction. To follow scrupulously her procedure would mean a wholesale re-lexicalizing of the field. Better surely to raise questions of contiguity, overlap, and identity of discursive resources at the appropriate moment. Stanley, much further into her text, pursues her argument further.

> ...telling apart fiction, biography and autobiography is no easy matter, for these forms of writing a life do not exist each in a hermetically sealed vacuum. (p.125)

To argue against a 'hermetically sealed vacuum', which in the matter of text is to state the self-evident is not the same as to conflate two or more kinds of text. Fiction, we notice, has now entered the problem, an abiding one for all taxonomies. There are other forms of autobiographical activity, especially those which occur in spontaneous speech which create a wide diversity, making it even more distinctive from biography.

Marcus (*op.cit.*) takes up a position similar to Stanley's. Having throughout her book used both terms, auto/biography and autobiography, on the last page she tells us why.

> Attempting to open up the modes of autobiographical representation, recent critics have coined neologisms intended to redefine extensionally and intentionally autobiography away from its component parts, self-life-writing. The term auto/biography which I have used throughout this book, is one such attempt to indicate the affinities between biography and autobiography as traditionally defined. (p.294)

But affinities exist between all kinds of written prose. Affinity is not identity nor is it even, necessarily, proximity. And the affinity referred to here, which undoubtedly exists, should not be invoked if it blurs or even erases valuable distinctions. It is also said by way of justification that autobiography frequently has within itself passages which relate to the lives of others and therefore overlaps with biography. I find this something of an absurdity. How is it possible to speak of one's past without also speaking of those who shared it? If that includes speaking of parts of their lives in which we did not participate directly it is because those reported lives became part of our sense of our own. When my grandfather spoke of his childhood while I was a child, his words merged into my experience of him. Lastly, it is also a trivializing of the issue to claim proximity because a biographer has a personal investment in his/her subject. So do the writers of all kinds of prose. Scientists writing a report of a lab experiment have that investment, too, although their training explicitly teaches them to keep it totally concealed (see Rom Harré, 1990). What singles out autobiographical practices from biographical ones is above all their dependence on *autobiographical memory*, a phenomenon which is only now being given serious attention and to which I devote the whole of Chapter Four.

I have perhaps laboured this point but, if I have, it is because it is likely that auto/biography will become the favoured term. However, I do not think it will prove helpful to those with an interest in autobiography or biography or both. A blurred boundary is still a boundary, as dialect cartographers found out a long time ago. On the other hand, I do not consider it as a contradiction to see very close affinities between autobiography and certain other forms which I describe in Chapter Two and which constitute one region of 'the map of discourse'.

* * * * *

What then is autobiographical discourse? We can be sure that this question was first posed by those with a passion for establishing literary genres, a passion going back to classical rhetoric and its categories of discourse. Here, in its written form, was a new sort of animal, elusive, not quite persona grata, wandering across well-established frontiers, a kind of duck-billed platypus in the natural history of discourse. Were there not similar twitchy anxieties about the novel as it proliferated? Definitions had to embrace both *Tom Jones* and *Ulysses*. This is more than just a pertinent analogy since autobiography has to disentangle itself from the novel. Think of *Sons and Lovers* or the *trompe l'oeil Moll Flanders*. Maybe it never will. Lejeune, to whom I shall return, accumulated a massive archive of French autobiographies. Small wonder then that he inspects sceptically other people's attempts to pin down this wriggling creature which is neither fish nor flesh. Olney (1980) in introducing his book looks at the critical literature and writes,

> All the foregoing books and articles ... look to the historical, psychological and social origins of a literary act that has been extended, altered, and redesigned in subsequent centuries but that for all its inward and outward transformations, has still retained some sort of constant essence. (p.13)

Note in passing that Olney assumes that autobiography is a *literary* act and I assume that in this context he means a *literature-like* act. It's true that – graphy means writing but it is an acceptable shift of meaning for me to make it include speech in much the same way as we talk of oral literature. The a-historical attempt to establish a body of work, 'true' autobiography, quite distinct from certain kinds of fiction which seem to be kith and kin, aspired to discovering the distinguishing features within the text. However, after careful analysis, Fleishman (1983) concluded that '... autobiography is not distinguished by its formal components, its purely linguistic register.'

Place side by side the stories in Mary McCarthy's *Memoirs of a Catholic Girlhood* (1957) and the fictional versions which originally appeared and subject them to intense grammatical, lexical and discursive analysis in order to discriminate between them and you will go away empty-handed. Lejeune was not daunted because he proposed an entirely different determinant which he called *the autobiographical pact*, a kind of implicit contract between author and reader in which the author commits himself to the sincere effort to come to terms with and understand his or her own life by means of a narrative of the events of that life. A hundred and one questions and challenges come tumbling out. Sincere? That raises more questions than it answers. How do we determine sincerity? And the contract? What precisely are its terms? And so on. However, Lejeune was prepared to chance his arm with a definition, a working definition:

> ... we shall define autobiography as the retrospective prose narrative that some-one writes concerning his own existence where the focus is his individual life, in particular the story of his personality. (p.14)

The tone and bias of this definition echo a view of autobiography which came to dominate European thinking and which I might call Rousseauism. It can only survive by excluding from its embrace autobiographies which are not the work of those who are intent on telling the story of the development of their personalities. Let me cite two examples. Facey's book *A Fortunate Life* (1981) is the story of an 'uneducated' man who in Australia had endured from the age of eight the life of an itinerant worker; he fought at Gallipoli, lost his farm in the Depression and in his eighties filled his life-story notebooks at the end of the kitchen table. The story of the publication is itself significant.

> Albert was not 'discovered' by established writers nor sought out by publishers. The manuscript sat in a cupboard for a couple of years, until a neighbour typed it for a fee of $300 from Albert's pension earnings. Then the Freemantle Arts Centre Press were asked to help by printing and binding twenty copies for the family... During a taping session [to comment on his text HR] the title for the book emerged as Albert reflected on his 'fortunate life'. (p.327/8 from Jan Carter's Afterword)

By 1985, three years after his death, 250,000 Australians had bought his book. Facey nowhere dwells on his own personality, though it's impossible not to speculate about it or derive it from the many stories of the events of his life. He shows no hunger for a search for identity nor a yearning to address an audience wider than his close circle. He makes very few direct reflective comments; there is no introspection nor lingering over what Lejeune calls the development of a personality. Nearly all his stories are about endurance and stoicism in a hostile world although the life story never brandishes such terms. It is above all about certain kinds of activity and how he engages in them.

A more obvious example of an autobiographical work which would be set aside by Lejeune's rubric is Sakharov's short (22 pages) autobiography ('How I came to Dissent' n.d.) Its opening paragraph reveals a motivation utterly remote from Lejeune's notion of the story of a personality.

> In giving autobiographical information I hope to put an end to false rumours with respect to facts which have frequently been misrepresented in the press because of ignorance or sensationalism. (p.115)

Sakharov's utterly unemotional account as a world-famous physicist of his entry into oppositional politics in the former Soviet Union is given in the measured words of an eminent and formerly privileged scientist and is uttered in the medium of dispassionate public discourse but it is also what he calls 'a moral and social act'. There is only one brief moment in the text which might meet Lejeune's criterion.

> But by then the time for the test had already been moved up to an earlier hour and the carrier aircraft had already transported its burden to the designated point for the explosion. The feeling of impotence and fright has remained in my

memory ever since and it has worked much change in me as I move towards my present attitude. (p.119)

Lejeune came to change his position radically after many years of developing the focus of his studies and regarded his early position as elitist.

Anyone exploring randomly will find other examples, sometimes very challenging, ones which are vigorously miscellaneous. I was intrigued to find Roger J Porter's essay ('In Me the Solitary Sublimity. Posturing and the Collapse of the Romantic Will in Benjamin Robert Haydon', 1993) on the early nineteenth century artist Benjamin Haydon. It turns out that Haydon kept a diary for thirty-eight of his sixty years and made almost daily entries amounting to twenty-four volumes. Porter's comments are a compelling reminder that autobiographical writing stubbornly resists any purist and prescriptive attempt to describe it.

> His writing... refuses to be narrowly focused; a partial list of topics might include meditations on the Bible; literary criticism of Homer, Dante, and Milton; discussions of human and animal anatomy; treatises on the Elgin marbles; character analyses of Wordsworth, Keats, and Napoleon; technical discussions of oil paintings; attacks on debtors' laws (Haydon was imprisoned three times for debt); stories of betrayal by those whose patronage he had expected; gossip about other artists, M.P.s, and critics; detailed descriptions of his progress on a given painting; critiques of English and Continental politics; meditations on fleeting fame; endless self-analysis; attacks on the art-establishment and its institutions; and long prayers to carry a painting to completion. But Haydon's *Diary* and *Autobiography*, despite their sprawl and catch-all nature, have an autobiographical plot; ...The themes reveal Haydon's motive for writing, and indeed he makes the impelling need to write the dominant theme of his autobiography. (p.169)

Is it possible to say what we are talking about – not necessarily the same thing as a definition – in such a way as to include my own sense of the ubiquity of autobiographical behaviour? Here's my attempt:

> Autobiographical discourse embraces all those verbal acts, whether they be whole texts or parts of texts, whether they be spoken or written, in which individual speakers or writers or two or more collaborators attempt to represent their lives through a construction of past events and experiences.

Whether or not this is a kind of fiction is hardly the point and that question betrays us into numbing and sterile debates. Every serious commentator now agrees that autobiography is in a special sense a kind of fiction in several quite different ways. However, without some firm hold on the real world i.e.

actual events, actual things, actual people, we cannot seriously consider it as all or part of a life story.

My apparently uncontroversial formulation is, as must be obvious by now, an attempt to throw wide the concept of autobiography in such a way as to make it a common social and discursive activity. It makes it possible to enter the world of autobiography not, as is usual, via long written works but via speech-about-one's-past and to point towards its much wider and deeper significance. It directs our gaze beyond the revered monuments created within the institution of literary criticism to the world at large where everyone in one way or another, prompted by diverse motives, drawing on a variety of discursive resources, speaks of a past life.

Once this shift is made it follows that we must include the phenomenon of collaboration, not simply as an attempt to be comprehensive but as the deliberate foregrounding of important forms of autobiographical acts which are either unobserved in the literature or given little more than a passing glance. It has become an urgent matter to dismantle the image of the lonely autobiographer totally immersed in the task of narrating the self. What this kind of attention reveals is that collaborative autobiographical activity is undoubtedly entwined in everyday spontaneous conversations in which two or more people join forces to recount an episode from a shared past; they complement, amplify, correct, contradict each other, jointly to produce a narration which is the outcome of their dialogic turn-taking. The participants are alert monitors of each other's versions, so much so that at times they agree to differ. The most remarkable instance in my own experience was listening to a husband and wife over the lunch table giving an account of the Entebbe Airport rescue of a hi-jacked Israeli plane in Kenya. The couple were amongst the passengers who, until the last moment, assumed they would be killed. And there they were less than twenty-four hours afterwards in a London restaurant. The telling of these indelible events was accomplished with a rare and perfectly symmetrical reciprocity and immaculate turn-taking.

Quite different is the collaboration in which one person sets out to elicit from another a life-story or part of it. The motive may be entirely worthy and above board to make room for hitherto unheard voices, to supply resources for the social historian, to provide a basis for therapy, to create a publishable text which might satisfy our insatiable appetite for other people's lives. Whatever the case, the interchange is rarely symmetrical since the interviewer usually speaks with the voice of superior education, expertise and power. I return to this theme when I discuss Oscar Lewis's *Children of Sanchez* and other elicited autobiographies in a later chapter. It is sufficient to note for the moment that, although the practice is not new (Mayhew's scrupulous work is justly famous), developments in the academic world and the technology of audio and video recording have transformed a pioneer and dedicated practice into a major form of commercial activity.

There are also collaborations in our day of a quite different kind which constitute a new phenomenon. They occur in groups which have been deliberately organised to create a space, either to speak of and therefore to tape-record and/or write about their pasts which they have in some sense shared, like living through world wars, the Depression, strikes, schooling, growing up, factory life ... Such groups are not spontaneous but usually emerge from adult education or higher education departments. They amount to a novel socio-political event, often having the deliberate political intent of showing a view of events and experiences unlikely to be represented in official or dominant versions. They stand in strong contrast to the 'exemplary lives' tradition. Collectively they constitute a kind of counter-narrative. The collaborators in these enterprises are institutionalising and taking to a higher level a practice which can be found as a spontaneous occurrence in families, friendship groups, reunions and the like. This has the promise of transforming ephemeral, fortuitous and fragmentary voices into texts available for dissemination and thus entering the public domain.

Paul Thompson (1988; see Chapter 6) has a lively discussion of the achievements of group autobiographical projects and singles out from the proliferation of oral history groups 'the most radical model', A People's Autobiography of Hackney, *Working Lives 1905-1945* (Centerprise, 1975).

> Any member could record anyone else. At the group meetings they played and discussed their tapes – sometimes also recording these discussions – and planned ways of sharing what was collected with a Hackney audience. For this reason they especially emphasised publishing and issued a series of cheap pamphlets, assisted by local library subsidy, based on transcriptions and written accounts of people's lives. (p.17)

Collaborative autobiography has a particular appeal to feminists who organise groups, the members of which present to each other the experience of being a woman. Liz Stanley (1992) cites her own participation in one such project.

> In a project entitled 'Our Mothers' Voices' I and a number of other working-class-by-birth sociologists focussed on our mothers' pasts and the intertwining of these with our own. (p.87)

Roland Barthes commented on the universality of narrative and its capacity to cross all boundaries, geographical, temporal, social, and cultural but he would have been the last to assert that there are not hugely important differences when we cross those boundaries. The same is true of autobiographical acts. So we must go further and follow Christa Wolf (1980) who insists that subjectivity is at a nexus of historical coordinates. It follows that prevailing modes of autobiographical acts must be understood as intimately entwined in their historical moments. This obliges us to ask

- who at a given historical moment may speak of the self and its past? and in what ways? Using what language?

- who may speak to whom of such things? where?

- what silences must be observed?

- what kind of discursive models are available? (conversions? confessions? picaresque novels? the literary canon? oral storytelling?)

- at what point(s) in another kind of discourse may autobiography intrude?

- how imperative are all these constraints?

The quest for incontrovertible criteria to pin down autobiography has led to interminable and obsessive attempts to corral it within a particular genre. As Leigh Gilmore (1994) writes,

> ...a variety of self-representational texts, many of which have not previously been called autobiography, have failed at being assimilated into pure generic classifications, and have thus resisted being coopted by autobiography's post-Enlightenment project of saving autobiography for the politics of individualism. (p.8)

This project is inseparable from the complementary effort to limit the concept of autobiography to what may be thought of as literature i.e. its passing a test designed by critics. However, once we shift the concept to embrace all kinds of autobiographical acts, as I have done, that effort becomes meaningless. And, we might add, the enterprise is also flawed because in practice it turns its gaze almost exclusively on male, white, 'Western' authors, and imperially declares autobiography to be a European invention, achieving a canonical form in the Romantic Movement. Any genre definition emerging from such myopic inspection can only be totally inadequate before it is under way. It will not, for example, be tested against Mumtaz Mufti's *Labbaik*, of which Barbara Metcalf (1993) writes,

> ...Mumtaz Mufti, one of Pakistan's most celebrated novelists and intellectuals, a self-proclaimed 'nominal Muslim', encountered, or so he tells us – a series of disconcerting events, not quite explicable, all of which worked together inexorably to bring him to the point of undertaking the pilgrimage to Mecca. Some time after he returned from Mecca, Mumtaz Mufti was prevailed on by friends to write out his experience. They first appeared in sixteen instalments in an Urdu journal. (p.147)

The text, Metcalf tells us, slides from fantasy into reality and back to fantasy, from reportage to visions, from drawing on Western literature to narrative in a South Asian manner, but 'its three distinctive themes have long histories in the biographical and autobiographical texts in Urdu and, preceding it, the Persian traditions' (p.156). Urdu and Persian traditions! Never a breath of them in the search for 'a First World genre of the dominant culture written by persons whose lives are culturally endorsed, i.e. 'worth' writing' (Julia Watson, 1993, p.60)

There is a strand in postmodernism which offers an alternative to the quest for an essentialist autobiography, an alternative which is unambiguously political. Chantal Mouffe (1993), for example, counterposes to the notion of the fully unified self

> ... a theory of the subject as a decentred, detotalized agent, a subject constructed at the point of intersection of a multiplicity of subject positions... Consequently no identity is ever definitely established, there always being a certain degree of openness and ambiguity in the way the different subject positions are articulated. (p.34/35)

The fluidity of the self chimes with the fluidity of contemporary society where narratives are both diverse and contradictory, political systems are subject to new kinds of crisis and the grand knowledge systems of the West are under stress and challenge. Resistance to old oppressions have reached new levels of articulation. Autobiography can now become a means not only for registering in new kinds of discourse ferment, fracture and doubt but also the dynamics of the self in the contemporary world. Nevertheless, the self and its verbalised past is not a mere ragbag of subject positions, constantly changing, internally contradictory, always open and ambiguous, but constructed at 'a point of intersection'. As Christa Wolf (1983) writes in *A Model Childhood*,

> The present intrudes upon remembrance, today becomes the last day of the past yet we would suffer continuous estrangement from ourselves if it weren't for our memory of the things we have done, of the things that have happened to us. If it weren't for the memory of ourselves.
>
> And for the voice that assumes the task of telling it. (p.4)

We, or others, may find our selves to be problematic or, indeed, a turmoil. We may find it difficult to answer, 'Who was I? What am I? How many Is am I?' Yet again and again we confront those questions knowing that all is not chaos. It is memory which repeatedly rescues us and makes it possible to speak with a comprehensible voice.

For anyone to undertake to speak or write of his/her own past is not necessarily to enrol compulsorily for a particular genre (however alluring certain models may be). It is no more than to declare, often implicitly, a topic, a theme, a preoccupation, rather than a predetermined choice of discursive resources. Available models are not easily ignored; indeed they may exert irresistible pressure. This is why so many autobiographies display a particular kind of intertextuality. It is also why, as soon as the rules and regulations are suggested, a case can be cited which defies them. The autobiographical impulse is not a synonym for authorial intention but is realised by a dialogic act which invites not only all kinds of responses but particularly a response in kind. Addressees are as much part of the process as addressers. To speak of one's past is always an invitation to others to think and possibly speak of their own. Any autobiographical venture has the potential of setting in motion a symposium of autobiographical responses. Nowhere is this clearer than in the life-story activities of everyday conversations. Each participant tests his/her reality in the course of such interchanges and may make a contribution which either nods in agreement or says, 'Yes, but ...' or 'No, life is not like that; it wasn't that way for me'. Narrative truths and counter-narratives. Microcosms and macrocosms.

The vast embrace of autobiographical acts reaches across centuries, cultures, classes and genders and, therefore, inevitably takes in the diversity of forms establishing a complete intertextuality of its own, that is to say whether we hear them or not, other autobiographical voices speak in the text. As diverse as those forms are they are always being added to, as I hope to show. Out of that diversity comes another, for now everybody has something to say about autobiography in general, or some particular instances of it, or even to interweave autobiography and theoretical analysis of it. So, in Jane Steedman's *Landscape for a Good Woman: A Story of Two Lives* (1986) she not only tells the story, some of the story, but through multiple articulations in the text watches herself doing the telling and appraises what she is up to.

> I see my childhood as evidence that can be used. I think it's particularly useful as a way of gaining entry to ideas about childhood – what children are for, why to have them – that aren't written about in the official records, that is in the text-books of child psychology and child analysis, and in sociological descriptions of childhood. The public assertion of my childhood's usefulness stands side by side with the painful personal knowledge, I think the knowledge of us, all my family, going as far back as the story permits, that it would have been better that it hadn't happened that way, hadn't happened at all.
>
> I stayed at school once ... (p.104)

The transition between the paragraph and the beginning of the next one shows us a new kind of autobiographical text in which the life-story narrator, the historian, the sociologist, the neo-Freudian psychologist (one and the same person) all enter the text and have their say.

Ronald Fraser (1984) researched his childhood and checked his own recollections against those he collected in interviews with all those he had known in his childhood. It is thus a many-voiced work as each contributor speaks of the same past. Ronald Fraser's struggle is to make valid sense of it all. His book ends with a conversation with his therapist.

> – I've always thought history served one purpose at least. By discovering the major factors of change one can learn from them. The same ought to be true of an individual's history.
>
> – Yes ... you want to be the subject of your history instead of the object you felt yourself to be ...
>
> – The subject, yes, but also the object. It's the synthesis of the two, isn't it?
>
> – The author of your childhood then, the historian of your past. (p.187)

The educated and often tortured voice rises above the story, clears its throat, to ensure that we understand the text as 'evidence' or as a 'synthesis' so that autobiography earns its keep. Yet as in every autobiographical act there is at work the urge to perceive life as a source of narrative.

CHAPTER TWO

THE LANDSCAPE OF AUTOBIOGRAPHY
I. WRITTEN AUTOBIOGRAPHICAL ACTS

My aim now is relatively simple. I repeat, the literature about auto-biography is dominated by a preoccupation with lengthy works. It ignores almost entirely spoken life-stories and there is a glaring neglect of many other forms. I propose to set out a classification of auto-biographical acts in order to wrest autobiography from the grasp of the literary theorists and academic critics and ultimately to show what an everyday thing it is. Once we see it in this light it becomes a common, even indispensable possession. It is, as Sidonie Smith (1987) says, 'both the process and the product of assigning meaning to ... experiences after they have taken place' (p.45/46). It is one of the most impressive products of the workings of human memory, perhaps the supreme instance of it.

I am well aware that the categories I have made could easily have been different since the criteria for separating one category from another are far from clear-cut. I am not unduly concerned about that, firstly because I believe this is the first attempt at the task and, secondly, because the very nature of the material I am slicing up so blithely means that categories must overlap and interpenetrate. I may well have missed some entirely. Finally, all these discursive practices have evolved as part of social and cultural history. At the very moment when they are being described they are changing; some forms are dying out and new ones are coming into being. Any taxonomy of this kind should be partly obsolescent. I am encouraged by Frow's comment (1986),

> The patron god of hermeneutics, the bearer of messages from the greater gods, was also the god both of boundaries and the crossing of boundaries. (p.1)

Types of written autobiographical discourse
1. The major literary work
There are certain works which have achieved recognition of the kind which canonises them. A few titles will suffice as examples. Rousseau's *Confessions* (1782); *Father and Son*, E Gosse (1907); The Gorky Trilogy (*Childhood*, 1913; *My Apprenticeship*, 1916; *My Universities*, 1923); *Words,* Jean-Paul Sartre (1964).

Usually these works are spoken of as 'a life' or 'the life'. Those which are permitted to enter the literary canon, according to Pascal (1960), have to pass the test of being 'a spiritual experiment, a voyage of discovery' or, more demanding still, to be art and therefore to be treated with that special form of respect given to certain novels. Those which do not meet the requirements are banished from the genre. Yet the full-scale works which are readily included differ from each other in important ways. There are confessions, conversions, stories of intellectual development, continuous narratives, broken narratives, the heavily reflective and interpretative as against the strictly narrative and descriptive, the impersonal and 'objective' as against the intensely expressive. There are those which are tightly organised into a coherent structure and there are those which happily indulge in 'imaginative ramblings, digressions, 'visions', reveries, unusual or drawn-out depictions of other persons' (Renza p.268 in Olney). We should not be unduly surprised by that diversity. It mirrors the ways in which people can be heard any day talking about their lives. Furthermore, it is worth stressing the diversity of written life stories since, to judge by the critical literature, there are certain kinds of works which implicitly at least, do not come up to scratch. This is most likely to happen when the writer has no special claim to fame and does not set about the work already adorned with laurels. One example – *The Christian Watt Papers* (1988). Christian Watt was a Fraserburgh fishwife who wrote the story of her life in pencil on foolscap sheets while she was in an asylum as a patient, on and off for fifty years. None of it was published in her lifetime. It is a deeply moving book recording the bitterly hard life of a clever, highly principled, radically-minded woman. Her life-story only sees the light of day by a fortunate act of rescue. There are other autobiographies of this kind and the net needs to be cast wide enough to include them.

Where do the discursive resources of an autobiography come from? Written discourse abounds in narratives of many different kinds, any one of which can be taken as a model, but the richest source waiting to be plundered is surely fiction, which is one reason, but only one, why we immediately see a family resemblance and at times find it difficult to distinguish between the two. There is a constant interaction between fiction and autobiography, though it has been pointed out that the European model begins by borrowing its resources from diaries, journals and letters. Rousseau believed he could 'invent a language' in order to write in what he saw as a completely new genre.

> For what I have to say I need to invent a language which is as new as my project: for what tone, what style can I assume to unravel the immense chaos of sentiments,so diverse, so contradictory, often so vile and so sublime, which have agitated me without respite... Thus I have decided to do the same with my style as with my content. I shall not apply myself to rendering it uniform; I shall always put down what comes to me, I shall change it according to my humour without scruple, I shall say each thing as I feel it, as I see it, without study, without difficulty, without burdening myself about the resulting mixture... my uneven and natural style, sometimes rapid, sometimes diffuse, sometimes wise and sometimes mad, sometimes grave and sometimes gay, will itself form part of my story. (p.82)

Yet you do not have to be a particularly perspicacious reader schooled in the practices of eighteenth century fiction to detect Rousseau's debt to the picaresque novel which typically is the story of a rogue looking back at his more or less villainous life. The whole of *The Confessions* is indeed a text of unique heterogeneity, the components of which are readily recognisable. In addition to the picaresque there is a debt to religious confessions and to the fact that 'since the middle of the seventeenth century a game of exchange between memoirs and the novel had little by little transformed the narrative in the first person' (Lejeune *op.cit.* p.145). Indeed, until the end of the eighteenth century, when the word autobiography was invented, *memoirs* and *confessions* were the most used terms.

2. Memoirs

The term memoirs has been used so loosely in the past that autobiographers themselves have chosen to use it: thus, Siegfried Sassoon's *Memoirs of a Foxhunting Man* (1928) and *Memoirs of an Infantry Officer* (1930). What I have in mind here is that kind of writing in which the author gives an account of a public life. Gusdorf (1980) somewhat sarcastically noted,

> ... as soon as they have the leisure of retirement or exile, the minister of state, the politician, the military leader write in order to celebrate their deeds (always more or less misunderstood), providing a sort of posthumous propaganda for posterity that otherwise is in danger of forgetting them. (p.36)

Later he says that this kind of writing 'is limited almost entirely to the public sector of existence'. Memoirs, good or bad, are performed under the eye of history. When attention is turned to memoirs by those devoted to what they conceive of as autobiography proper, they are very cool about them. Mary Warnock (1987), for instance, says of memoir writers,

> They are more concerned with the great events of which they are a part, or the great people with whom they consort. Their diaries are and are meant to be contributions to a publicly accessible history. (p.104)

The boundary between this category and what I have called literary autobiography is a purely taxonomic construct. In fact both kinds of text contain passages, frequently extensive, which taken alone would place them in the neighbouring territory. When they oscillate throughout, we can say without scruple that they are, in fact, either in both categories at the same time or, for those who have an irrepressible devotion to classification systems, yet another category. I am thinking of Makarenko's *Road to Life* (1934-36, trans. 1951) the story of his experiences as a young teacher in the early years of the Soviet Union. He sub-titles it *A Poem of Education* and in the text, though inevitably he frequently speaks as the pioneer educator, he also recounts with passion and with narrative skill the extraordinary events in his school.

I am attempting to make a non-hierarchical list. I am not trying to deposit in separate steel containers all the works I know of. It would make better sense to treat memoirs and literary life-stories as on a continuum, at the poles of which judgements can be made with confidence. A case in point, Herzen's monumental four volumes of memoirs would be placed somewhere in the middle though it frequently moves towards either pole (*My Past and Thoughts: the Memoirs of Alexander Herzen*, (1861-66, trans. 1968). Herzen, brought up in a Russian upper-class family, was imprisoned as a young man and sentenced to internal exile for his radical views. He eventually, in 1847, exiled himself to Western Europe where he launched himself into the turbulent political life of the great radicals of that time. His memoirs have none of the smug, self-congratulatory tone of establishment successes. They are 'an amalgam of memory, observation, moral passion, psychological analysis and political description, wedded to a major literary talent... '(I. Deutcher, Introd. p.xxxv). '...all that he touches in which things, sensations, feelings, persons, ideas, private and public events, institutions, entire cultures, are given shape and life by his powerful and coherent historical imagination' (p.xxxvi). Yet the memoirs, veering as they do from his experience of the great upheavals of European history to the most intimate tragic events of his own family life, are not edited into a smooth text but instead are fragmented into stories, anecdotes, reflections, political descriptions and characters. They also contain many sequences which we have come to think of as the characteristic discourse of autobiography, his experiences of loves and deaths. Looked at in one way, *The Memoirs* is a miscellany but it is certainly not a ragbag, for such is his intellect and vitality that everything contributes to our sense of the man. Herzen himself in his 1855 Prologue wrote

> In order to write one's reminiscences it is not in the least necessary to be a great man or an adventurer who has seen the world, a famous artist or a statesman. It is quite sufficient to be simply a man who has something to tell and who has the ability and wish to do so... Memoirs, of course, can be boring and the life that is related in them can be poor and insignificant...there cannot exist any specialised guidance for the writing of memoirs. The *Memoirs* of Benvenuto Cellini are interesting not because he was a great artist but because he deals in them with questions that are interesting in the highest degree. (p.186)

3. Diaries, Journals, Collections of Letters

These kinds of writing could be dealt with separately but I choose to place them together to avoid over-elaboration, for what they share is their system of composition. Both diaries and journals, when published or when they come to light, consist of a sequence of entries composed very close in time to the events and moods they record. They constitute an autobiographical assemblage, the separate items of which are usually produced over a lengthy period of time. Separate entries may constitute complete little stories but juxtaposed as they are they can establish an extended discursive meaning. Readers trying to discover that meaning are left with more to do than with a straight autobiography. Linda Peterson in *Victorian Autobiography* (1986) discusses the anomalous *Autobiography* (1877) by Harriet Martineau.

> We might consider some versions of autobiographical writing that Victorian women did compose, in part to sketch an unknown segment of nineteenth cen-tury history, in part to define the social and generic restrictions that women writers faced when they chose the form of spiritual autobiography. Martineau wrote when the available forms of self-expression for women were three, (1) the private diary, (2) the family memoir – including that peculiarly Victorian form, the memoirs of a clergyman's wife and (3) the autobiographical novel. The most common of these was the private diary ... (p.124)

She goes on to show how, by the mid-nineteenth century, editors ritually denied that the women authors themselves had any intention to publish. A compilation called *The Earnest Christian*, which contained the journals and letters of Harriet Maria Jukes is editorially rendered acceptable.

> ... the Letters and Journals ... were never intended by the writer to meet the eye of any but near and dear friends.

In the twentieth century women writers turned this censorship and self-censorship on its head and made a virtue of the discontinuities of a diary and its closeness to day-to-day switches of interest and mood.

When I place letters here, I am, of course, thinking of letters in the auto-biographical mode (e.g. Cowper's Letters). Since letters were often written with publication in mind, they often took on a literary cast especially when recounting framed episodes from the life of the writer. The clearest lesson to be drawn from this collection of closely related forms is that as soon as we begin rooting about in written discourse we find forms which are not only clearly autobiographical but also in many, perhaps most, instances which have been readily seized upon as an outlet for the same kind of impulse as that which drives the most imposing full-scale autobiography, declaring itself without reservation.

Diaries, letters and similar documents are often used as the raw material of the autobiographer. Michael Fischer (1994), discussing the special charac-teristics of the autobiographies of renowned, innovative scientists contrasts Rita Levi-Montalcini's methods with Irene Fischer's. The former 'perceived diaries and journals (and life histories?) as vanities, and yet at the same time is thankful for the return of letters that allowed her to relive intense periods of her life and to construct key portions of her autobiography'. Fischer juxtaposes these contradictory postures.

> I never developed the habit – nor do I regret never having done so – of keeping any kind of record, still less a diary, because I believe that, if memory has not taken the indelible imprint of a given event, then it could not and should not be brought back to life by mere written witness. I believe, in fact, that the very act of recording an event causes, if only unconsciously, a distortion resulting from the blatant desire of the diarist to make use of it as an account to be exhibited to third parties, as a way of reliving in old age a particular moment, and of making one's descendants partake in it or even, if one is especially vain, for its value to posterity. (p.115)

Yet some sixteen pages earlier she had written,

> Having never kept a diary, I was very pleased when, in June 1980, Viktor Ham-
> burger sent me a large envelope containing all the letters – carefully preserved
> for so many years – that he had received from me during the period I spent in
> Rio, from September 1952, to the end of January, 1953... In reading them, I
> have relived one of the most intense periods of my life in which moments of
> enthusiasm and despair alternated with the regularity of a biological cycle.
> (p.115)

Irene Fischer, on the other hand, is unhesitating in her use of a personal
archive.

> Unlike Levi-Montalcini's ambivalence toward diaries, this text is built on rich
> documentation of diaries, correspondence, and publications, allowing a textured
> interlacing of stories... (p.116)

Arnold Wesker, in his autobiography, *As Much as I Dare* (1994), not only
uses his diary ('The Diary of Jon Smith') as a resource but also quotes from
it (p.336-9, 342-8 and 363-71).

4. Autobiographical Writings

I am using this term to accommodate *groups* of stories of personal experience, each one of which is self-contained and has its own structure, so
much so that it can stand on its own feet. In fact many of them have been
published separately before being gathered together. They are often published as collections which unambiguously invite us to establish connections
between the stories which might transform them from a mere miscellany
into a meaningful whole. I have in mind such works as Mary McCarthy's
Memories of a Catholic Girlhood (1957), John Clare's *Autobiographical
Writings* (Robinson, 1983) and Maxim Gorky's *Fragments from my Diary*
(1940). I think of them as collages, since the meanings emerge from juxtapositions, interconnections and a consistent prose narrative voice.

And what are we to make of Kafka's *Letter to a Father* (1976)? Was it
actually a letter or a cry to the whole world or both? It certainly is the autobiography of a son's relationship to his father. The letter opens with a justification of his sustained mourning for their relationship.

> Dearest Father
> You asked me recently why I maintain I am afraid of you. As usual I was unable
> to think of any answer to your question, for the very reason that I am afraid of
> you and partly because an explanation of the grounds for this fear would mean
> going into far more details than I could even approximately keep in mind while
> talking. And if I now tried to give you an answer in writing, it will still be very
> incomplete because even in writing this fear and its consequence hampers me

in relation to you and because [anyway] the magnitude of the subject goes far beyond the scope of my memory and powers of reasoning. (p.557)

The letter continues for twenty thousand words approx! It not only explores their relationship but inevitably is full of stories of humiliations and failures of communication. In addition to this very long letter we have its complement, *The Diaries*, (*op.cit.*).

Mary McCarthy's *Memories of a Catholic Girlhood* (1957) illustrates to perfection the elusive nature of stories of this kind, particularly if we would like to place them with confidence. The collection is composed of stories which had already been published separately and which were assumed by many people to be works of fiction. In a kind of preface ('To the Reader') McCarthy writes,

> These memories of mine have been collected over a period of years. Some readers finding them in a magazine have taken them for stories. The assumption that I have 'made them up' is surprisingly prevalent, even among people who know me. 'That Jewish grandmother of yours...!' Jewish friends have chided me, sceptically, as though to say, 'Come now, you don't expect us to believe that your grandmother was really Jewish?' Indeed she was... (p.9)

The whole of 'To the Reader' is a splendid case study of an autobiographer reflecting on her enterprise.

> ...I have given real names and, wherever possible, I have done this with neighbours, servants and friends of the family, for, to me, this record lays a claim to being historical – that is, much of it can be checked. If there is more fiction in it than I know, I should like to be set right; in some instances, which I shall call attention to later, my memory has already been corrected. (p.10)

Scrupulously she adds to each chapter her very full revisionist notes in which can be found remarks like:

- This account is highly fictionalised (p.8)

- There are several dubious points in this memoir (p.45)

- The reader will wonder what made me change the story (p.45)

- The most likely thing I fear is that I have fused two memories (p.73)

- This story is so true to convent life that I find it difficult to sort out the guessed at and half-remembered from the undeniably real (p.108)

- There are some semi-fictional touches here (p.146)

The addenda taken collectively transform the original stories, not only by revealing them as autobiography but also by giving us a sight of the auto-biographer at work. Moreover, it takes up an issue which I shall return to and which haunts all discussion of autobiography, namely, the debate about truth and fiction.

Gorki wrote a full-length autobiography (the trilogy, *My Childhood, My Apprenticeship* and *My Universities*) which is so well-known that it has found its way into the texts used by English teachers. Less well-known is his *Fragments from my Diary* (1940) which Gorki put together in 1922. He assembles the book from material he'd been gathering for many years. The word 'fragments' must be taken as almost metaphorical since they are only fragments in the sense that no explicit interconnections are made between them. The book reads as a set of moments in one man's journey across Russian space and time, a journey in which he stops to pick out people he has known. Gorki keeps himself very much in the shadows, refusing to be drawn into comment by the people and events he is describing and yet esta-blishing himself as a presence. Typically, when he encounters an ex-doctor tramp, one exchange goes like this, after the tramp has denounced literature as 'a gangrene, poisonous to most people and a mania as far as you writers are concerned':

> In this tone, but quite good-humouredly and with evident pleasure, he continued to talk for a long time. As for me, I listened to him patiently without interrupting him.
>
> 'You don't contradict me?' he said.
>
> 'No.'
>
> 'Then you agree?'
>
> 'No, of course not.'
>
> 'Ah, then you don't think me worth contradicting. Is that it?'
>
> 'No, not that either. But I place the dignity of literature too high to wrangle about it'. (p.51)

I give as a last example of the wide range of writing which needs to be brought together here John Clare's work, collected by Eric Robinson as *Autobiographical Writings* (1983). Robinson put together all those writings which fall under the rubric of his title: Sketches in the Life of John Clare, More Hints in the Life, etc (sic); Autobiographical Fragments; Journey out of Essex. The splendid material in this edition reminds us that, if we are looking for examples of autobiographical writing which do not conform to the by now accepted format, we have to look for it in the less-than-obvious places. The next category obliges us to look almost everywhere!

5. Embedded Autobiographical Writing

Perhaps nothing better illustrates the fact that any serious consideration of the nature of autobiography must take into account its pervasiveness than the way it crops up in the midst of other texts, even the most unlikely ones. None of us expects the life of the author to intrude itself into a physics textbook, although in principle, and perhaps one day in practice, there is no reason why it should not. Certainly much more often than is generally supposed, autobiographical material can be found in texts where we might least expect to come across it (see Rosen, 1993). Given the powerful control exerted by the policing of texts and the veto on personal intrusions into impersonal prose, the frequent occurrence of embedded autobiographical material is all the more remarkable. Yet the practice is a venerable one. William Harvey, the discoverer of the system of the circulation of the blood, did not hesitate to take up the autobiographical stance in *An Anatomical Disquisition on the Motion of the Heart and Blood in Animals* (1628). For him the account of an experiment meant telling what *he* did – a *he* undisguised by liberal use of the passive voice which any contempory apprentice scientist will tell you is mandatory.

> When I first gave my mind to vivisections, as a means of discovering the motions and uses of the heart and sought to discover these from actual inspection, and not from the writings of others, I found the task so truly arduous, so full of difficulties, that I was almost tempted to think, with Fracastorius, that the motion of the heart was only to be comprehended by God

> ...some chid and calumniated me, and laid it to me as a crime that I had dared to depart from the precepts and opinion of all anatomists; others desired further explanations of the novelties which they said were both worthy of consideration, and might perchance be found of signal use.

In Steven Rose's *The Making of Memory* (1992) we have a remarkable switching of modes which only a scientist of his breadth and discursive daring would undertake. He tells us,

> I've wanted to write this book – or at least a book like this – for many years now. The ways in which many non-scientists, friends and colleagues often regarded me as a laboratory scientist – with incomprehension and awe, tinged, I sometimes feel, with faint patronage – engendered in me a sort of apologia for laboratory life. Could I explain what I did day by day in the laboratory in a way which would give a sense of this arcane activity? (Preface)

We can see in the phrase 'what I did from day to day' an autobiographical glint in his eye which gets brighter when he says, 'I want to describe what it feels like to be a neuroscientist' and he is as good as his word. Very quickly we are taken through a day in his life in the lab 'going through routine tasks of experimentation, training chicks'. Something of the flavour of this chapter may be judged by this extract:

> As I pass through the doors I find myself singing. I don't sing often, for I am, I must make clear, practically tone deaf; listening to my singing is, I am told, an excruciating experience. But leaving the office for the lab always cheers me; first formless hums and finally snatches of mixed song, of verses which clutter the recesses of my memory like undisposed-of garbage break out. Catching myself singing, I am amused. I know what it signifies; it's a day for real experiments not just paper-shuffling. (p.16)

Light-hearted as that might seem, Rose rapidly moves in the account of his doings, including a subtle analysis of who wears what kind of coat in the lab, to what he as a scientist actually does to pursue his research on this particular day. Scarcely a chapter is without the injection of autobiographical moments; what it's like to attend a high-powered academic conference or to go through the process of writing 'a paper' and getting it published. They become an essential part of the orchestration of Rose's scientific score. Remember, this book is sub-titled 'From Molecules to Mind' and its goals are 'To chronicle an adventure in research, illustrate the nature of doing so and reflect on a theory of mind'. Rose forswears what he calls 'biologese' and in the process creates a new form of sustained discourse which, without apology, has woven into it the texture of the author's own life, stitched so dexterously that no censoring pen could excise it and leave a meaningful whole. For him the inclusion of autobiographical material is a matter of explicit principle.

Once alerted to embedded autobiographical material, you will find it everywhere. If I had not chosen Rose, whom I read with immoderate enthusiasm very recently, I might have chosen the work of Oliver Sacks, especially *The Man who Mistook his Wife for a Hat* (1985), a touchstone book for me which can be read not only as a set of case studies of his patients but also as the writer's autobiography

> Constantly my patients drive me to question and constantly my questions drive me to patients – thus in the stories or studies which follow there is continual movement from one to the other. (p.ix)

Autobiographical discourse, nudging its way into texts of all kinds, implicitly justifies its intrusion because the author feels the need to draw on extra power, extra authenticity, reality even. But there are great variations. A friend sent me recently an article by EP Thompson called the *Liberation of Perugia* (1985). It is the story of a military action near Perugia in the last war and, as the commander of a tank unit, Thompson finds himself witnessing the deaths of some of his men in the leading tank for whom the whole piece is a kind of lament. It is a sad and deeply moving tale. It might well have been left as yet another story of the miseries of war of which there can never be too many, 'the resigned complicity of military life,' as Thompson called it. But then comes the transition as, asking himself why he writes this forty years after the event, he moves into a political analysis of modern warfare and from there to the theme for which he became so well-known – the need to resist nuclear preparations for another war. A concluding passage begins,

> I have strayed far from my theme and Europe herself has come a long way since that day in June, 1944, when I drowsed in my tank on the outskirts of Perugia. It's not easy to join into a single theme those episodes from the last war and the strategies for preventing another. (p.198)

The stern and unforgiving laws of genres, that is to say of prose genres, demand that they should have clear boundaries, and countless students have been schooled to observe them and to censor from the discourses of academic subjects all markers which signal the presence of the writer, of which the first person pronoun is only the most obvious example. Yet these laws, though they are obeyed by most of those who practise academic writing and its close relatives, who have learned to remove themselves from a text, are also defied by writers who, though they may be law-abiding discursive citizens for most of the time cannot resist sometimes the impulse to pop up as persons in the text. Others like Rose, as we have seen, commit themselves quite explicitly to braiding together quite different modes as a matter of principle. A person's knowledge can only exist by virtue of a vast range of past experiences which have been lived through, often with the most intense feelings. These experiences, including textual experiences (books, lectures, lessons, conversations, etc.) we have been taught to disguise so that our utterances are made to seem as though they emerge from no particular place or time or person but from the fount of knowledge itself.

Instructions on the necessary discursive strategies are nowadays laid out in some detail. Carter (1990) cites the Sail Project with restrained approval and offers as 'useful' the advisory document for teachers on a kind of writing called reports.

> The major requirement of this type of writing is for the writer to write him or her self out of the text and to concentrate on the subject matter. Mention of personal feelings or reactions will indicate lapses in control of the writing. Students are required to distance themselves from 'what I did' and write about what took place. (p.178)

It continues in this advisory vein, setting up a model which comes close to parody and ignores the fact that a huge volume could be compiled of examples taken from the works of renowned scientists and scholars of all kinds who use 'what I did' to buttress, enrich or clarify their texts. These sometimes surprising irruptions are almost always subordinated to the overall function of the text which enfolds them. But they often nestle there as stories so well told that they can command attention in their own right. Rom Harré (1990), in his analysis of scientific discourse, which he describes as 'untouched by human hand,' says,

> Students as apprentice scientists are trained in this rhetoric (i.e. the elimination of personal pronouns, even the academic 'we' and the adoption of the passive voice. H.R.) from schooldays on. Everything that is personal is leached out of the discourse. Looked at as a narrative convention, this choice of grammar enables the author to tell a story not, I think, in the person of Everyman, but Big Ell himself. (p.86)

Big Ell for Harré is Logic itself. Of the typical scientific 'story' of hypothesis, results of experimentation and inductive support for the hypothesis, he comments,

> Anyone who has ever done any actual scientific research knows that this is a tale, a piece of fiction. The real life unfolding of a piece of scientific research bears little resemblance to this bit of theatre. The first point to note about it apart from its empirical falsity as a description of events is that it is a 'smiling face' presentation. All has gone well. The apparatus has worked and/or the questionnaire's been fully understood and the answers properly encoded. No fuses have blown and no one from the sample population has fallen ill, gone away or inconveniently died. If anyone tried to publish a story more like real life, in which hypotheses were dropped for lack of support, apparatus couldn't be made to work within the parameters of the original experiment, and so on, it would be turned down. (p.86)

In Umberto Eco's book, *Interpretation and Misinterpretation* (1992) there are several instances of the contributors' use of autobiographical material in the process of debating a key question in literary theory. I have chosen just two examples because they illustrate contrasting uses of autobiographical interpolation. In the first, Eco is attempting to deal with what he calls 'the empirical author' in order to understand better the creative process, and the growth of textual strategies. He goes on to tell at some length an auto-biographical story which has a relationship to the mysterious poisoned manuscript in *The Name of the Rose*. He tells how one day he started writing a technical description of a book in his home library, a 1587 edition of Aristotles's *Poetics*, which he had forgotten that he had. In the process he suddenly realised that he was rewriting *The Name of the Rose*.

> The only difference was that from page 120 when the 'Ars Comica' begins, the lower not the upper margins were severely damaged; but all the rest was the same, the pages progressively browned and stained from dampness, and at the end stuck together, looking as if they were smeared by a disgusting fat sub-stance. I had in my hands, in printed form, the manuscript I had described in my novel. I had had it for years and years within reach, at home... I had bought the book in my youth, skimmed through it, realised it was exceptionally soiled, and put it somewhere and forgot it. But by a sort of internal camera I had photo-graphed those pages, and for decades the image of those poisonous leaves lay in the most remote part of my soul, as in a grave, until the moment it emerged again (I do not know for what reason) and I believed I had invented it. (p.87/88)

The story's moral, Eco tells us, is that there are unfathomable mysteries in the history of a textual production. But it is clear that Eco is relishing his story as a story for it is told at greater length and with more calculated narra-tive skill than its use to support his argument warrants.

In the same book, Richard Rorty responds to Eco's arguments as is customary in such jousting, but notice how Rorty sets about it. What he does is to tell us the story of his reading of Eco's piece and his thinking as he engaged with it. He dares to be playful, too. It is a brief exercise in intel-lectual autobiography inserted into a book-text where we probably would not expect it.

> So much for the Pragmatist's Progress – a narrative I often use for purposes of self-dramatisation, and one into which I was charmed to find myself being able to fit Professor Eco. Doing so enabled me to see both of us as having overcome our earlier ambitions to be code-crackers. This ambition led me to waste my twenty-seventh and twenty-eighth years trying to discover the secret of Charles Sanders Peirce's esoteric doctrine of 'the reality of Thirdness' and thus of his fantastically elaborate semiotico-metaphysical 'System'. I imagined that a similar urge must have led the young Eco to the study of that infuriating philosopher and that a similar reaction must have enabled him to see Peirce as just one more whacked-out triadomaniac... I was able to think of Eco as a fellow pragmatist. This agreeable sense of cameraderie began to evaporate, however, when I read Eco's article. (p.92/93)

Autobiography surfacing in apparently unpropitious contexts from which we have every reason to expect it to have been banned should suggest to us that it is always lurking in the sub-text of our language and thinking and can break through at any moment. But in writing much more than in speech it requires a bolder effort to resist the controls and, in Bakhtin's terms, to assert the centrifugal against the centripetal. I believe we need to take further a consideration of these practices. Surely the time has come for a comprehensive study of these parenthetic, usually momentary shifts of discursive position of all kinds. It would serve as a superb means of examining the management of discourse and attempts to subvert it. Such a study would have to acknowledge at the outset that it was confronted by an elusive and many-faced creature, as many-faced as full-scale autobiography.

Shifts of codes exhibit a functional diversity. They may be moments from the writer's experience which illustrate in a compressed and plausible manner a generalised point in the text, a kind of fable. They may illustrate the writer's personal involvement in his/her impersonally presented subject matter. They may lurk in introductions as metanarratives which comment on the grander and more remote narrative of the main text. Moreover, in any given text the extent to which the code shift occurs can be significant. It may be one daring insertion in which the writer steps forward from the shadows and then disappears forever, or frequent, possibly lengthy, accounts of personal experience which may be a deliberate attempt to compose a layered form of discourse. Length and frequency in such instances are qualitative rather than merely quantitative matters.

A comfortable home for the blending of the personal and impersonal is a popularising work by an expert in the field. The writer has to be someone with a certain kind of pedagogic intent, a desire to engage as closely as possible with his or her 'pupils' by attempting to mesh their experiences and his. Richard Fortey in his *The Hidden Landscape: A Journey into the Geological Past* (1994) tells us straight out that his 'intention is to enrich the reader's awareness of our extraordinary past' which 'makes my geology a more personal account'. A page or so into the text we are reading,

> Most geological hammers have a square, bashing side and a chisel side. A gentle tap with the latter is often all that is needed to break open a bedding plane, and awake the sleeper. So tapping and tapping at the Cleddau rocks I obtained a good break along the bedding; every time such a crack opened up the two sides of the rock were parted impatiently: inside could be who-knows-what treasure. When nothing was revealed and the rock split into two to show only the grey speckled face of a barren Silenian sea floor, I plucked a new piece of rock

from the rock face and split it and then, suddenly, a trilobite! No longer than my thumb but crouched in the rock as if waiting to be released from his sleep in stone. I cried a shout of pure joy at the discovery. I can still remember my antici-pation as the rock piece parted company in my hand, almost as one might cut a deck of cards: no strain or grinding. Then there was astonishment in suddenly finding this complex creature so perfect, yet so old, with a pair of petrified eyes visible to the naked eye even in the misty light of a Welsh afternoon, eyes that had last seen the world more that four hundred million years ago. (p.4)

As Fortey takes us on a long geological walk across Britain he repeatedly draws on his own experience:

- When I was a child I was given a copy of Arthur Mee's Children's Encyclo-paedia. (p.175)

- One of the first brick pits I visited in search of fossils .... (p.191)

- Several years ago, in the Suffolk seaside town of Southwold, I overheard a young woman in a shop say how her husband had found a skull in the cliffs nearby. (p.278)

The overall effect for me, certainly an appreciative reader, is a sense that I am being permitted to listen to a scientist in action, talking to me and, since he is broad in his comments and generous with his stories, a scientist who popularises tellingly partly through autobiographical interpolations.

The best popularising traditions will no doubt come to influence more specialist texts. The tightly controlled generic terrains are becoming de-stabilised. Phelps (1990), for instance, argues,

Against the powerful tides towards specialising and technologising knowledge (but driven by the same forces), post-modern ideological transformations constantly operate in contexts characterised by disequilibriums, heterogeneity, greater range of variability and diversity, labile boundaries, ambiguities and complexity, gaps and discontinuities, unpredictability, mystery laminated con-structions of reality, paradox ... (p.63)

The confident prescriptive tone of the school manual rings very hollow in this context. Phelps perhaps overestimates the extent to which the rigid codes of certain genres are dissolving under this bombardment but it reminds us that the right to resort to the autobiographical is broadly a poli-tical matter as are all attempts to establish alternative discursive practices and to create different or new cultural codes.

It remains only to add that there are interpolations which flicker in a text for no more than the twinkling of eye. In Homi Bhabha's *The Location of*

Culture (1994), which is, to put it mildly, a demanding theoretical work, I come across,

> Listen to my friend, the Bombay poet Adil Jussawalla writing of the 'missing person' that haunts the identity of the post-colonial bourgeoisie ... (p.45)

I deliberately choose a minimalist example. The fact that Jussawalla is the writer's friend is, we might say, neither here nor there, but the whole injunction – listen to my friend – leaps from the text as generically alien in its intimate beckoning of the reader. 'My friend' is the merest trace, a metonymic reminder that hidden from us is a huge chunk of autobiography and the admiring analysis of Jussawalla's poem which follows puts a retrospective gloss on 'my friend'.

A broad spectrum exists from Richard Fortey's cheerfully interventionist stories to Bhabha's style, words or phrases. Writers in practice frequently chafe under and refuse to submit to the rule which demands that they write themselves out of the text and concentrate on the subject matter. They persist in the heresy that there are times when they are themselves legitimately part of the subject matter.

6. Autobiography in Canonical Literary Genres
6.1 *Autobiographical fiction*
It's a matter of common practice to refer to some novels as autobiographical or as 'thinly disguised' autobiographies: Proust's monumental *Remembrance of Things Past*, for instance, or DH Lawrence's *Sons and Lovers*. The Murdstone chapters and the job in the blacking factory in *David Copperfield* are so frequently cited as to make them a paradigm of autobiographical fiction. We take for granted that novelists draw extensively on their own life-stories and the immediate acknowledgement of that fact makes it tempting to leave the matter there with the awareness that we have evidence to prove or substantiate the point. But that would leave certain interesting and problematic matters ignored, matters which touch on some major critical questions about autobiography.

First there is the obvious question: how much autobiographical material needs to be placed within the pages of the novel for us to call the novel autobiographical? On the one hand the question is unanswerable as long as it is left as a purely quantitative matter, as though once the score crosses a certain threshold we can easily make the decision; on the other hand, if we ask whether a novel told as a *bildungsroman*, a life story, comes close to the life, up to that time, of the author, the question is more easily answered. At least it is so as long as we do not ask why, if the answer is a confident yes, we do not call it an autobiography straight out and leave it at that. It all becomes more complicated when we recall that there is now general agreement that all autobiography is a construct, a fabrication we might say non-perjoratively, and, further, that in a direct sense there are inventions, pure and simple, which occur in all autobiographies, such as elaborate conversations, apparently recalled across half a century or more. The ghosts of fiction and fabrication stalk through all autobiography. Barrett Mandel (1980), writing of Edmund Gosse's *Father and Son* notes the fabrication in that autobiography:

> Gosse records minute details in the novelist fashion. He provides visual meta-phors, allows us to feel through tactile images, provides convincing dialogue, plays omniscient narrator. But we do not mistake the passage for fiction... when I read what Gosse's father said to him I know that he cannot actually remember what his father said to him. (p.60)

Now turn to the novel. 'The great events of my life are my works' said Balzac. All novelists are autobiographers in two distinct ways. First, they may draw directly on their life experience in a sustained way, allowing it to dominate an entire work, or, second, in fabricating whole stories, they must, at a deeper level, stay in touch with their life experience. However, in writing a novel, a novelist is attaching himself/herself to a form of discourse which has evolved its own demands and resources, one of which is to give a certain shape to the whole. Autobiographers, on the other hand, find themselves in a much more open and discursive space. The history of their chosen form makes it available for much more anarchic play than even the 'polyphonic' and 'carnivalesque' nature of novels permits.

The fact that autobiographical fiction can, or may be, distinguished from autobiography in its more conventional forms does not mean that a nice formula will always enable us to distinguish between them. I remember my late and somewhat embarrassing discovery that Defoe's *Journal of the Plague Year* (1719) was a work of fiction by one of the most skilled journalists of the day, writing some fifty-seven years after the events of 1665 which he would have us suppose he lived through as an adult.

Most autobiographies are not only large over-arching stories but subsume many little stories, every one of which owes its form to the writer's reservoir of textual experience, especially that of written fiction, borrowing from its strategies and tactics, its choice of openings, its use of dialogue, its selective structure, its sense of an ending. I think we may say with some confidence that autobiography and fiction, especially autobiographical fiction, are symbiotic, plundering each other both for detail and overall patterning, be it confession, conversion or the picaresque.

In the critical literature the distinction between autobiography and fiction is returned to again and again. In fact no serious work on autobiography avoids it. The topic is usually explored in an almost nervous attempt to define auto-biography in such a way as to give it a recognised and honourable place in the canon of literary genres and thus concede to it a passport into the academy. But for Paul John Eakin in *Fictions in Autobiography: Studies in the Art of Invention* (1985), autobiography is necessarily a kind of fiction and makes its entry on that account, particularly in its twentieth century forms.

> I shall argue that autobiographical truth is not a fixed but an evolving content in an intricate process of self-discovery and self-creation and, further, that the self that is the centre of all autobiographical narrative is necessarily a fictive struc-ture ... I seek to identify the fictions involved in autobiography and the sources – psychological and cultural – from which they derive. (p.3)

I will not attempt to repeat his development of that theme which is based on the study of autobiographies by Mary McCarthy, Henry James, Jean-Paul Sartre and finally a small group of very recently published works. For all his reiteration that the self in autobiography is fictive, he comes to the con-clusion that he does not mean to conflate the fictive and the fictional.

> ... I have emphasised the presence of fiction in autobiography, yet in speaking of the self as an artefact I have not meant to confuse autobiography with other works of the imagination. (p.277)

Perhaps not. In spite of all his sensitive analyses and some tortuous explora-tions of the notion of the self, ending with the banal despair, 'I regard the self finally as a mysterious reality', he never resolves what makes the self an artefact in autobiography different from the self in novels and other works of fiction. I shall return to that question in a later chapter. What Eakin does not acknowledge is Olney's point:

> Autobiography, like the life it mirrors, refuses to stay still long enough for the genre critic to fit it out with the necessary rules, laws, contracts, and pacts; it refuses simply to be a literary genre like any other. (p.25)

The difficulty is that Olney, concerned solely with fat-book autobiographies, cannot see that its Protean nature and prickly resistance to confident defini-tion, derives its character from its organic connections, not only with other fat books, but with human discourse itself and its multiplicity of autobiographical acts. Autobiographical fiction has its own similar connections with that multiplicity which includes, of course, spoken autobiographical acts to which I shall be turning my attention shortly but which never seem to arouse the interest of critics like Eakin, Olney and many others.

There can be no simple relationship between our experience of the world and the sense of a self which begins by emerging from experience and very soon partly shapes how we perceive that experience. Even more resistant to simplicities are the way we attempt to verbalise that relationship in written texts. Let me conclude this section by taking one work which illustrates perfectly that teasing process, Maxine Hong Kingston's *The Woman Warrior: Memoirs of a Girlhood among Ghosts* (1976). In this book Brave Orchid, the mother, is constantly telling her 'talk-stories'. ('My mother funnelled China into our ears'). Is it an autobiography or a novel? Certainly there are those who are content simply to label it as autobiography in an unproblematic way (see, for example, Susan Friedman in Benstock (1988, p.52, 53). Yet a reading of it reveals there are intricacies here which make such facile labelling an impossibility. Only Sidonie Smith (1987) in a very full analysis

(*A Poetics of Women's Autobiography*) provides a more challenging view.

> ... Considered by some a novel by others an autobiography, the five narratives conjoined under the title, *The Woman Warrior*, are decidedly five confrontations with the autobiographical possibilities embedded in cultural fictions, specifically as they interpenetrate one another in the autobiography a woman would write. (p.151)

Hers is an analysis of the book which puts it into a category of its own and refuses the choice of novel or autobiography. It is, she tells us, 'an autobiography about women's autobiographical storytelling' and 'an occasion to consider the complex imbroglios of cultural fictions that surround the autobiographer who is engaging in two sets of stories: those of the dominant culture and those of an ethnic subculture with its own traditions, its own unique stories'. I leave to Sidonie Smith the elaborations of those perceptions.

It seems right to end this section with the instance of *The Woman Warrior*, an autobiographical act which does not belong precisely here but which does not belong obviously anywhere else.

6.2 *Autobiographical Poetry*
It seems so obvious that poetry is often inevitably and very directly autobiographical that it is surprising that this literary form has not been

given serious attention by the theorists of autobiography. A quick search of my own collection of critical and theoretical work turned up no more than a few lines in Lejeune who, with typical perspicacity, takes on poetry without hesitation when he revises his view of the 'autobiographical pact'.

> ...who can say where prose ends? ...instead of proposing a definition that, curtly, excludes verse, I should have designated as the centre of the present system, this tension between referential transparency and aesthetic pursuit and shown ...that on both sides of a point of balance, there existed a continuous gradation of texts going, on one side, towards the banality of the *curriculum vitae*, and on the other, toward pure poetry. (p.128)

I will make life easier for myself by putting aside all those poems in which the use of 'I' is only a dramatising convention of lyric verse, as in Shelley's 'I met a traveller from an antique land'. I have in mind something much narrower than this, poetic narratives which directly present part of the story of the poet's life. My son, Michael, is much taken with this kind of poetry.

Newcomers

My father came to England
from another country
My father's mother came to England
from another country
But my father's father
Stayed behind

So my dad had no dad here
and I never saw him at all
One day in spring
some things arrived:
a few old papers
a few old photos
and – yes –
a hulky bulky thick check jacket
that belonged to the man
I would have called 'Grandad'
The Man Who Stayed Behind

But I kept that jacket
and I wore it
and I wore it
and I wore it
till it wore right through
at the back

We could all assemble a little collection of poems which we've carried around in our heads, some going back to schooldays which work in that kind of way. Or we could thumb through an anthology and make a fresh collection of similar kind. My own choice would be sure to include some of Tony Harrison's poems (1984). I read those poems and construct a someone as I go, a someone who puts his past straight in front of me. I stop writing this and browse through my shelves of poems and find, as I knew I would, a ubiquitous 'I' who turns up in nearly every volume, who considers how his light is spent or is young and easy under the apple boughs. I remind myself that this 'I' speaks in many different ways and that a separate study would soon produce a tricky and controversial taxonomy, as complicated, if not more so, as the superordinate one I am in the process of constructing for autobiographical discourse. This is no place to attempt it. Perhaps, for all I know, someone already has, deconstructing the poetic 'I' and its disguises. I wanted here simply to signal its presence among other autobiographical acts. Moreover, lest anyone should think that the personal experience poem was invented by the Romantics, here is a Chinese poem from the First Century A.D. (Waley, 1946)

> At fifteen I went with the army,
> At four score I came home.
> On the way I met a man from the village,
> I asked him who there was at home
> 'That over there is your house,
> All covered over with trees and bushes.'
> Rabbits had run in at the dog-hole,
> Pheasants flew down from the beams of the roof
> In the courtyard was growing some wild grain;
> And by the well some wild mallow.
> I'll boil the grain and make porridge,
> I'll pluck the mallows and make soup.
> Soup and porridge are both cooked,
> But there is no one to eat them with.
> I went out and looked towards the East
> While tears fell and wetted my clothes. (p.45)

However, I cannot quite leave it there, for everyone will say, 'What about Wordsworth? What about *The Prelude*?' It is a full-length autobiographical poem. No-one in English verse had attempted anything like it, so ambitious was it in its scope. It is a poetic intellectual autobiography, the story of the formation of his mind, in that, as he said, he 'set out to record, in verse, the origin and progress of his own powers as far as he was acquainted with them'. He was well aware that 'it was a thing unprecedented in literary history that a man should talk so much about himself'. But what was unprecedented was not its preoccupation with the self but, as Wordsworth probably knew, Rousseau's *Confessions* had done that before him. What was truly novel was that this preoccupation was expressed in poetry. His must, without question, be the monumental instance of autobiographical poetry.

6.3 *Autobiographical Drama*

I have perhaps laboured the point that we should be ready to find autobiography wherever language is being used. Even so unlikely a literary genre as drama shows this to be true. I am not speaking of that resolute and earnest pursuit of those who catch sight of Shakespeare's boyhood in *Henry IV Part One* and speculate on deep parallels between his late plays and his entry into a pessimistic phase. I have in mind more straightforward examples like Arnold Wesker's *Chicken Soup with Barley* (1959). The play is a dramatisation of his own family's devotion to communism (Jewish East End version) and the disillusion of the late fifties.

> Ronnie: What has happened to all the comrades, Sarah? I even blush when I use that word. Comrade! Why do I blush? Why do I feel ashamed to use words like democracy and freedom and brotherhood? They don't have meaning anymore. Remember all the writing that I did? I was going to be a great socialist writer. I can't make sense of a simple word. You look at me as if I'm talking in a foreign language. Didn't it hurt you to read about the murder of the Jewish anti-fascist committee in the Soviet Union? (p.71)

Wesker's own autobiography, *As Much as I Dare* (1994) puts the matter beyond doubt.

> My memory of how and why I wrote the play is clear. I had quarrelled with my mother over politics, raging at her continued adherence to communism... On two memorable occasions, after bitter exchanges, I wrote down what she said feeling them to be remarkable and moving declarations of faith. Written on different types of paper they must have come to me on two different occasions. I fused them into one speech... It's difficult to be certain which are her lines and which are mine. (p.495)

He goes on to quote the speech he wrote for the character Sarah which occurs in the last minutes of the play.

Let that suffice. I cite autobiographical drama as yet another instance of Sidonie Smith's insistence that, 'Autobiography is not so much a mode of literature as that literature is a mode of autobiography'.

7. Autobiography as Travellers' Tales

As a fourteen-year-old grammar school boy I read with my classmates RL Stevenson's *Travels with a Donkey*. And then we read Kinglake's *Eothen*, an account of travels in Egypt and the Middle East, a book of such huge reputation that in 1900 it was published in OUP's World Classics and in 1908 in Dent's Everyman's Library. Today you may easily find copies in second-hand bookshops but scarcely any secondary school student will have heard of it. We even had to read the opaque, for us, Elizabethan prose of Sir Francis Drake's *World Encompassed*, baffled as to why and how it had become a set text in a matriculation exam. As a Sixth Former I had to read Prosper Merimée's *Voyage en Espagne*. Somehow the processes of canonisation had given certain books of travel proper status as literature rather than declared to be in the twilight world of light-weight ephemera.

Today there is a vast corpus ranging from weighty tomes to brief articles, all of which are personal accounts by the authors of their travels. What in their diversity they share is that they are all parts of life-stories, whether portentous or trivial. They are licensed discourses, alluring their readers by virtue of their exoticism or authority. They all have stories of their own to tell, vouched for through personal experience. Some contemporary works have achieved the status of 'classics', like the books of Paul Theroux, Jonathan Raban and Bill Bryson. In Old English literature we find detailed accounts of the voyages of Othere and Wulfstan, but a new kind of travel literature is the account of the voyager himself. The Romantic Movement gave us a new figure, the walker in the countryside, like Wordsworth and Hazlitt, who strides across the hills and fields and tells us all about it. The Eighteenth Century established the travel book as serious literature and the Englishman and woman abroad became familiar figures (See Arthur Young's *Travels in France*, 1792; Smollett's *Travels through France and Italy*, 1766; Sterne's *A Sentimental Journey'* 1768); and, later, Mary Kingsley's *Travels in West Africa* (1897). Very soon we have the stories of globe-trotters and adventurers or sober accounts like Darwin's *Voyage of the Beagle* (1845).

8. Journalism as Reportage

Travel literature is often journalism in the sense that it sometimes appears in the daily/weekly press where personal accounts (first-hand, as we say) are legitimised as intimate insights into social and political reality. Journalistic accounts of personal experience, however, are not limited to travel, for journeys can invade any sphere. So acceptable is the first person account of almost anything that it sometimes becomes a formula for entering a topic. I reach for today's *Guardian* newspaper:

p.4 (A Dirty Day in Georgia)

By the time we hit the Interstate heading out of Atlanta my cabbie, Chuck, is in full flow. He tells me how four years ago he was shot in the head by a teen-age passenger who later said he had just wanted something to do. 'They gave him life plus twenty years'.

I learn about his own crack habit, his estrangement from his son and how his ex-wife is suffering emotionally 'in a pit of hell' over her loveless marriage to a richer man.

p.7 Last week I rang the American phone line by the Klan's subsidiary White Aryan Resistance and was startled to hear a recording of Bernie Grant, MP...

p.8 (One of its series on holiday romances) When I first saw Vincent, I was scooting around the Eastern Pyrenees, trying to find a way for its reputedly spectacular views. (continues for six columns).

p.6 An addict serving a long prison sentence sent this account of drug-taking in prison to *The Guardian*.

Despite many efforts to bring my addiction to an end, the sheer availability and the large number of addicts in prison mean that I consistently fail...

p.19 (from 'A Country Diary')

The first of this group (i.e.of hawk moths HR) with which I became familiar, was the Elephant Hawk which used to come to my bedroom when I was a boy... I saw my last specimens from a local garden a few years ago but my first adult specimen, with a wing span of five inches, was smitten fatally by a bedside bible when it entered a bedroom.

Not one of the products of a quick trawl in my copy of today's paper pretends to be a major piece of reportage. On-the-spot reporting from, for example, battlefields or natural and other catastrophes takes up the autobiographical mode. It can be very powerful and even influential. Journalists sent to a country as the paper's correspondent are expected to cover the important news stories but from time to time they will send in a personal piece about, let us say, their family's doings or daily living, which brings out the differences between their host country and home. There are political axes to grind and Causes to serve but many of these pieces are of the sort which are now dubbed 'human interest'.

It does not take long, a quick scanning, as I have shown, will suffice to establish the fact that the autobiographical now constitutes the very stuff of contemporary journalism

9. The Curriculum Vitae

At first glance the CV, turning up at this point, must seem like a very odd and boring outsider. Since it has been my intention all along to demonstrate that autobiographical activity embraces practices which had hitherto not been generally remarked upon, let me try to make clear why the CV is properly considered here. I have already cited in another context Lejeune allocating to the extreme pole of autobiography 'the banality of the curriculum vitae'. By banality Lejeune means to contrast it with 'poetic' autobiography. He makes the remark in passing, but for my purposes here the CV deserves much more serious attention. It has become an important, sometimes sinister and oppressive, institution, elicited at a seat of power from an applicant who is also a supplicant. It is for many an instrument for deciding life-chances and part of the process which has come to be known as gate-keeping.

Back in 1985 I presented a paper in Georgetown called 'The Autobiographical Impulse' (Rosen, 1988). It was my first attempt to open up the theme which I have been exploring in this work. I was very enthusiastic in arguing for the centrality, force and pervasiveness of autobiography, advocating it 'as one means of asserting our authority against institutionalised power'. I am now glad that I didn't let my advocacy run away with me completely and, in a concluding passage, I wrote:

> I do not wish to forget that alongside the autobiographical *impulse* there is the autobiographical compulse, of the courtroom, of the government inspector, of the attitude test, of the curriculum vitae, of the torture chamber. There are some very sinister people engaged in hermeneutics! We are not left free to limit our pasts to unpoliced crannies and congenial moments. Stand and deliver. There are many ways in which power attempts to wrest from us our past and use it for its own ends. Our autobiographies also figure in dossiers wrung from us as surely as were confessions by the Inquisition. Such invitations do not coax and tempt memory, for they surround it with caution, fear and even terror. (p.86)

All autobiography operates within very specific constraints – the reluctance to give offence to living persons, the deliberate omission of sensitive material, the effort to conform to an image, and so on. The autobiographer is always a self-censor and sometimes a very skilful one. But these constraints are as nothing compared with the hyper-careful composition of a CV, dominated as it is by an intense awareness of a particular kind of reader and what turns on its reception. If all autobiographers are concerned with what the world may think of them, the CV writer can think of nothing else. Broadly speaking the autobiographer engages in an optional activity. Yes, there are pressures such as when the great are called upon to give an account of themselves, usually towards the end of their careers when they are pressed to take off their masks. The call for a CV is, however, quite different. It is a peremptory demand to an applicant to compose in writing the course of his/her life within certain elaborate conventions which have become acceptable as a means of recruiting employees or screening those who are being appraised in their posts, perhaps for possible promotion. It has become part of the huge array of bureaucratic practices in institutions, ousting informal ones, moving, as ever, into codification and elaboration. Moreover, unlike the practices I have considered so far, it is always only the first phase in a longer process, possibly culminating in an interview. The interview extends the autobiographical process into an oral exchange which is usually a very asymmetrical occasion, sometimes grossly so (many interviewers, one candidate). It is worth remembering that to be asked about our pasts can be an innocuous or even a friendly gesture, whereas we need to be intensely aware of the fact that a single question on an immigration form, such as, what is your place of birth? or, at social security, who is the father of your child? can determine crucial decisions about your future made by the inter-rogators. It is no exaggeration to say that in our social world we are all subject to very modern forms of interrogation to which we must respond in writing, whether it is the CV, the application for a driving licence or an insurance company's probings into our medical histories. I am therefore taking the CV as paradigmatic.

In the CV process there is a disparity between reader and writer which is clear to both. The writer is under considerable pressure to outwit the reader and plays this serious game by suppression and possibly lying just as the reader plays his/her part in the game by trying to penetrate the writer's disguises, evasions, distortions and highly calculated displays. It is a war of wits in which each side needs to deploy special skills. but one in which the interrogating side is usually better armed and better trained.

The CV, until very recently, scarcely received a mention in the studies of autobiography mainly because of the tunnel vision of those studies. When in 1993 the British Sociology Association devoted a special issue of *Sociology* (vol 27, no 1) to what they call 'auto/biography' it signalled, somewhat late in the day, that institutional sociology had become fascinated by a topic which had preoccupied workers in other disciplines for twenty years or more. In the 1993 collection there is a short paper on the CV entitled, 'Called to Account: the CV as an Autobiographical Practice' by Nod Miller and David Morgan. They approached the topic through the study of academic CVs and, as they emphasise, the specific contexts in which they are elicited. The authors' view of the CV is that it is, 'part of an overall system of institutional surveillance and rationalisation' and therefore must be seen as functioning within 'the dialectics of power in modern institutions'. They draw heavily, and perhaps inevitably, on Goffman (1971) and his ideas of 'the presentation of self and impression management'. This leads them to say,

> ...the CV like any other administrative document is never complete: it is always open-ended. Others are encouraged to read the gaps or listen to the silences. (p.135)

Their analysis proposes that CVs are 'clearly and increasingly rule-governed' and that they are different from the conventional structure of auto/biographies in as much as they break from conventional accounts.

> ...conventional understandings of a life course are fragmented according to administrative considerations. (p.136)

Looking at the CV from the writer's end, they quote Goffman (1971),

> ...many performers have ample capacity to misrepresent the facts; only shame, guilt or fear prevent them from doing so. (p.65)

Further, of a little experiment, they write,

> In questioning each other on our respective CVs, we invited ourselves 'to spot the whopper'. While we both failed in this task, further questioning did reveal some economies with the truth and one of the authors revealed being given the, doubtless, informal advice that 'what you need is some whopper training'.

It is above all the radical change of context which makes the CV and its bureaucratic cousins sharply contrast with the kind of life histories which routinely receive attention. It is one of the best examples of how diverse are the practices of telling our pasts. No full account of autobiographical acts can ignore CVs. Further, it may be that works I have called memoirs have a distant resemblance to them, however slight, doctored as many are to evoke assenting admiration for public deeds. But they do not, it is true, serve the writer as a manoeuvre for a job or promotion but rather for a path to glory itself.

10. Professional Testimony

Makarenko's *Road to Life* (1951) is an account of the foundation and highly successful development of a residential school for delinquents ('the colony'), set up with minimum resources in the midst of the famine and the chaos in the Ukraine immediately after the Russian Revolution of 1917. It is above all an educational work. Makarenko is centrally concerned to vindi-cate and promote the kinds of methods he developed with youngsters who had murdered and engaged in banditry on trains, in fact been involved in every conceivable kind of crime. He could easily have written, and written well, an educational work of the familiar kind which set out his principles and their origins in pedagogic, social and political theory. An impersonal account of the colony might have followed which documented the process of putting these principles into practice, obstacles encountered and overcome, changes of direction. The pattern of that genre is immediately recognisable. There are whole libraries full of that kind of work. Makarenko's account is of another kind, just as recognisable and particularly suited to a man of his literary talent. It's an intensely personal account of the running of the colony, developed through a set of highly dramatic narratives and marked by restraint in the use of purely educational discussion and routine drawing of conclusions. Post-revolutionary Russia and Bolshevik officialdom in particular is always knocking at the door and the colony is never presented as an oasis of utopian practice in a dangerous and bureaucratic world.

Makarenko sub-titled his book *A Poem of Education*. It certainly is, but within certain significant autobiographical limitations. His own involvement is intense. Nevertheless there are major aspects of his personal life which are never mentioned since they are clearly not considered relevant to his account.

This kind of autobiographical writing is not rare, that is, people writing of their working lives with deliberate didactic intent, but this intent is realised by virtue of the means they deploy. They are saying to us, this is what it is like to live through the experience of being a doctor, a miner, a nurse, a research scientist. There must be a special meaning behind the fact that many of the best known of these accounts are by teachers. I would guess that they are demonstrating what many teachers can be heard saying: that grandiose pronouncements and impressive theorising must be ruthlessly tested in the lived-through complexities and unpredictabilities of the classroom and of school life. Though beliefs may be made explicit (often they are not) and impassioned arguments may burst into the text, they usually let their stories, descriptions and intimate observations deliver their philosophies, intellectual credos, educational stance, leaving them inscribed in a continuous sub-text.

CHAPTER THREE

THE LANDSCAPE OF AUTOBIOGRAPHY:
II. SPOKEN AUTOBIOGRAPHICAL ACTS

The character of autobiography, wrote Todorov, 'comes from the speech-act which is at its base: to tell a story about oneself'. When writers set out to trace the origins of autobiography, naturally they follow the procedure of combing through written records. They may take us back to St Augustine or, like Bakhtin, as far back as classical times. It is always assumed, as far as I can tell, that autobiography is yet another intellectual and literary triumph for European man (eventually woman, too). This blinkered view which we meet in other fields goes much deeper than a kind of Ptolemaic cultural geography. The love of libraries, archives and manuscripts has turned many scholars stone deaf, for they do not hear the autobiographical acts which are an abiding feature of everyone's conversation the world over. Perhaps they do hear but, if so, they cannot believe them to be of any great importance for they never speak of them. It is an unfortunate deafness, for the birth of autobiography must surely have been in the discourses of conversation. The 'articulate mammal' must speak his/her past and listen to others doing the same, frequently exchanging pasts with others. This may seem like a narcissistic indulgence, but it is beyond doubt a working resource for a community, indissolubly incorporated in the bedrock of social interaction.

Linguists have always insisted on what they call the primacy of speech, pointing out that it takes precedence over writing, phylogenetically and ontogenetically. In practice, scriptism dies hard and the exemplar sentences which they used as data were usually written forms, often concocted by themselves. Nevertheless, serious concern for the spoken rather than the written did start with linguists even if, for a long time, they were so dazzled by the grammar of the sentence that they ignored the structure of texts, including spoken ones. It goes without saying that literary scholars have cloth ears in this matter. Small wonder, then, that autobiographical speech received so little attention in spite of the fact that a short spell of listening to any group of intimates busy with their spontaneous interchanges uncovers for us a frequent shifting into autobiographical mode. Any anatomy of conversation must include this feature of it. It needs no academic ear to hear this. Indeed, just as we all learn to engage in conversation with minimum explicit instruction, so, as an intrinsic part of that very process, we acquire the essential skills for kinds of oral autobiography from substantial mono-logues to fragmentary irruptions in the flow of talk. It is an indispensible part of what Dell Hymes (1971) called 'communicative competence', a mostly tacit awareness of the social rules governing the production of speech. You need to know how your own community handles such things. Shirley Bryce Heath in *Ways with Words* (1983) showed that the black com-munity of Tracton and the white community of Roadville had quite different ways of telling stories of personal experience. Tracton believed in the inventive embellishment of the facts and Roadville in the sanctity of them.

It is a nice question to ask what social rules permit us to elicit autobiography, to make what amounts to the invasive request, 'Tell me about your life' or, more simply, 'Tell me what happened'. And what are the rules which allow someone to proffer the autobiographical 'Let me tell you about my life' or 'This is what happened to me'? By the same token *how* we choose to tell of our pasts or elicit the pasts of others changes as the situation changes, when, for example, the level of formality shifts up or down or when the setting becomes more public or when there is a marked asymmetry of power among the participants. Lapel-grabbing threatens social equilibrium. The Ancient Mariner was taking chances. Most of us cannot rely on the mesmeric power of a long grey beard and glittering eye.

Everyday speech is common stuff, by definition. To accord it respectful attention seems almost a perversity to those who believe that only the written language can carry the highest order of the articulation of the socio-personal self. For others, myself included, there is a potential for a remarkable demotic eloquence which can be triggered at certain critical moments (see Rosen, 1975). There is no need to be naively romantic about this. There is solid evidence. No less a person than the socio-linguist, William Labov, (1972) whose book, *Language in the Inner City*, has become a definitive starting point of vernacular language studies, remarked of the stories of personal experience told by black teenagers,

> Many of the narratives cited here rise to a very high level of competence; when they are quoted in the exact words of the speaker, they will command the total attention of an audience in a remarkable way, creating a deep and attentive silence that is never found in academic or political discussion. The reaction of listeners to these narratives seems to demonstrate that the most highly evaluated form of language is that which translates our experience into dramatic form. (p.396)

The tape recorder provided the technology for his close analysis of those stories. It gave a special and widely available impulse to *elicitation*, that is, as a research tool or a political act of faith or both. For whereas autobiographical acts crop up spontaneously and die out in thin air, the tape recorder, it turns out, has made possible the highly conscious drawing out and preservation of life stories from people who have never before articulated these experiences or encountered those willing to listen to them with respect. In a simple phrase we say, they are finding their voices. But often they are breaking through a tongue-tied silence, an act of massive social significance. Voices are not found easily by all those oppressed and muffled in their world. It is the oral historians above all who have opened up the politics of oral life stories; to them I shall return.

A final introductory remark. I have at this point shifted from the written to the spoken, from the permanence and prestige of the printed page to the ephemeral breath of speech. It must seem I have crossed a frontier from one universe to another. Yet some written language easily converts to spoken forms. Spoken words can be taped, transcribed and appear in print. Whole books have been created in that way. I myself have written personal stories and then delivered them as spoken ones. I have also told stories of my childhood for many years and recently made written versions of them. The solid wall between the two modes often dissolves, once again warning us not to be too respectful of boundaries even if we have drawn them ourselves. Bearing that in mind as an important caveat, I shall now set out the major forms of oral autobiographical acts, noting where there are parallels with written ones. It is in the very constitution of the written language that it is more easily patrolled, policed and determined by authorities. The genre guardians do their best to bully and cajole. Speech is less susceptible to control. Categories are looser and more easily mixed.

1. Attempts to speak a life

There are not many occasions when, in the course of spontaneous conversation, a space is cleared by common consent for someone to tell his/her life story. Conversational time is rationed by subtle, tacit (for the most part) understandings and procedures. This does not mean that everyone gets an equal share but it does mean that no one can lay claim to much more than the cultural code normally provides for. Is there room for someone settling down to tell the whole of a life story? I suppose we get close to it when a refugee, a survivor, an exotic is accorded special licence. The rare spellbinder gets a special dispensation. Substantial spoken life stories are told in particular circumstances, though it is a common device of fiction from the eighteenth century onwards to have a character telling a novel's worth of life story. It may be that I am wrong and that more often than I supposed or have observed it does occur. However, there have arisen certain contemporary practices, made possible by technical gadgetry, which have produced life stories of considerable length. We are, in short, encountering new forms of autobiography. The *Face-to-Face* format of the BBC makes it possible for Michael Grade to sit opposite the novelist Joseph Heller and, with minimal gentle probing, have him tell his life story in about an hour, taking us through his childhood in Brooklyn, to his war years as a bombardier and on to university education, a job as a copywriter for an advertising agency and finally, after severe illness, to fame as an internationally-known novelist. There are well-known TV variants in which famous people offer us their lives, revisiting in talk and image the places where they grew up, worked and played. So-called chat shows often contain truncated versions. There are even moments when these new forms make it possible for voices or voices with images to enable us to hear someone who is very non-famous telling a life story. At the same time someone like Heller, not lacking a huge potential audience of readers, is happy to use the new form to tell his life orally.

Lejeune notes the contrast between Jean-Paul Sartre's autobiography, *Les Mots* (1964), and Sartre talking about his life on film in *Sartre par Lui-meme,*

> I especially noticed that, when Sartre was recounting his life orally, he was talking like everyone else. (p.132)

The new form, the recorded and transcribed oral life story, inevitably raises problems. A paternalistic transcriber easily slips into 'editing', shifting the thrust of the narrative and tampering with the meanings of the speaker. Studs Terkel, a deservedly celebrity figure nowadays, undoubtedly has a very high degree of sympathy with those whom he records. Nevertheless he clearly feels obliged to turn their speech into written prose (see, for example, *Division Street America*, 1966, and *Working,* 1972). And Lejeune cites the instance of a left-wing academic editor who massages the story of a militant who has not quite conformed to the orthodoxy of how a militant should behave and think. 'The controlled classes,' says Pierre Bourdieu pessimistically, 'do not speak, they are spoken.' I think many of the oral historians, socio-linguists, ethnographers and others have shown him to be wrong. He does, however, pin-point the hazards of sponsored texts and the mid-wifery of those who have their own motives for manipulating the spoken texts.

The Children of Sanchez (1962) is one of the most celebrated and successful instances of the publishing of oral autobiography. It contains certain unique features. Firstly, it consists of five oral autobiographies by members of a Mexican family who are described as being from the urban poor. Secondly, there is a special system of dealing with the taped material. The editor/scholar, Oscar Lewis, offers this description of it.

> In this volume I offer the reader a deeper look into the lives of one of these families (i.e. the five families he has already documented in an earlier study H.R.) by the use of a new technique whereby each member of the family tells his own life-story in his own words. The approach gives us a cumulative, multi-faceted, panoramic view of each individual... (p.xi)

I am inclined to believe that Lewis did everything in his power to respect the testimony of his autobiographers, but we have to note that he feels obliged to use his editorial powers in order to turn his tapes into acceptable written prose, as he scrupulously tells us.

> In preparing the interviews for publication, I have eliminated my questions and have selected, arranged, and organised their materials into coherent life-stories... I believe this in no way reduces the authenticity of the data or their usefulness for science... The editing has been more extensive in some cases than others. (p.xxi)

That makes very clear the extent to which the tapes have been 'managed'. Lewis is over-optimistic in thinking that this intervention has not affected the 'authenticity' of his material. Whose notion of coherence is being used as a criterion? In any case, incoherence, or an alternative kind of coherence is itself a significant part of the data. It is as though oral material is essentially deficient but can be made to conform to certain criteria of literate prose before it can pass through the admission door. Some of Lewis's emendation is, no doubt, a consequence of the heavy loss of the rich resources of the human voice, though he does not say so. The most scrupulous transcription leaks. 'Selected, arranged and organised' is heavy treatment which leads to important features of the orality of the original being eliminated, though no doubt this made for a much more readable book.

I have brandished oral history several times and I propose to deal with it more fully later when I discuss the main contributors to our understanding of autobiographical acts. For the moment I want to note that it is the oral historians who, more than any other group, have put before us spoken life stories. They are, of course, researcher historians who began by seeing their work as the tapping of a new rich source of evidence from the mouths of hitherto unheard witnesses. Joanna Bornat in 'Is Oral History Auto/bio-graphy' (1994) offers us Frisch's definition (1990) as her preferred view of oral history.

> ...a powerful tool for discovering, exploring and evaluating the nature of the process of historical memory – how people make sense of their past, how they connect individual experience and its social context, how the past becomes part of the present, and how people use it to interpret their lives and the world around them. (p.188)

A good working definition perhaps but nowhere does it touch on what might be uniquely *oral* about oral history. Further on in her paper Joanna Bornat does so in order to 'value aspects of performance within oral history.'

> Narrators play out what are dramatic roles. They 'take the floor' and act as if the tape recorder is not there while they tell their stories, develop narratives or simply answer questions. (p.23)

There still seems to be something missing. Talking is not writing. It arises from a face-to-face interaction with the questioner, provoker, eliciter and, however little the latter contributes, what emerges is powerfully affected. We know, too, that speakers have at their disposal a rich repertoire of resources, not dwelt on by Oscar Lewis, with which to deliver ideas and feelings which are not available to a writer – rate of speech, pauses, pitch, volume, intonation, forms of articulation (throatiness, etc) and a body language with its repertoire of gesture and facial expressiveness. Even that does not exhaust the possibilities; consider humming and hawing, kinds of laughter and the range of sounds which we call exclamations. Many more people can draw on all this than can draw on a confident literary expressiveness, particularly those for whom the written language is elusive and even threatening. Writer's block, sadly, is a very common ailment. Oral historians, therefore, can draw on testimony which is articulated through a medium that has its own special resources for orchestrating meaning. We must ask, too, as Frisch hints, what the providers of oral history believe they are doing when they consent to speak their autobiographies. What's in it for them? It took oral historians some time to become aware of the need for an honest reciprocity rather than a self-serving tapping of a new reservoir of documentation. There are many oral historians who see the very act of telling a life as a liberating means of changing oneself. In the early stages of their enterprise both they and their detractors were preoccupied, obsessed even, with the reliability of the evidence accumulating on tape. The question always hovering over autobiography of all sorts has now been changed as the transformations worked by tellers are recognised as important and creative ways of composing myths.

I return to Joanna Bornat's paper. She offers a political view of oral autobiography as it was conceived in the late Sixties.

> The origins of oral history in Britain lie in that period of the late 1960s with those who, in the main, identified themselves with social and political change. It traces its roots back to areas of research and teaching which challenged the established order of things... (p.24)

> Oral history developed under the influence of a modernist belief in the possibility of future change and with commitment to a particular kind of change. To give it the label 'socialist' today is to pronounce an academic exclusion order. However its leading protagonists clearly identified themselves with socialist traditions of explanation and change, and most probably still do. (p.25)

It is just that commitment which puts a vast distance between the kinds of understandings developed around oral life stories which emerge from the oral history movement and those which we encounter in the analysis of written autobiography. The politics of the written mode are just beginning to emerge (see, for example Julia Watson, 1993). It is only to be expected that a discourse which is preoccupied with the self would have a special allure for those who see it as the licensed medium for predominantly individual rather than social concerns. To be attentive to the comparison and assessment of texts of identity in the modern western world is to be engaged in a struggle with a single dominant kind of text which gives centrality and sovereignty to the individual.

I have given precedence to committed oral historians and their project of collecting oral life stories not simply as an historical research tool but as a means of changing political and social life. However, they are not the only ones to collect spoken life stories. You could perhaps say that we all do it, interested as we are in what people have done and how they see their lives. Some like to collect oral stories of the past as a teaching resource and there are those who collect them in much the same way as others collect physical bygones, shepherds' crooks, bread crocks and Dinky toys. Which is innocent enough but there are now scholars who are interested in how people *speak* of their lives. We can find in *Texts of Identity* (1989) not only an approach which breaks new ground but a diversity of contributors from psychology, sociology, the philosophy of science, Jungian analysis, interdisciplinary social sciences and folklore. There are others, too. Psychoanalysts set out to listen to a life story and perhaps to change it. Roy Shafer (1976) claims that psychoanalytic therapy involves a restructuring of a person's sense of the past so that it would make a more cohesive narrative.

The spoken-out-loud life story is the antithesis of the locked diary and the stored-away hand-written text. It is public and interactive and 'requires linguistic skills derived from the traditions of explanations and storytelling within a culture, and which issues in a narrative that owes its meaning ultimately to the interpretative practices of a community of speakers'. (p.219).

2. Framed episodes
In our waking lives most of us spend a lot of time in talking with others. Call it spontaneous conversation or just talk. The word spontaneous suggests there is an absence of a fixed agenda and defined goals and that what is spoken is unrehearsed and free from constraints, which might operate to make it inhibited and, to use Labov's word, careful. We compose as we go. It's a matter of degree, of course, but there are obvious differences between talking with a group of close old friends and a group of fellow students encountered for the first time in an adult education class. All talk has its constraints but it's not for nothing that we speak of loosening our tongues. Loosened tongues busy with conversation take to telling anecdotes, stories of personal experience, which are taken for granted as a move in the talk because they are socially endorsed features of it. Nevertheless they are also perceived as being in some important ways different from the talk in which they are embedded. To embark on such narratives usually means that we must signal our intention to do so, may be with a prefatory marker ('I've never told anyone this before...'); or it may be by the semantics and grammar

of an opening utterance ('When I was ten I did a wicked thing to my brother...'). Once launched, we must operate within the structures, strategies and tactics which our community thinks proper for this kind of telling. The story is strongly framed and the episode drawn from the past takes the listeners into another world, just as fiction does. Mostly these stories could, as it were, be snipped out and presented as free-standing tales. They are the oral equivalent of the short story.

Tellers of these stories have often told them many times before and polished them lovingly. In this way they achieve canonical form, changing only minimally from performance to performance in the light of feed-back from many tellings. Whole utterances remain unchanged. In families these stories become part of the household folklore and are retold by other members. Nevertheless it may be that the story is being given its first airing and it may prove to be the last one. There is an important aesthetic at work here, for listeners always have a keen awareness of the degree of virtuosity the teller is deploying. The 'gift of the gab' often means a talent for storytelling. Yet there's a crucial corollary needed here for the understanding of auto-biographical discourse. Recognised virtuosi there may be, but anyone may command rapt attention, especially if the tale touches the deepest feelings of the listeners or speaks with the sharpest relevance to their social condition.

The teller must also take chances, for he/she has to challenge for conversa-tional space and interrupt the normal flow of turn-taking. Moreover, there are always potentially hostile listeners. So it is that anecdotal storytellers deploy a range of tactics to avert rejection, boredom and inattention. Once again we can note the difference between the oral and the written. Impro-visation can place a speaker, as distinct from a writer, at a disadvantage but paradoxically it can also be a strength.

> The tactics of the *oral* storyteller, whose audience is in *praesentia*, are deter-mined by the phenomena of feedback: thus, the 'same' story may be long or short, elaborate and digressive or brief and to the point, ornamented or plain, according to the narrator's sense of audience reaction. In this sense the story is truly the result of a collaboration or at least of a negotiation, and the good story-teller is one who has the flexibility to make necessary adjustments in different circumstances, for different audiences and − for the same audience as the narrative proceeds. (Chambers, 1984, p.220)

The feedback, ranging from small indications of response like mutters, chuckles and fidgets to out-and-out interruptions, makes adjustments pos-sible in the very process of telling. There is a whole world of discourse with subtle variations which surrounds the story of personal experience. Everyone has some awareness of how it works or fails to work but, as yet, it has not had the detailed attention it deserves.

3. The oral story subordinated to conversational goals

The stories I have called Framed Episodes belong in conversations with no fixed agenda or defined goals. They are therefore different from stories which are entirely subordinate to the general goals of a conversation. It is no longer a matter of the storyteller presenting a tale believed to have intrinsic interest, a kind of offering in the midst of a conversation which could take any direction and wanders unpredictably, though it may serve powerful social functions like knitting the group together or contributing to its collective memory. A story under the rubric in this section, personal though it is, may further an argument, furnish an instance, shift a debate from the abstract to the concrete, provide evidence of personal involvement in the topic being pursued. It enters under the banner of authenticity and the validity of life experience but in this context it is always, in Kenneth Burke's phrase, a representative anecdote, standing as it does for its subtext of general statement. It is one contribution to a general collaborative effort.

The oral story of this sort, is commonly encountered in group interchanges of many different kinds. I think at once of families or groups of friends trying to settle controversial questions of the day, interpersonal practices, party politics and the like. We can recognise them immediately as having a strong resemblance to a personal experience story which also occurs in monologic discourse, an institutionalised holding of the floor – lectures, speeches, moral harangues. In sermons it has been at home for a very long time: the personal experience becomes a parable. Goffman in *Forms of Talk* (1981) adopts a sceptical, if not cynical, tone as though every tactic employed by a lecturer is cunningly calculated and manipulative.

> Take as a heavy-handed example the parenthetically interjected anecdote. It is told in a manner to imply that its telling was not planned, but that the story has now become so a propos that the speaker cannot forbear recounting it even at the cost of a minor digression. (p.178)

Goffman takes no account of speakers who make no pretence of digressing but whose strategy is unapologetically anecdotal and for whom it is a normal part of their idiom and rhetorical strategy. It is their way of speaking, often inherited from and endorsed by their cultural community. Nor does he make any attempt to relate the lecturer's 'interjected anecdote' to the common discursive practice of using stories of personal experience as a resource available to any participant who is aware of its persuasive power. In any discussion in which ideas and decisions are being explored and where disagreements can flare up, speakers persist in believing their individual experience to be relevant, happily unaware that 'anecdotage' in academic circles is thought to lower the level of discussion and to be insufficiently theoretical. There is a clear analogy here to genre control in written forms.

4. Oral personal story on demand or under duress

The curriculum vitae, a written form of life story which I have already discussed, has as its complement the interview. Like the CV, the interview is now a practice experienced by many more people than hitherto. There are two contending forces at work in an interview which is most often felt by interviewees as a gruelling experience. The interviewers in pursuing their goal try to read the CV in such a way as to delve below its surface in order to get at matters not yet revealed to them, especially if, as is normally the case, they have some awareness of how CVs can be manipulated and doctored. They try to detect silences, distortions, exaggerations and downright inventions. They may, however, feel that the interviewee has not done him or herself justice and try to probe for unstated achievements and relevant experience. On the other hand, knowing full well that the initiative in the dialogue is in the hands of others, the interviewee has still to struggle to keep presenting a favourable image. The dialogue is often a battle of wits in which one side is usually more heavily armoured than the other.

In the course of this now very ritualised procedure the interviewees may be called upon to tell the story of a particular period in their lives. Let me invent an example.

> Mr Robins, in 1989 you left a senior post with Mummerset County Council to take a much less responsible one with a small authority. How did that come about?

or

> I notice, Mrs Simmons, there is a gap in your CV from 1986 to 1987. Could you fill that in for us?

If such instances make too much of the oppressive elements there should be added to this category of life story contributed under demand or duress the formal religious confession, courtroom testimony and official interrogations of all kinds. All are reminders of how widely and deeply autobiographical discourse penetrates the fabric of society and ranges from gift to extortion. There is a nice irony in the fact that when we say someone 'has a past' we mean there is something disreputable or shady in it which will only be revealed when the sinner repents or force majeure elicits it.

The minimal autobiographical utterance

The least regarded, the least studied form of autobiographical acts is the single utterance, which while it is itself not a story, points to a larger narrative. Although it scarcely gets a passing mention it is the most pervasive of autobiographical acts, exemplifying more than any other kinds of text the inescapable, always present autobiographical-ness of spoken discourse. While some would see this as the ego asserting its right to have its say, I see it rather as a speaker's claim to valid membership of some kind of community or even paradoxically, in some instances, rejection of it.

We could perhaps say that these utterances are the shortest, most compressed and compact tales. They are the single crucial lines of a song that never gets sung. They are cryptic, inasmuch as they can only be deciphered by a strong intuition of the invisible tale which has not been told, the shape of which is a ghost, positioned behind the solidity of a handful of words. If I say, as I often have done, 'My grandmother was a steely woman', friends listening will know, narrative-minded creatures that they are, that a whole cluster of tales is yet to be told, a set of sub-texts which are the storied instances of my grandmother's steeliness. Yet on this occasion I do not tell a single one of them, which leaves this utterance reduced to an almost subliminal flicker in the talk. How does this come about?

It may be that is all the speaker wants to say at the moment, i.e. my grandmother's steeliness is a sufficient comment to counterpose to other remarks which have tended to glorify the grandparental role. Or the speaker does not get a chance to say more. The talk sweeps past and leaves no room for him/her to get into full stride. Or the speaker had hoped for signals of encouragement which were never hoisted. Or the speaker is simply not ready to develop the full story or is not certain how to do so. Perhaps memory has not yet done its work and delivered the detail and may never do so: all the speaker has available is the precipitation from memory of a general summarising word or two.

These apparently light-weight words which come and go so quickly can only be accorded their proper importance by placing them at the end of the broad spectrum of all autobiographical acts. There they serve to remind us that they too demonstrate, however infinitesimally, the human disposition to narratise personal experience using its own unique methods to contribute towards the creation of nothing less than a cognitive, emotional, moral and social world.

* * * *

I have divided the terrain into spoken and written forms, an accepted way of looking at language. We speak nowadays of oracy and literacy. Yet we know that the written is often spoken – speeches, lectures and even apparently spontaneous talk which is in fact a reading from a text, from notes or from the autocue. Similarly what was originally spoken may end up as written text, with or without editorial tampering. Autobiography is no exception, for it can easily slip across the frontier from one modality to the other. I can vouch for that, since I have myself done some frontier crossing, putting into print (Rosen, 1993) autobiographical stories which I have told for many years and recrossing by telling those stories, influenced inevitably by the written version. Audio and video recordings have created a new means of presenting autobiography. Transcriptions from tape can be published to create whole books, as I have shown above.

As I established my categories I was always mindful of Derrida's warning words

> ...as soon as the word 'genre' is sounded, as soon as it is heard, as soon as one attempts to conceive it, a limit is drawn. And when a limit is established, norms and interdictions are not far behind. (1978, p.4)

So my laying out of the field with its suggestions of boundaries should be read as an invitation to others to make adjustments and challenge its distinctions.

CHAPTER FOUR

KEY STUDIES OF AUTOBIOGRAPHICAL DISCOURSE

Who owns autobiography, academically speaking? For a long time there were no eager claimants. On the contrary, in the nineteenth century there were scholarly voices which warned against the vanity and banality inherent in the activity and the danger of its being invaded by mercenary mountebanks, including, of all people, members of the lower classes, women 'and an innumerable host of hungry pretenders'. Laura Marcus (1994) cites a Blackwood's reviewer who attempted to curdle the blood of respectable folk:

> ...the very name of autobiography will, we apprehend, erelong, be loathingly rejected in the drawing room as fit only for the kitchen or the servants' hall (p.32)

The only way to hold at arm's length this growing band of trespassers was to single out a few works of genius whose authors' names occur and re-occur in the long history of the discussion of autobiography. The problem has always been, 'How can we define it in so tight a manner that we could keep out the hoi-polloi and recruit it as a worthy object of discussion?'. The disreputable penumbra which surrounded it, its infuriating diversity and elusiveness postponed until recently its full acceptance in the academy in spite of the fact that individual scholars had given it weighty attention.

'Autobiographical Studies' as they are now called are a recent invention but in spite of the apparent interdisciplinary promise of that title most studies emerge from the English departments of universities, almost always in the United States. Many of these studies have been published only in the last five years or so and some of them are major contributions to the subject but this academic location of autobiographical acts has skewed the attention to certain works and led to a total neglect of many acts, especially spoken ones. Academic departments are notoriously expansionist, perhaps none more so than in the discipline we call English which has absorbed autobiography with scarcely a hiccup.

In contrast, it is my purpose in this chapter to show that autobiography has become a preoccupation in other disciplines – psychology, sociology, ethnography, and oral history. Indeed, some of the most recent work proclaims that the field is now devoted to an increasingly trans-disciplinary practice. However, the well-established near-monopoly exercised by scholars in English is not easily breached. Laura Marcus's book, *Auto/biographical Discourses* (1994) is the most comprehensive analytical survey of the history of the study (mostly in English) of autobiography and the state of contemporary discussion. She describes the scope of her work in this way:

> The focus is primarily on work in literary studies, although the boundaries between this area and more historical, cultural and sociological work, loosely grouped under the category 'life studies' has become more open. (p.179)

The focus on literary studies is not surprising, for that is exactly where she is coming from. It would be ungenerous not to acknowledge that her book shows a breadth of resources not normally found in literary scholarship. Yet, in a frank admission, she tells us that 'recently Paul Thompson has introduced me to the world of oral history and life stories'. Small wonder then that oral history earns no more than a paragraph in her book – this in 1994!

Even in a would-be avant garde work like *Autobiography and Post-Modernism* (Gilmore and Peters, 1994) eight of the eleven contributors are professors of English. Yet in this very book, the mostly challenging piece by a long way comes from an anthropologist, Michael Fischer, 'Autobiographical Voices (1,2,3) and Mosaic Memory: Experimental Sondages in the (Post)modern World':

> Sondage is the archaeologists' Francophone term for 'soundings', for the search techniques of an exploratory dig...efforts to listen to the many kinds of voicings in autobiographical forms that might on the one hand be the ways genres of autobiography are recognised (beyond for instance the fairly narrow master

narratives of Western individualism, or universalising theories of individuation-maturation, which studies of autobiography are so often used to celebrate, innocent of any effort at serious cross-cultural validation) and on the other hand provide clues for keeping social and cultural theory abreast of a rapidly changing and pluralising world. (p80)

Fischer's sondages lead him to look at the autobiographies of five scientists and a philosopher of science. Fischer's 'voicings' should be heard as one of the other ways of talking about autobiography, in this case from anthropology.

* * * *

That preamble points the way to my strategy in this chapter. I want to present to readers those studies which give a clear indication of the breadth of current work that must inevitably include literary theory but go far beyond it to works of quite different provenance which look at autobiographical acts rather than just autobiographies from other vantage points. It is not my intention at this point to survey the literature in a comprehensive manner for which the best starting point is Laura Marcus. Instead I have selected four areas and from each of them selected a study (in one case, two) which I believe to be good launching pads for looking at related work. The layout of the chapter from now on looks like this:

- *Literary criticism and literary theory*: the work of Philippe Lejeune in the volume *On Autobiography* (1989) which is a selection from his work, originally in French, edited by Paul John Eakin.

- *An ethnographic study*: Richard Bauman's *Story, Performance and Event* (1986) which is based entirely on a corpus of contemporary oral stories.

- *A psychological study*: Jerome Bruner's *Acts of Meaning* (1990) and his related papers.

- *Cultural studies and oral history*: R. Samuel and P. Thompson,eds, *The Myths We Live By* (1990) and P.Thompson *The Voice of the Past* (1988)

1. Literary Criticism/Theory:
Lejeune P. 'On autobiography' (1989)

I have already drawn briefly on the work of Philippe Lejeune but here I want to single him out for closer attention. The short history of his sponsored insertion into the world of literary criticism/theory might tell us something about which non-Anglophone scholars are selected for translation and promotion at a given moment. As Edward Said (1993) insists,

> The modern history of literary study has been bound up with the development of cultural nationalism, whose aim was first to distinguish the national canon, then to maintain its eminence, authority and aesthetic autonomy. (p.384,1993)

The first and only attempt to put before an English-reading public Lejeune's work was not a translation of one of his books but a substantial selection from them edited by Paul John Eakin and this in spite of the traffic (mostly one-way) in French literary theory and its gurus which so intoxicated the English-speaking world of literary studies – Barthes, Genette, Derrida and others. – from the Seventies onwards. Yet he had published five major studies of autobiography and many papers from 1971: *L'Autobiographie en France* (1971), *Le Pacte Autobiographique* (1975), *Lire Leiris* (1975), *Je Suis un Autre* (1980), *Moi Aussi,* (1986). In the proliferating literature on autobiography since 1980, it is customary to refer with admiration and reverence to Olney's *Autobiography: Essays Theoretical and Critical* (1980 Princeton University Press) and to designate it as a major landmark in autobiographical studies. This must be because in it there were gathered together for the first time commissioned essays by scholars of great repute. Yet in it there are only the briefest references to Lejeune's work which are no more than honorific and bibliographic, a line or two here and there.

I choose to single out Lejeune from the tradition of autobiographical studies not because he is typical but, on the contrary, because, although he began by being deeply entrenched in the world of literary criticism, unusually his studies took him towards a wider and wider view of what constituted autobiography. This gives a reader the pleasure of the rare sight of an academic repeatedly revising, adjusting, changing until he emerges as the only writer in the field with an embrace which is hospitable to every kind of autobiographical act. Lejeune cured himself of that dominant disposition to regard autobiography as an intensely restricted literary practice. Step by step he radically revised his position until he eventually saw it as a universal creative human activity, taking many different forms. Finally he arrived at the position where he observed that what some do with their pens others do with their mouths and he committed himself enthusiastically to everyday manifestations of life-stories. How great a leap this was may be gathered by juxtaposing the dominant view and Lejeune's. Here is John Sturrock in *The Language of Autobiography* (1993),

> If it is the case, then, that the twenty-five or so canonical autobiographies studied here in extenso reveal a certain convergence, in what does that certain convergence lie? Above all, in the determination with which everyone of these writers marks him or herself off from other people, as an individual who has come to distinction in his life by his or her own efforts and the exercise of an essentially natural endowment. The autobiographical hero rises and in order to do so breaks ranks with the stage army of the anonymous, or that un-differentiated human mass whose members may be assumed to have no story to tell. (p.289)

Readers will have noticed that my book pursues exactly the opposite thesis, namely that the 'human mass', that telling phrase, is made up of people, every one of whom may be assumed to have a story to tell, as brilliant recordists like the late Charles Parker and Studs Terkel have shown. Indeed, Charles Parker once said to my own students, 'Everyone has a story to tell. The only matter in doubt is whether they are willing to tell it to you. I could stop any passer-by in the street and he would have a story'. When chal-lenged, he went out into the street (we were on the ground floor, and watch-ing), took the first passer-by, a uniformed University messenger, and demonstrated his point. When Parker asked him, after five minutes of desultory chatter, why he never smiled, there followed a lengthy account of a series of mismanaged operations around his mouth. 'How can people know I'm smiling inside, if they can't see it on my face?' he asked. Lejeune left behind the Sturrockses and ended up alongside the Parkers.

> I loved the immensity of the field that was opening up before me... Nothing about the field is narrow or limited. Around 1972 I was interested almost exclusively in masterpieces. Today I am involved with something quite different which surely I could not have foreseen. I had become democratised: it is the life of everyone which interests me; no longer sophisticated texts but the elementary forms, the most widely known, of autobiographical discourse and writing. (p.132)

The encyclopaedic ambition to track down every possible written text which might be classified as autobiography, we can see at its most monumental in the work of Georg Misch (*A History of Autobiography in Antiquity*, trans, 2 vols, Routledge and Kegan Paul 1950. Original German, 1907) who worked his way through writings which ranged from tomb inscriptions to mediaeval work. His intention, never realised, was to continue this staggering enter-prise, 'to assemble a corpus of all the autobiographical texts written in all times and in all countries' (Lejeune p.259). Lejeune, too, had an ambitious project in mind when he made his entry into the world of autobiographical studies. Though he too toiled in the archives, his attitude to Misch was gently ambivalent.

> Most of the critics who devote themselves to the autobiographical genres take part in the ideology of our society and adopt an attitude favourable to the auto-biographical phenomenon, in which they can take a personal interest. This is true for G. Misch, who tries to trace the remote origins of this birth of the human person, and for me when I state, keeping an admiring distance, that autobio-graphy is 'one of the most fascinating aspects of one of the great myths of occidental civilisation, the myth of the self'. (p.162)

'Keeping an admiring distance' warns us that for all the apparent affinity between Misch's project and his own there are crucial differences between them. For Lejeune does not scrutinise his own archive in order to peer through it, as did Misch, to cite some grand historical truth nor to treat it as a reservoir of historical information but rather as a source of a particular kind of social fact, that is, the history of discourse. Autobiography for him never has at its heart a universal and everlasting essence but is rather a constantly changing expression of social practices which are themselves always mutable and diverse.

Lejeune began with two projects in tandem. The first was to sift out from the archives a unique corpus of autobiographical texts and the second, obviously complementary to it, was the study of present day autobiographical activity. *Autobiographie en France* (1971) was his first stab at compiling an annotated list of all French autobiography, but, as he was soon to realise, his original criteria, highly literary ones and 'purist' (his word), excluded so much that any account based on them would be an historical absurdity. Having arrived at this conclusion he parted company with such autobio-graphical theorists as Pascal and Gusdorf whose approach is based precisely on the conscious attempt to find ground for the exclusion of what Lejeune now wanted to include. He embarked on the project of compiling a compre-hensive 'repertoire', or list with comments, of all French language autobio-graphies written in the nineteenth century. Just how daunting was this un-remitting trawl can be appreciated by the fact that his former exclusiveness has now turned into inclusiveness and that Lejeune's habitat was now La Cote Ln 27, the relevant shelves in the Bibliotheque Nationale. This puts Lejeune in a class apart, not only because of the sheer size of his self-imposed task but also because of his resolute intent to see autobiography as a richer, wider and more socially significant phenomenon than literary critics before him had done. One important consequence, which it is not likely that he saw when he took this route, was that it opened up for him a new set of exciting topics to which I shall return later.

Something of the scope of the discoveries he unearthed can be gathered from his notes on his publications at the back of *On Autobiography (op.cit.)*.

> *Bibliography of Studies in French on Personal Literature and Life Stories* (Biennial bibliography, taking into account, from a multidisciplinary perspective, studies in French that deal with the following genres: autobiography, journal, correspondence, self-portrait, memoirs, witness accounts, biography, oral and audiovisual life-stories; preceded by a thematic inventory.) (p.273)

There is also the *Inventory of Autobiographies Written in France in the Nineteenth Century (1789-1914)*, which has as its programme a general study of the inventory itself and sectionalised studies, four of which have appeared in journals.

Section I   Commercial, Industrial and Financial Lives 1982

Section II   Lives of Teachers 1985

Section III Lives of Criminals 1986

Section IV Lives of Homosexuals 1987

Section I appears as Chapter 8 in *On autobiography*. The central interest of his toil in the Bibliotheque Nationale lies for me in the fact that it schooled him through a unique formation for someone who began as a literary critic. From over ninety thousand possible texts he waded through 63,000 and finally selected and annotated 23 industrial or commercial life-stories and this just for one section of his inventory. This formidable labour ensured that his view of autobiographical activity grew broader and broader, eventually taking in oral life-stories and other forms hitherto ignored. Examining the sociology of his few chosen texts, he speculates on the possibility of a future category, the life-stories of honest men! It had already been proposed in the 1880s

> Frightened by the political instability born of the French Revolution, and especially by the social conflict that was brewing, some of Le Play's disciples tried to find a remedy (indirect!) for the social problems in certain practices of autobiographical writing... 'Why? Because the traditional family is falling apart (the family as social and economic cell, heritage and enterprise). To check this decline, let us restore the old practice of keeping the family record book'. This was perhaps to confuse the effects and causes but it led these historians to

publish, beginning in 1869, texts that had hitherto been totally unknown: family record books, accounting books, journals, memoirs of private life dating from the sixteenth, seventeenth and eighteenth centuries... Charles de Ribbe had compiled a synthesis of all these documents in order to draw up a model... *Le Livre de la Famille* (The Family Book), 1879 is a sort of manual or practical guide for the familial autobiography. (p.168)

From such explorations and archaeology, Lejeune transformed his own consciousness and became a Michelet of autobiography. It was Michelet, the most renowned of French nineteenth century historians and another toiler in the national archives, who became chief of the historical section of the National Archives of France and who said of his collection,

> ... I was not slow to discern in the midst of the apparent silence of these galleries, a movement and a murmur which were not those of death. These papers and parchments, so long deserted, desired no better than to be restored to the light of day: yet they are not papers, but lives of men, of provinces, and of nations... (cited in Thompson, 1988, p.47)

When Lejeune's work is accorded some attention nowadays, it is most likely to be not for his Inventory but for his proposal that there existed an 'autobiographical pact', a kind of implicit contract between writer and reader. Yet this proposal grew directly out of his attempt to create a coherent corpus of texts. If his hunt was meant to track down autobiographies, he had to be using a definition, implicit or explicit, as a principle of selection. Therefore the definition he arrived at is literally a working definition. What he proposes deliberately excludes non-European texts and is meant to apply only to post-1770 works. I have already quoted it but must repeat it here

> Retrospective prose narrative, written by a real person concerning his own existence where the focus is his individual life, in particular the story of his personality. (p.4)

He glosses this definition by drawing attention to its underlying different kinds of criteria: the form of language used, i.e. prose narrative; the subject treated, i.e. an individual life, the story of a personality; the situation of the author, i.e. author and narrator are identical; the position of narrator, i.e. narrator and protagonist are identical and the narrative is retrospective. At this early stage in the development of his ideas, he tells us which closely related forms he is excluding, namely memoirs, biography, personal novel, journal/diary, self-portrait or essay, all of which, with the exception of biography I have included in my view of the autobiographical landscape.

There are numerous problems raised by Lejeune's definition. It excludes, for no clear reason, poetry, but more importantly it also rules out the autobiographical novel in spite of the fact that there is no way, when we are confronted by the text and the text alone, by which we can distinguish it, especially as it can plunder with ease any textual feature of autobiography including its title page. It also begs the huge question of what constitutes fiction. It has become a cliché that all autobiography must in some sense be considered as a kind of fiction. Caught in this mire, Lejeune sought to extricate himself by drawing up the autobiographical pact, a kind of invisible agreement between the autobiographer and his readers, an unspoken promise by which the autobiographer vouches for the sincerity of his work and his attempt to reach an understanding of his life. Then Lejeune, nothing if not a perfectionist, recognising that the notion of sincerity creates more problems than it solves (he himself calls it 'a sterile problematic'), makes a strange and unexpected move. It is the proper name and the title page which establish the authenticity of an autobiographical work rather than that slippery contender the first person pronoun. So we return to a criterion located within the text – only just! – which determines how we should read it. Typically, Lejeune could not leave it at that but returned to his pact in a lengthy discussion 'The Autobiographical Pact (bis)' (p.119-137) in which he begins by wryly reviewing his original definition of autobiography, having realised that 'experience shows that it is better to begin with the analysis of a corpus rather than immediately to propose a definition' (p.122). One of Lejeune's great strengths is what I may call his talking tone which we can hear clearly in his rueful second thoughts when writing off his earlier dogmatic attitude to anonymous autobiography.

> Instead of proceeding with a more exhaustive analysis of different possible cases (and of the different possible reactions of readers), I'm stuck. Feeling that I am quite in the wrong, I get out of it by being angry with my readers: 'Surely by asserting that it is impossible to write an anonymous autobiography, I am only stating a corollary to my definition not 'proving' it. Everyone is free to assert that it is possible, but then it will be necessary to start with another definition' . There! I decline responsibility, I wash my hands of it... (p.122)

Though the original pact seems to show us a Lejeune anxious to banish from consideration much that almost anyone might consider to be autobiographical, his second thoughts show him to be uniquely aware of the possible range of texts which he might have accommodated within another definition. No one else has this comprehensive familiarity, both historical and generic. For him the literary term autobiography must, like all literary terms, of necessity be elastic, plastic and polysemic and therefore promote dialogue amongst critics. His self-criticism extends to a blunt rejection of his original normative notion of identity (as he had said, 'an identity is, or is not. It is impossible to speak of degrees') based as it was on the confessional mode. By thinking of texts as located in his 'autobiographical space', he makes room for 'the free play that is inevitably related to identity' which gives rise to so wide a diversity that it produces at one pole banality and poetry at the other.

The essay is disarming and mercurial. He faces his deconstructionist critics who argue that he legitimises only surface phenomena, that his pact ignores the unconscious, class struggle and history and that he is therefore complicit with the ideology of the genre.

> How do I answer this?... It's better to get on with confessions: yes, I have been fooled. I believe we can promise to tell the truth: I believe in the transparency of language, and in the existence of a complete subject who expresses himself through it: I believe my proper name guarantees my autonomy and my singularity (even though I have met several Philippe Lejeunes in my life); I believe that when I say 'I', it is I who am speaking; I believe in the Holy Ghost of the first person. And who doesn't believe in it? But of course it also happens that I believe the contrary, or at least claim to believe it... We *indeed know* all this; we are not so dumb, but, once this precaution has been taken, we go on as if we did not know it. Telling the truth about the self, constituting the self as a complete subject – it is a fantasy. In spite of the fact that autobiography is impossible this in no way prevents it from existing. (p.131)

In sum, Lejeune very deliberately tells us that it is possible for him to have his cake and eat it, to stand by his original definition of autobiography and his unveiling of the pact and at the same time to depart from it by acknowledging its weaknesses. Though he makes no response to the explicit charge that he ignores class struggle and history, when he comes to consider oral autobiography these themes are at the forefront of his analysis. As for the self, that giant bogeyman of post-modernist anxieties, it needs to be given much more sustained attention than Lejeune ever gets round to.

Lejeune does not abandon his first enthusiasms, continuing to ransack primary sources and to refine his original formulations, but what makes reading him so rewarding is that he also branches out into other aspects of what has become his life's work. He becomes fascinated by autobiographies which abandon the sine qua non of the first person pronoun and resort to 'he/she' and 'you', or even a mixture of them. Sophisticated games, he calls them, seeing them as borderline cases which are particular forms of the play of persons and pronouns. There is the instance of an autobiography, Daniel Guérin's *L'Autobiographie de la Jeunesse*, in which the author tells the story of his youthful years in the first person and then adds an appendix as if he were a doctor studying the author's case. And there is Gide, who invents a travelling companion called Fabrice who is himself, and Gertrude Stein's *The Autobiography of Alice B. Toklas* which consists of both the autobiography in the third person concerning Gertrude Stein and the biography in the first person concerning Alice Toklas. There are others. These are borderline cases indeed. Most autobiographers, for all their diversity of tone and deployment of literary resources, are utterly dedicated to the long established hidden codes of autobiographical prose. Inevitably we are intrigued by writers who defy those codes, whatever the discursive regime they work within. Lejeune positively relishes the outlaws and devotes long essays to Sartre's *Les Mots* and Leiris's *L'Age d'Homme* which radically break the mould of chronological order by inventing new structures which instantiate a different model for describing and explaining human beings.

> Actually, a narrative form is not improvised. At the moment when we pick up the pen to write our life story everything has already been played out; thus if we question ourselves for the first time about what form to give the narrative, we will fall again, after some naive reflections into traditional methods... The very rare autobiographers who have succeeded in inventing a new narrative order are those who have tackled autobiography after having spent part of their life, of their work as a writer, in research or in attempts that have made them question all that the methods of traditional biography imply, and who have formed a new vision of human beings and new practice of writing. Because they do not rely on such previous research, almost all autobiographers end up falling back, after some qualms, some complaints, or some attempts at innovation, into the rut of chronology.... (p.73)

Rut of chronology? It is unfortunate, or worse, that Lejeune, anxious to pay tribute to innovators, finds it necessary to denigrate a method which elsewhere earns his approval. For he writes in the same context, 'Up to and including chronological order, it is *meaning* finally that organises the narrative'. The rut of chronology is by no means a straight and smooth furrow and can be managed in many different ways, all of which are very familiar to literary theorists of the novel. Even a teenager can work within its constraints in a highly creative fashion. Some years ago I ran into this centrifugal piece by Martin, aged fourteen, about his infant days,

There was nothing.

And I was two. Rabbit is my very best friend. I sat in a corner and we were playing with a thing and then there were reds and yellows and browns. My brother is Gonofan and he told Mummy (whose real name is also Mummy) to come and see the pretty colours. Mummy did not like them and hit the pretty colours.

The deers in the park are brown. I like deers and I touched a deer and it ran away and I ran after it into the woods but she did not have a broom stick. She wanted to eat me so I ran back to Mummy. I ran and ran like Johnny Rabbit ran from the farmer's gun....

I ran up the stairs with Rabbit. My bottom hurt and I needed the potty but I cannot run as fast as Rabbit and I had to leave the brown gunge on the stairs and I wet my eyes but I started to read and so was happy.

Mummy made me some red and blue shoes and

he played nic nac on my shoe

And I was three

He played nic nac on my knee

My Daddy (whose real name is also Daddy) is a good wizard. He did magic on the house and made it change. I went for a ride in the car and when I came back it had changed but there was no room for Daddy in our new house. He should have made it bigger

And I was four

He played nic nac on my door

I was with Rabbit on the pavement and we were waiting for Daddy to make us be on holiday and a young man, really the Giant up the beanstalk, made the door sing like Penny Penguin. She says, 'Michael row the boat ashore.' I was taken to be mended in hospital.

Chronological that most certainly is, covering those momentous years from two to four. The surface texture is the pseudo-voice of the infant which changes subtly as the passage progresses. It is a deceptive representation by a young chronologist who knows how to manage the juxtaposition of images, abrupt transitions and montage. This double-voicing and complex verbal play is managed easily within the chronological frame. Lejeune knows this well enough for in his essay, 'The Ironic Narrative of Childhood', the analysis concludes that his chosen writer, Ernest Pitou, uses a voice that no longer makes any 'natural' (that is to say, believable) sound but that perhaps invents a new form of the natural.' (p.69). And all that within the chronological rut? Reading Lejeune, we must be prepared for such contradictions and even at times a supercilious, judgmental tone.

It is Lejeune's adventures into quite new territory which further enlarge and transform the scope of his work. The new territory has features which are just the sort he likes to inspect and pronounce upon. If the ground under his feet is somewhat treacherous, so much the better. The first sortie takes him into a consideration of 'collaborative' autobiography. Since he is investigating 'autobiography by those who do not write' (not, note, cannot write), he first turns his attention to ghost writing. This well-known phenomenon of autobiographical writing sometimes openly acknowledged on title pages, sometimes secret, has existed in writing for a long time. His interest directs us once more to the conceptual minefield of autobiography, especially when we inspect its more baffling instances. An autobiography by a ghost writer is clearly no autobiography at all: or is it? Suppose the writer is very faithful to the supplied material, teased out perhaps in lengthy interviews. Lejeune refuses to be scandalised and concludes, since the author and the actual person referred to in the text are not one and the same in orthodox autobiography, 'anyone who decides to write his life story acts as if he were his own ghost writer' (p.188). Nevertheless. ghost writers themselves live on the frontier and can easily slip across to either side of it.

> The modern developments of interview techniques, while leaving room for rewriting and editing, make the person asking the questions and the one who is being questioned intervene in an explicit way in the final text, and have opened the possibility for new intermediate solutions: we are coming closer to biography if the intervention is critical and creative, or rather to autobiography if it tries simply to relay the model by discreetly effacing itself. The public really likes these acknowledged positions with which radio and television have familiarised them; they can in this way consume the object of this desire (the life of a famous person) in a presentation that is, in a way, stereographic, and both auto- and hetero-biographical. (p.190)

The real quarry in discussing 'the autobiography of those who do not write' is the published version of a taped autobiography. (I discuss some of the problematics of this kind of life-story in the comments on Oscar Lewis in Chapter Three). Lejeune is here at his most political, deploying a language which has an unmistakably Marxisant French accent, pinpointing the imbalance of power relations between the taper and the taped. Many of those who have been taped and subsequently published in one kind of version or another (conversations with X; extracts from transcripts edited by Y; etc.)

are not illiterate. Yet they do not write their own life-stories. This fact leads Lejeune into a digression on 'proletarian' writing in France, a somewhat bleak account. He uncovers what he calls the silence – the absence of any established corpus of working-class or peasant autobiographies which pre-date the last sixty years. This he attributes in the main to the fact that 'the network of communication of printed work, and of the function of the texts and discourse that are exchanged through its channel is in the hands of the ruling classes and serves to promote their values and their ideology' (p.198). In spite of the fact that he asserts that there was virtually no published popular autobiography in France in the nineteenth century, he nevertheless tells us that in the second half of the century there appeared autobiographies of militants. The practice of action, political and trade union commitment, allow a working life to have identity. The life-story becomes an arena where class-consciousness takes shape and is used to inspire it in others.

The contemporary situation is a dramatic contrast and in France, as in other countries, social scientists are systematically collecting oral documents influenced by Oscar Lewis's *Children of Sanchez* (1963). The burgeoning of oral testimony and oral history which followed was particularly concerned, as it was in England, to record working-class life histories and to penetrate to the other side of the 'crust of writing'. As Lejeune weighs up the outcome of this contemporary devotion to the oral life-story, though he has a host of reservations, he is drawn towards it himself and fascinated by 'the picked-up or surprised speech of someone who does not write'.

> ... it is a kind of *underside* of the autobiographical text that is produced: what would come to light is the truly lived memory, the spontaneous word, everything that writing uses but transforms, and finally hides. (p.207)

However, he always remains sceptical even at the moment of his recruitment. For him the investigator is invariably tainted, no matter what his political position, by his affiliation to the universe of writing and publishing and academia which, in the final analysis, belong to the ruling classes. The recording of oral life-histories is indeed a form of rescue or help but nevertheless, at the same time, it is an act of violation or voyeurism. He argues that, no matter how scrupulous the recorder, this remains an essential feature of his work. This scepticism in practice leaves out of account the intense awareness of the hazards which now permeate the oral history movement. Surprisingly, Lejeune makes scant reference of any kind to oral history in Great Britain; all of his Anglophone awareness is confined to the United States. He might otherwise have found in Paul Thompson's *Voice of the Past*

(1988) a highly developed consciousness of the effect of power relations and of consequent kinds of bias, a consciousness which is derived from a continuous practice of oral history over many years.

> ...there have been many telling criticisms of a relationship with informants in which a middle-class professional determines who is to be interviewed and what is to be discussed and then disappears with a tape of somebody's life which they never hear about again – and if they did, they might be indignant at the unintended meanings imposed on their words. (p.190)

Part of Thompson's strategy is to show how the dangers of middle-class takeover can be circumvented and how much of substance has been achieved in spite of asymmetries between interviewer and subject. Eventually Lejeune, too, sees the productive possibilities of taped life-stories, putting his hopes in the scrupulous work of the Ecomuseum of Creusot which has assembled a corpus of audio-visual life-stories. He takes us back to a stormy symposium there in 1977 on the theme of collective working-class memory which had the explicit aim of bringing together historians and workers, to persuade historians to abandon their role of professional listeners and workers to assume the task of constructing their own memories. It was an effort to defy the process by which, as soon as life-histories become trans-formed from the oral to the written, they pass out of the hands of the creators and become a middle-class commodity. For Lejeune the Ecomuseum has the solution of the future since it has abandoned the written and edited transcript and produced instead audio-visual life stories. In the end he is reconciled to the oral life-story and really does become the democratised scholar he told us he had become amongst the shelves of the Bibliotheque Nationale.

2. The Ethnographic Tradition:
Richard Bauman: 'Story, Performance and Event' (1986)

Since it is oral autobiography which tends to be marginalised, it makes sense to give close attention to the work of a scholar who enters the terrain by the ethnographic/anthropological route or, as he puts it, 'the perspective of the folklorist and linguistic anthropologist'. Richard Bauman, in a major essay *Verbal Art as Performance* (1977), gives centrality to the notion of perfor-mance.

> Fundamentally, performance as a mode of spoken verbal communication con-sists in the assumption of responsibility to an audience for a display of com-municative competence. This competence rests on the knowledge and ability to speak in socially appropriate ways. Performance involves on the part of the performer an assumption of accountability to an audience for the way in which

the communication is carried out, above and beyond its referential content. From the point of view of the audience, the act of expression on the part of the performer is thus marked as subject to evaluation for the way it is done, for the relative skill and effectiveness of the performer's display of confidence... Performance thus calls forth special attention to and heightened awareness of the act of expression and the performance with special intensity. (p.11)

Bauman is the inheritor of the remarkable work of Dell Hymes who, though not the originator of the concept of performance, developed it fully and exemplified it in *'In Vain I Tried to Tell You'* (1981); in Chapter Three, 'Breakthrough to Performance' (p.79 et ff) he shows that storytelling events, including traditional ones, are on the one hand unique but also operate with underlying rules and regularities. Because of Chomsky's well-known use of the term, he is at pains to make clear the distinction between himself and Chomsky. The latter's performance is a given realisation, probably imperfect, of an underlying set of internalised grammatical rules. For Dell Hymes it is the form of presentation of traditional stories as centres of a social event: eventually he applied it to all storytelling. Performance in this perspective puts the emphasis on the structure of that social event: it is situated in context and emergent from that context

The concern is with performance, not as something mechanical or inferior, as in some linguistic discussion, but something creative, realised, achieved, even transcendent of the ordinary course of events. (p.81)

The rest of Bauman's essay is his own elaboration of the notion of performance, showing how it works in different kinds of communities and describing specific features of it (e.g. metanarration, that is the storyteller stepping out of the story to comment on it). Performance for Bauman is what turns speech into art, 'a unifying thread tying together the marked, segregated aesthetic genres and other spheres of verbal behaviour into a general unified conception of verbal art as a way of speaking' (p.5). His repeated and emphatic deployment of the term verbal art is a marker of commitment. He is not a purely descriptive scholar but a champion of the artistic powers of speakers of stories. His argument is, further, that these performance powers are culture-specific and the only way to discover them is through ethnographic investigation in particular communities. And this is exactly what he did and reported in his major work, *Story, Performance and Event* (1986).

The book is based on thirty texts collected from Texan oral storytellers over fifteen years: they range from obvious fictions to autobiographical tales. Some are more difficult to place. Once again we see in action Bauman's belief that performance is the enactment of the poetic function in the actual conduct of an artistic verbal performance. The general significance of his preoccupations lies in the fact that he does not refer only to outstandingly skilful, even professional performers, nor does he confine himself to tellers of traditional tales, though he does not exclude them. His interest lies in the fact that anyone may engage in oral storytelling without any special social accreditation. Thus it is that he comes to embrace the oral storyteller in auto-biographical mode.

A brief digression. In the normal traffic of ideas those with an interest in oral narrative are more likely to plunder the conceptual apparatus of literary theory than vice versa. Bauman himself argues that that is an essential operation and he draws on Kenneth Burke, Stanley Fish, Genette and narratology in general. However, the concept of performance travels in the opposite direction. Marie Maclean's study of what she calls 'the Baudelairian experiment' is entirely based on the notion of performance, as her title, *Narrative Performance* (1988, Routledge), clearly shows. Unusually for a literary academic, she says boldly at the outset that 'the basic problems of narrative can, in the first instance, be better understood in relation to oral narration' (p.2). Although she offers some lively thoughts on oral narratives she neither puts before us nor analyses a single one. Nevertheless she offers a clear description of what she sees as oral performance before she goes on to apply it to the experimental narratives of Baudelaire. For her, all narrative is the site of an interaction, where every performance is unique and always retains what is present in the minimal 'recounting of story events in every-day life', that is, the features of performance in it.

> While many stories in traditional societies are not only sanctioned but enforced by the rules and conventions of the culture, it must be remembered that the most lasting authority is that of the performance itself. Performance generally works on the basis of shared expectations, whereby power is granted to others, to the hearers as well as the teller in this case, in the expectation of certain results. Oral performance is not just an act of saying something, it is produced by all the different acts in saying something. What is said is less important than the *saying*, an interaction which... involves purpose, energy, and effect as well as the 'message' conveyed. (p.7)

There is an overlap here between Bauman and Maclean, though neither refers to the other. Maclean here has as her focus 'traditional societies' and their practices but is at pains to suggest that performance is salient in all oral storytelling. The interactive approach to all narrative, even printed words on the page, must surely be foregrounded in oral autobiographical stories where the teller is engaged in the most direct I-you discourse, an extreme of self-exposure which proposes at one and the same time vulnerability and intimacy, incorporation and exclusion, seduction and rejection.

To return to Bauman and his Texan storytellers, it is only to be expected that his analyses, performance-based as they are, never look at the story text as the sole material but at the total social action of the storytelling event in which the chief components are 'the setting, the institutional context, the occasioning principles'. We could predict that a disciple of Dell Hymes would give the closest attention to situational features. He locates them in:

- participant identities and roles i.e. listeners' relationships to the teller and to each other

- the expressive resources used in performance, the voice, the body, the selection of language and the deployment of silences

- social interactional ground rules, norms, strategies for performance, criteria for interpretation and evaluation (every storyteller operates in an arena of cultural assumptions and practices)

- the sequence of actions that makes up the scenario (at what point in the scenario is the story told?)

Bauman, for all his intense awareness of the teller located in the centre of powerful cultural forces and strongly affected by them, is no cultural determinist. None of his storytellers is a mere recording instrument of the voice of the culture. Aware that the stories can be dropped very easily into conventional categories (wonder tale, trickster tale, tall story, narrative jokes, etc), he is insistent that each teller establishes an individuality and produces something unique. Dell Hymes (1973) once described a native American storyteller telling the traditional story of skunk, in this way,

> All this in detail, with voices for different actors, gestures for the actions, and always, animation. For that, as people will be glad to tell you, is what makes a good narrator: the ability to make the story come alive, to involve you as in a play... each is a voice. (p.15)

In some ways Bauman's book is a manifesto. He not only studies oral narrative, he champions it. Oral narrative, he tells us, displays an indissoluble unity of text, narrated event and narrative event (the distinction between the two latter categories is between the events a story is telling us about and the event which constitutes the telling itself). Like others before him he believes that narrative is a primary cognitive instrument for making experience comprehensible. Yet, for all the subtext of advocacy and delight in his chosen performers, he is not blind to the fact that tellers can use their stories as an instrument for obscuring, confusing and questioning what went on.

So much for a very brief account of Bauman's view of oral storytelling. However, the main reason he figures here is that he turns his attention to autobiographical oral storytelling in Chapter Three of his book (and briefly elsewhere in it) which is entitled, 'We was always pullin' jokes: the management of point of view in personal experience narratives'. The chapter contains three stories which recount practical jokes in which the teller is either the perpetrator or the dupe. His analysis demonstrates the need to distinguish between different kinds of personal experience stories according to the relationship of the teller to the events being narrated. Does the teller have direct experience of them or are they known partly through the stories of others? Does the phase structure of the events determine the narrative or are the events retroactively constituted by the narrative?

Bauman is by no means the first to focus on oral stories of personal experience, nor the first to record some in order to offer us a very rich, detailed analysis of them. But he makes a unique contribution to this tradition. Labov's pioneering study, already referred to, is treated, quite rightly, as a locus classicus. Bauman points out that personal experience stories imply both (a) a particular class of reported events i.e. ones in which the narrator was personally involved and (b) a particular point of view adopted by virtue of that participation. Labov, he reminds us, makes no distinction between a story in which there is intense focus on the narrator as a protagonist of the original event and another in which the narrator is solely a witness. Sandra Stahl in three carefully worked papers (1977a, 1977b, 1983) showed herself to be a rare student of stories of personal experience. Bauman notes the two broad categories into which she divides these stories, *other-oriented* and *self-oriented.* The other-oriented stories are those in which the tellers underplay or eliminate entirely their own personal role. They become more of a witness than a participant. The self-oriented stories are those in which the tellers emphasise their own involvement, their own self-image, the motives and values behind their actions. Stahl's distinction between other-oriented and self-oriented bears a certain resemblance to the distinction I have made between autobiography and memoir. Bauman applauds Stahl's distinction but points out the limitation from which it suffers is that her analysis cannot distinguish the two categories in formal terms. This is precisely what he does in his study of oral autobiographical practical joke stories.

We must remember when reading Bauman's protocols and discussion of practical joke stories of personal experience what he has already said in respect of dog-trading stories ('a study of expressive lying') which focus on the negotiation of sales.

> The narratives that are the instruments of these negotiations do not fall into clear-cut categories of factual and fictional, truthful and lying, believable and incredible, but rather weave a complex contextual web that leaves these issues constantly in doubt, ever susceptible to strategic manipulation... (p.32)

Then Bauman turns his attention to a particular class of fabrications, those event-based fabrications we call practical jokes. His interest is in the stories of personal experience which relate the course of these jokes and which are told by a participant in them. Thus the tale involves a particular point of view which the narrator must manage. Point of view has long been recognised in literary studies, but before Bauman's work it had not been an object of attention in the analysis of personal experience stories, in this case stories of practical jokes. He poses the question, 'How does one construct a story about a practical joke in which one has been involved?' To answer it he examines closely a set of autobiographical acts (he does not call them that, of course), three stories told by a West Texan in his early eighties, who has lived all his life in a close community and is a member of a small group of men 'who drank coffee, fished, hunted and played dominoes together'.

The narration of the events of the practical jokes is complementary to the perpetration of the jokes. What is the joy of the joke if it cannot be narrated to others and, of course, relished in the retelling by the participants themselves, whether tricksters or their victims? Practical jokes are manipulations of the social environment and they involve differential access to and distribution of information. So, the trickster knows what is going on, the victim does not and there may be others whose inside information varies according to how the trickster is working the situation. Bauman's storyteller in some stories is the trickster and in others the dupe. Key questions, therefore, are how a storyteller goes about handling the audience's access to information and how he deals with and organises what he knew then and what he knows now. The narrator, when he has been the trickster, is in a doubly privileged position by virtue both of his original role and of his knowledge of how it all turned out.

What the story does is to place the hearers at an intermediate point, somewhere between the trickster and his victims. The victim's view is false, the trickster's view is formed by full knowledge about what he has already done, what he is doing in the particular scene, and what he expects will be the consequences. The narrator, whether trickster or dupe, leaves us to guess about vital details, such as whether what someone in the tale is telling us is the truth or not.

Bauman's analysis (p.48/49), which puts the story performance under a microscope, concluded that there is a specific five-phase structure to them:

- *Orientation* The where, when and who

- *Set-up* which narrates how the dupe is inveigled into the trap

- *Trick event* The practical joke is perpetrated

- *Discrediting the fabrication.* A kind of denouement when the chief victim realises he has been fooled

- *Evaluation* A closing statement which comments on the story.

In following this routine, which Bauman suggests is present in other kinds of tales, the storytellers do not rely exclusively on events they have personally experienced. When the teller is the dupe, for example, he must tell of the stratagem being set up, an event he knows of only through hearsay

> ... the personal involvement of the narrator as protagonist is subordinate to the structure of the event; it is the phase structure of the event that gives structure to the narratives, not the personal involvement of the narrator in the original action... These considerations raise a point of considerable significance in narrative theory, namely, in what way events may be taken to be prior to and determinative of the narratives that recount them and in what way the events may be seen as retroactively *constituted* by the narratives. (p.51)

What we have come to know as the relationship between story and event in narrative theory Bauman demonstrates on the levels of content and structure in personal experience stories.

In another set of analyses Bauman focuses on the use of direct and indirect speech. Some stories of personal experience centre on direct speech and are concerned with other people's words or, I would add, one's own. They add a special heightened quality to the story inasmuch as they become 'the object of interpretation, discussion, evaluation, rebuttal, support, further development' (Bahktin 1981, p.337). The punchline of many told stories is a citation, supposedly exactly as originally said. To call it a punchline is to draw attention to its power and by the same token, the frequency of the use of direct speech presupposes its special force. Bauman notes how, at retellings of certain stories, separated by as much as ten years, the quoted punchline is repeated word for word. These closures re-key all that has been recounted before. However, the use of dialogue throughout the telling 'enhances the re-enactment by transposing the past to the present', moving the telling from diegesis to mimesis (telling as opposed to showing and enacting). The oral storyteller has here a resource which gives an advantage over the writer. He purports not only to be giving us the exact words but the very way they sounded. The piquancy of the situation lies in the fact that to cite the words of another in a newly fashioned context is to change their meaning, perhaps only minimally but possibly grossly.

Bauman explores these matters through what he decides to call anecdote, for which he proposes a definition.

> A short, humorous narrative, purporting to recount a true incident involving real people. (p.54)

This is, of course, his own idiosyncratic definition of the word 'anecdote' for such narratives: one might choose others. The anecdote is, he adds, 'one of the least studied of oral forms'.

> The characteristic formal features of the genre include a focus on a single episode and a single scene and a tendency to limit attention to two principal actors... anecdotes also tend to be heavily dialogic in construction, often culminating in a kind of punchline, a striking, especially reportable statement, rendered in direct discourse. (p.55)

This brings together the autobiographical anecdote jokes, urban legends and the routines of stand-up comedians. Indeed, many stories of this kind, told in autobiographical mode, may well borrow resources from other kinds of performances but it is just as likely that the latter in their turn depend on the skills of the everyday practitioner. There is a fascinating symbiosis to be explored here.

Bauman sums up the importance of his enterprise in this way,

> When one looks to the social practices by which social life is accomplished, one finds – with surprising frequency – people telling stories to each other, as a means of giving cognitive and emotional coherence to experience, constructing and negotiating social identity; investing the experiential landscape with moral significance in a way that can be brought to bear on human behaviour... (p.113)

3. A Contribution from Psychology:
Jerome Bruner 'Acts of Meaning' (1990)

If I ask myself who in addition to the more obvious candidates, historians, literary critics, etc., would find autobiography a compelling, perhaps essential, interest I answer that it must be psychologists. I know that memory, identity and self have long been their conceptual and empirical preoccupations and that in therapy, life histories are the all-important resources of their consultations. Surely, I tell myself, in autobiography, written or spoken, they must find an inexhaustible treasure or, as they might say, data bank. When I set about a search I very quickly noted that as Brewer (1986) wryly informs us,

> The study of autobiographical memory is one of the least well-developed areas in the study of human memory. (p.25)

That is not altogether surprising in a mainstream tradition which outlawed introspection, sought explanations which took no account of meaning-making and ended up with information-processing models of cognition. In that tradition a life story would have been discarded as distracting noise, irrelevant or, in a favourite perjorative rejection, anecdotal. We may leave it to psychologists to explain their failure or unwillingness to examine as profound evidence of the working of memory, the ubiquitous phenomenon of people's construction of their past lives. Moreover, how did it come about that they put in cold storage for so long the pioneer work of Bartlett, reported in his *Remembering* (1932) which established that autobiographical memories are not in some sense a true copy of the past but a special kind of reconstruction of it? I go into these matters more fully in Chapter Five.

Freudian psychoanalysis is quite another matter for its raw material is autobiography, searching as it does for a latent autobiography beneath the one first given to the analyst.

The old assured approaches are now beginning to dissolve very rapidly. There are psychologists now who turn eagerly to real life-stories and show a daring willingness to offer their own in order to shed light on the working of memory. This is now called 'remembering in natural contexts'! (see Neisser, ed., *Memory Observed; Remembering in Natural Contexts*). Salaman (1970), not a psychologist, in *A Collection of Moments: a Study of Involuntary Memories*, unashamedly treats her own memories as valid evidence and is cited respectfully and at length in Conway (1990), an academic work on autobiographical memory, which marks a significant turn amongst certain psychologists.

Following the procedure I have adopted, I want to examine the contribution of one psychologist who, in recent years, has made autobiography a salient feature of his work. Jerome Bruner in *Acts of Meaning* (1990) goes far beyond others. He does not see autobiography as one among many possible interests for a psychologist but as the major phenomenon in what he calls cultural psychology which is in fact the theme of his book. Bruner is also a practitioner, having some years before written *In Search of Mind: Essays in Autobiography* (1983). There he traces his intellectual journey from cognitive psychology to cultural psychology (a term unheard of not many years ago).

> The main stream of psychology I entered as a student was dominated by sensationalism, empiricism, objectivism and physicalism. But when I was an undergraduate, my heroes and my mentors were almost to a man swimming against the main stream. My heart was with them – Gestalt psychology, Sigmund Freud, the cultural anthropologists, even McDougall. (p.59)

He eventually discovers that he must accommodate fully the cultural component: 'Speaking as an 'intellectual autobiographer', I find 'myself' not just inside but outside as well.' In the Eighties he was more and more drawn to the study of autobiography and produced in rapid succession a series of papers on the subject, including 'The Autobiographical Process' (1993). There followed *Acts of Meaning* which is devoted to 'the nature and cultural-shaping of meaning-making' and 'how human beings interpret their world and how we interpret their acts of interpretations'. In the book we were promised for 1992 another work, written in collaboration with Susan Weisser, *Autobiography and the Construction of the Self*. Unfortunately it has, so far, failed to appear, a great disappointment, for it was due to give a full account of the experiment with oral autobiography dealt with briefly in one chapter of *Acts of Meaning*.

Bruner sets out to rehabilitate folk psychology, for so long a pejorative term. The organising principle of folk psychology which deals with the stuff of human action is narrative through which are expressed beliefs, desires and hopes, implicitly and explicitly. Bruner's culturally oriented psychology may be summed up in this declaration,

> ...there is a publicly interpretable congruence between saying and doing and the circumstances in which saying and doing occur. That is to say there are agreed canonical relationships between the meaning of what we say and what we do in given circumstances and such relationships govern how we conduct our lives with one another. (p.19)

The book is a long complex argument to sustain this standpoint. But how did it lead Bruner to the culmination in the final chapter which is devoted exclusively to autobiography? More specifically, how does it lead him and his colleague, Susan Weisser, to a project in which they elicit half-hour oral autobiographies? At its simplest they wish to deepen their understanding of self in practice, the self as an actor and talker, a doer and sayer.

> By the late 70s and early 80s, the notion of Self as a storyteller came on the scene – the Self telling stories that included a delineation of the self as part of the story. (p.111)

It becomes clear that autobiography is being seen as a window onto a particular view of the self. Bruner enters the autobiographical field because he sees it as a supreme instance of cultural psychology. He also applies it to the concept of the self 'which is as central, classical as any in our conceptual lexicon' (p.99). After tracing the erosion of the idea of self as 'an enduringly subjective nucleus' through work outside psychology in historical and anthropological studies, he concludes,

> What all these works have in common is the aim (and virtue) of locating Self not in the fastness of immediate private consciousness but in a cultural-historical situation as well. Nor... are contemporary social philosophers far behind in this regard. for no sooner had they begun to question the previously accepted hold of positivist verificationalism on the social sciences – the notion that there is an objective and free-standing reality whose truth can be discovered by appropriate methods – than it became clear that Self too must be treated as a construction, that, so to speak, proceeds from the outside in as well as from the inside out, from culture to mind as well as from mind to culture. (p.108)

For someone like myself at some distance from today's intellectual and ideological battles among psychologists it is a significant moment when we find some of them using as basic data the recognisable activities of human beings rather than the distillations of narrow empirical enquiries. Let me cite just two of them. First, Gergen K. J. (1982) argues for two psychological universes. As Bruner paraphrases him,

> The first is human *reflexivity*, our capacity to turn round on the past and alter the present in its light, or to alter the past in the light of the present... The second is our dazzling intellectual capacity to envision alternatives. (p.109)

Next there is Polkinghorne (1988) who rejects what he calls the traditional research instruments 'designed to locate and measure objects and things' and turns to an alternative.

> We achieve our personal identities and self-concept through the use of narrative configuration and make our existence into a whole by understanding it as a single unfolding and developing story. We are in the middle of our stories and cannot be sure how they will end. (cited in Bruner, p.115)

Bruner draws on both these scholars and many others, but that will suffice to indicate the discourse he finds congenial and who are his intellectual companions.

In a chapter called 'Entry into Meaning' he shows how soon young children start telling autobiographical stories, above all in soliloquies. There is, for example, Emily, of whom he says, 'About a quarter of her soliloquies were straightforward narrative accounts about what she had been doing'. By the age of three, infants can use the simple narrative forms of everyday speech – an orientation, a linear depiction with a precipitating event, a resolution and sometimes a coda – about a quarter of which are the child's own doings. But, 'telling the right story' means presenting actions and goals as justified and legitimate. Young children's stories are not merely recountings but also a form of rhetoric. That all-too-brief indication of the thrust of Bruner's book should show why he was poised for the final chapter, 'Autobiography and the Self'. It is not so much that he wants to unravel what autobiography is as that he wants to use it as a means of observing the Self in action. He had already explored the nature of narrative as both a kind of text and as a mode of thought in his influential *Actual Minds; Possible Worlds* (1990). It had led almost by serendipity to the collection of some spontaneous oral autobiographies. From them he learned, he says, that people always seem to be engaged in constructing the self. These oral stories were built up from smaller stories which drew their meaning from their being located in a large scale story.

This led him and his colleague, Weisser, into a study 'with requisite interpretive rigour' of half-hour autobiographies elicited by the simple request, 'Tell us the story of your life'. To some of us this might seem a very unproblematic procedure, accustomed as we are to basing ideas on genuine texts elicited in specific contexts just as Bauman's were. Yet to appreciate its novel simplicity we can contrast it with all the experiments reported and discussed in Rubin's *Autobiographical Memory* (1986) and Conway's *Autobiographical Memory* (1990), not one of which was based on asking people to tell their life stories. It is therefore refreshing that Bruner not only makes this direct request but also takes the unusual step of asking for an oral response though he himself does not make anything of this nor does he tell us why he did not ask for a written response. Almost by default he is acknowledging that this is the way most of us tell the story of our lives, however piecemeal that story may be. It has to be said that even this 'natural' mode of collecting life stories takes place in exotic circumstances. Nearly all sustained oral tellings of this kind are scarcely spontaneous events, uninfluenced by the research stance of the elicitor. However, astute researchers like Bruner and his colleague, with life-long experience, are unlikely to be unaware of such matters.

> ... once into the task [they] have little difficulty with telling their stories. No doubt the stories we heard were designed in some measure for our interest in how people talk about their lives. Nor were we under any illusion that an interviewer could be neutral during the interviews... Obviously 'the story-of-a-life' as told to a particular person is in some sense a product of teller and told. (p.124)

The full account of the interview procedure (p.123-126) suggests a relatively relaxed atmosphere. Together with some colleagues in the London Narrative Group we found that in replicating Bruner's procedure we could without difficulty obtain oral life stories just as he says. However, some of the storytellers construed the task quite differently from others, some choosing to tell their life stories in an other-oriented manner, as though they were creating a document for the historical record. They assumed, no doubt, they were expected to provide a contribution to the social historical record. We are taken by Bruner through a set of life-stories told by members of the Goodhertz family whom he selects from his corpus. The analysis shows how they all independently make a sharp distinction between their public and private worlds, 'home' and 'the real world'.

Bruner concludes that 'intra-psychic forces have fashioned the selves which emerge from them' but at the same time they are also expressions of society, of history.

> But to let the matter rest there is to rob the Goodhertzes of history and to impoverish our own understanding of their lives and their plight...Whatever view one may take of historical forces, they were converted into human meanings, into language, into narrative and found their way into the minds of men and women. In the end, it was the conversion process that created folk psychology and the experienced world of culture. A cultural psychology takes these matters as its domain... On the other hand, it insists that the 'methodology of causation' can neither capture the social and personal richness of their lives in a culture nor begin to plumb their historical depths. (p.136/7)

Bruner here is trying to resolve a debate that runs through most discussions of autobiography. What force writes or tells autobiography, the self or society and history? This debate, of course, extends far beyond autobiography. His resolution suggests an active interplay between the two forces but gives priority to the culture of the given society. He does not attempt to show or discuss how it is that each one of us experiences the culture differently. Moreover, each person is located in the culture in a particular way, not only being part of the process of reproducing and possibly changing it, but also experiencing it in ways which differ according to one's ethnicity, class, gender, religion and other crucial components of our life experience. Within those all-powerful forces the individual always remains in certain respects unique. Metaphorically we might say that we all have hands and fingers but each of us has unique fingerprints.

A certain set of principles emerges from Bruner's argument. A life is created not recorded by autobiography. It is a way of construing experience and re-construing and reconstruing to the end. Most lives are accounted for in patches which are glimpses of a more general narrative about life, a total narrative, much of which is left implicit. It has been widely recognised that in literary autobiographies there are usually key passages which mark conversions, awakenings, turning points. They have a particular salience in people's life stories. Bruner is the first to find that exactly the same is true of oral life stories.

It is a matter of methodological interest that Bruner did subject his corpus to detailed linguistic analysis, looking for revealing words, signature expressions, counting deontic (i.e. obligative and permissive) and epistemic (about knowing and believing) modals to see how each person leaned on contingency and necessity. But he found, as others did before him, this yielded nothing substantial. In the end he turned to literary theory and discourse linguistics. Bauman's performance-centred approach might have proved even more useful but, as so often happens, that school does not earn itself even a passing reference. Moreover, Bruner's assertion that autobiography actually creates a life and is not a straightforward record of it is an extreme position which imperiously avoids the obvious fact that, while the totality is always a special kind of construction, there are many elements in every autobiography which are clearly registering features of, and events in, the autobiographer's life. Bruner here is echoing the voice of much post-modernist thought which often takes up a logocentric position. It can also be seen in some views of autobiographical memory.

There is one important and recurrent theme in Bruner's book which I will touch on briefly. At several points he argues that autobiography functions as a force maintaining social stability or, as he puts it, 'an essential base not only of personal meaning but of cultural cohesion'. A life story, then, keeps the peace. I can give ready assent to the idea that in a thousand and one ways, even the most rebellious life stories, visibly and invisibly , take up the dominant postures of the society in which they are set. Nevertheless, they can at the same time be par excellence, instruments of opposition and even subversion. Another kind of cultural cohesion can be created by separate groupings in a society fissured in many different ways. The trouble is that Bruner has two serious blind spots, ideology and the implicit assumption at times that culture is in some ways a single uniform phenomenon. Ideology is a slippery term, but Eagleton (*Ideology*, Verso, 1991), while acknowledging as much, puts the matter succinctly

> Dominant power is subtly, pervasively diffused throughout daily practices, intimately interwoven with 'culture' itself, inscribed in the very texture of our experience from nursery school to funeral parlour. (p.114)

Dominant power is not in Bruner's lexicon. Dominant power does not speak with a single voice and the dominated have their voices, too – the voices of the working class, of women, of ethnic minorities, of the gay community. Bruner's 'folk psychologist' has to be located with as much precision as possible in this vast conversational space.

For Bruner, each culture favours a canonical form of autobiographical texts which is specific to it. Our culture favours the chronological and centres on emblematic events and stages. Yet there are autobiographies and even more autobiographical writings which make a clear break from the chronological – Michael Leiris's *Manhood*, for example, cited by Lejeune (*op.cit*) as the paradigm case. In Shirley Bryce-Heath's *Ways with Words* (*op.cit.*) there is a very sharp contrast between child oral storytellers in two neighbouring working-class communities in Carolina – one black, the other white. In Roadville's white community when children tell stories they are expected to be utterly non-fictive, 'to stick to the truth'. 'Adults listen carefully and correct the children if the facts are not as the adult remembers them.' Fictive elements are plain lies. In black Tracton, by contrast, when children base stories on actual events, they are expected to 'creatively fictionalise the details surrounding real events' and their embellishments may be so substantial as to render the story more and more remote from what actually happened

> Tracton's stories, on the one hand, are intended to intensify social interactions and to give all parties an opportunity to share not only the common experience on which the story may be based, but also in the humour of wide-ranging language play. (p.188)

Thus there are huge differences between Roadville and Tracton in form, occasions, content and functions. Heath sums them up dramatically,

> For Roadville, Tracton's stories would be lies. For Tracton, Roadville's stories wouldn't even count as stories. (p.189)

Bruner's contribution has to be admired for he makes it in an intellectual milieu which can be very hostile to his kind of thinking. He invites us to look closely at folk psychology which operates through 'narrative culture – stories, myths, genres of literature'. Always he gives priority to meaning-making through which, by interpersonal processes, we construct our social selves. As a psychologist he stands out as one who always seeks explanation in terms of culture and history as his study of autobiography shows. We may disagree with his view of culture and history but to put them at the forefront of psychology is a bold step.

4. Autobiography in Social and Cultural History, with Special Reference to Oral History:
Samuel R. and Thompson P. eds. (1990) 'The Myths We Live By' and Thompson 'The Voice of the Past' (1988)

Oral historians, as we have seen, have for several decades been listening to life stories from people who have in the past been rendered silent and almost invisible by history. The original impulse for recording these stories lay in the discovery that, because of the nature of their lives, ordinary people could illuminate aspects of the past which no historian had, up to that time, either been aware of or cared about. In this way, to use E.P. Thompson's memorable phrase, they could be rescued from the condescension of history and could be disinterred from under the stacks of statistics, the reports of government officials and the resonant generalisations of learned observers. Oral history is much older than the oral history movement with its impressive national organisations, conferences and publications. Take Henry Mayhew, for example, of whom Paul Thompson (1978) writes,

> His comments show both emotional sympathy and a willingness to listen to their [the interviewees'] views. No doubt his attitude helped him to be accepted into working-class family homes and receive their life-stories and feelings. And, significantly, it was linked to an unusual concern with their exact words. He normally went to interviews accompanied by a stenographer... And in his reports he gave very substantial space to direct quotation (p.35)

Paul Thompson's book, *The Voice of the Past*, (1988) is a passionately committed and sparkling exposition of the raison d'etre of oral history. In spite of its being a smallish book it is encyclopaedic in its scope: a kind of atlas of varied developments and also a users' manual for new recruits. But it remains essentially, and properly, an historian's book. It is not part of its purpose to ask the makers of oral history, the tellers themselves, what they think they are doing, what they believe to be the value of both the process and the product. And what place do these oral histories occupy in the totality of their autobiographical utterances? Such matters are not entirely ignored. Mostly they are signposted or have to be heard as a subtext throughout.

> Oral history gives history back to the people in their own words. And in giving them a past it helps them towards a future of their own making. (p.226)

In his final chapter, 'Evidence', which confronts the touchy question of truth and reliability in oral recollections, Thompson undertakes an appraisal of memory, seeing it not as a purely intra-individual psychological phenomenon but as an active social process. Oral history throws up in particularly sharp form two issues which surface in any substantial examination of autobiography, whatever form it takes. How 'true' is it? And what does it reveal about the functioning of human memory? To these questions I return several times. Further, oral historians are often hovering on the brink of another question which is a matter of aesthetics. Do some life histories have value not only as a special form of historical evidence but also as a kind of art, oral literature, in fact? Here is the end of a chapter in Thompson's book.

> Oral evidence, by transforming the 'objects' into subjects makes for a history which is not just richer, more vivid and heartrending but *truer*. And that is why it is right to end with Theodore Rosengarten's *All God's Dangers*, the autobiography of Nate Shaw, an illiterate Alabama sharecropper, born in the 1880's, based on a hundred and twenty hours of recorded conversations: one of the most moving, and certainly the fullest, life story of an 'insignificant' person yet to come from oral history. (p.99/100)

'Richer', 'more vivid', 'most moving'. These are just the traces of an aesthetic response which enables us to hear the tone which lies behind the whole passage. His historian's restraint prevents him from adopting Bauman's unequivocal celebration of what he calls 'appreciation of oral literature' and 'verbal art'. His intention, he tells us, is to 'illuminate and celebrate oral narrative for the artful accomplishment that it is'.

The tape-recorder transformed dramatically the study of speech, making it available for careful scrutiny and analysis. It is, of course, the oral historian's essential tool and has, indeed, produced a vast archive only a tiny fraction of which has been transcribed and published. However, it creates its own problems. To have access to oral life-stories most of us have to resort to the published transcriptions. Representing speech in a completely faithful written form is impossible and leakage of performance features inevitable. So we engage in the paradoxical activity of reading oral stories which have been tinkered with one way or another to make them readable. Scrupulous scholars (Bauman, for instance) diligently describe their principles of tran-scription. Elinor Ochs, in her landmark paper, 'Transcription as Theory' (1979) shows how the systems adopted for transcription imply theories of language. Is there such a thing as a paragraph in spontaneous speech? Bauman writes in his 'Note on the Text',

> My representation of spoken language is, frankly, intended to have more ex-pressive than linguistic accuracy in a strictly technical sense. I am more interested here in the narratives as oral literature than dialectological data.... I have attempted to convey that this is a record of language in a spoken, not a written, mode and to preserve something of the quality (however vague and im-pressionistic that term may be) of oral discourse. (p.x)

It is well known that a transcribed story on the page may appear banal and flat and yet spring to life in the sound recording. It is partly an awareness of this phenomenon which leads transcribers to resort to devices which may compensate for the stultifying loss of power in their versions. Others go much further and engage in 'creative' editing to produce an acceptable written work. They may even doctor their material to make it match their own intentions. Always there is the force of internalised literary models and written grammatical structures. The emenders of spoken texts are parti-cularly likely to make such changes when they aim to produce a popular work and their transcribed texts hover in a no-man's-land between the written and spoken. I have already mentioned Studs Terkel. His intro-ductions do tell us a great deal about his procedures but there is not a word about the editing of his transcriptions. For me, Studs Terkel remains one of the greatest collectors of autobiographical material, a modern Mayhew, but he exemplifies the compromises that have to be made to achieve a readily accessible version of spoken lives. Ronald Blythe's *Akenfield*, so hugely successful that a film version of it was made, goes even further, for his village turns out to be a composite one, constructed from transcripts ob-tained in several different villages. Again we are not told about the kinds of procedures which were used to assemble *Akenfield*.

These books and others like them are each in their own way very successful, even important, works. But they are essentially, for all their links with living speech, a special form of literary work, thriving in the space somewhere between the written and spoken, a kind of hybrid form of autobiographical discourse, firmly helped by an editor on the way to becoming verbal art.

Oral historians are not the only ones to record and transcribe life-stories and stories of personal experience. Sociolinguists have their own interests in doing so and Labov has already been referred to. In his pioneer study, now considered a classic, he recorded black working-class speakers and, after analysing their stories, using a model drawn from narrative theory, he proposed that 'black English vernacular' was 'the vehicle of communication used by some of the most talented and effective speakers of the English language' and this at a time when in educational circles some were asserting that black speech was a linguistically deprived argot. Others followed Labov's lead. There were educationists who countered the deprivation description and championed working-class speech, arguing that a special place could and should be found in the classroom for stories of the pupils' and their families' lives. The National Oracy Project drew on these practices and reported favourably on them. The stories of teachers' experiences of teaching have also been seen as a unique means by which they can reach a deeper understanding of their working lives. There is a whole history here of how oral autobiography has entered the classroom and it has yet to be written. (See Cambridge Journal of Education, Vol 20 No3 1990, and Okazawa-Rey et al., 1987).

I have already indicated that amongst oral historians there was for a long time almost an obsession with the reliability of what they recorded as historical evidence. Could a speaker be depended on to deliver the true facts, not to forget crucial material, and not to embroider it, not to change it whether wittingly or unwittingly? In this regard, historians shared a preoccupation with other writers on autobiography and, indeed, some autobiographers who are concerned with the question 'Is it true?'. Now, however, the validity of the question itself has been challenged by a counter-question, What kind of truth have they in mind? There is one book which registers unambiguously an important shift away from the preoccupation with a particular concept of valid record.

The Myths We Live By (1990) is a set of papers from the Sixth International Conference of Oral Historians. The editors, Raf Samuel and Paul Thompson, in their introduction, show how far they have travelled from the earlier preoccupations of oral historians. They argue that we must learn fresh ways of 'reading' and interpreting life-stories.

> When we listen to a life-story the manner of its telling seems to us as important as what is told.

That is the long-established idiom of literary critics who have for so long insisted that form and content are inseparable. It is also almost word for word what other commentators on oral stories have said. But the editors want to go much further: for them now the study of life-stories is inter-disciplinary territory and that has, of course, been the burden of this book. They urge us to acknowledge the subjective element in the depositions we study. Once we follow their advice we are plunged into the emotions of the speakers, their miseries, their hopes, their desires, their fantasies. We eavesdrop on the potent metaphors of memory. They recognise that each life-story has its own individuality and constitutes a vital document in the construction of consciousness. What was easily assumed to be a homo-geneous group turns out to contain, when once its members have told their stories, wide and even contradictory versions of the same experience and this in spite of the fact that a shared culture runs through them all. This interplay of the public and private has been a theme running through all of the approaches I have singled out so far. It constitutes nothing less than a preoccupation with self and identity. Recent work, including those works I have already cited, has refused to make a choice between seeing autobio-graphy as essentially an expression of the individual psyche or as the realisa-tion of the inexorable forces of the culture speaking through the voice of one person. The attempt now is always to perceive both forces interpenetrating.

Samuel and Thompson set out a basic proposition which registers the new course which oral history has set for itself.

> [Life-stories] should be seen, not as blurred experience, as disorderly masses of fragments but as shaped accounts, in which some incidents were dramatised, others contextualised, yet others passed over in silence through a process of narrative shaping, in which both conscious and unconscious, myth and reality played significant parts. (p.5)

This is to go to the heart of narrative in general and to see the oral narrator not simply as a mouthpiece which may conveniently drop some data in the path of the lurking historian but as an active constructor of the past. The authors have indeed been to school and made themselves willing students both of literary theory and memory itself. For the oral historian this must mean that their task has become more complex, more exciting and much more likely to be profoundly illuminating. Let us see how this works out in other contributors to the volume.

There are studies which add something fresh to the understanding of oral autobiography derived from the analysis of extremely diverse speakers on equally diverse topics: Rosanna Basso's study of children's accounts of their 'strike' in a middle school – a protest against inadequate heating; Alistair Thomson's examination of the Anzac legend via interviews with Australian veterans of the First World War; a University of Turin project which involved interviewing survivors of deportations to Nazi concentration camps. It is a compendium of testimony and memories. Always there is an awareness that myth and memory intertwine. For example, in Alistair Thomson's study, he reports on the as yet unpublished work of the Popular Memory Group in Birmingham.

> The 'popular memory' approach, devised by the Popular Memory Group at the Centre for Contemporary Cultural Studies in Birmingham is useful precisely because it rejects the notion of memory as historical record – though it does not reject the use of memory out of hand like the traditionalists who condemn oral sources for their distortion. Instead the 'distortions' produced by the effect of 'public' upon 'private' memories become the key to understanding the powerful role of the past in the present. (p.77)

> From the moment we experience an event we use the meanings of our culture to make sense of it. Over time we re-member our experience as those public meanings change. There is a constant negotiation between experience and sense, private and public memory. (p.78)

As the Anzac paper brings out clearly in 'our' society, 'our culture' will always offer different meanings, different legends and anti-legends, which is why even speakers whose experience may seem virtually identical never produce identical texts.

Remembering is firmly anchored in the present moment which asserts its own colouring, its light and shade in our vision of the past and which affects not only what we select and what we elaborate but also the very way in which we structure our stories to produce 'a construction of a coherent narrative, whose logic works to draw the life-story towards the fable' (*op.cit.*). A life-story or a story from life, therefore, is always in the broadest sense a moral tale and the tellers should be thought of as storytellers rather than 'informants' to be milked for historical data. The history lies not so much in the facts behind the myths and fables as in the historical significance of the mythical narratives themselves. The past of decades ago is not simply summoned up like a ghost or restless spirit so that it is made to re-happen in words or appear to us like the re-running of a film. The teller is speaking in a way which registers his/her present social and cultural location. Past events are seen as illuminated not only by the kinds of intervening experience which immediately come to mind (marriage, jobs, the experience of old age, deaths) but also, possibly, massive upheavals – shifts in class position, changes in political allegiance, religious conversion or loss of belief, the effects of education prolonged into adulthood, emigration/immigration. In my recent reading of the autobiography of a woman of seventy I encountered her story of her schooling as working-class child, but she sees it all through the lens of higher education, embarked on when her children had grown up, feminism and political activity.

Conclusion

It remains only to add a final comment on this chapter. Autobiographical discourse, as I have seen it, in all its pervasiveness and variety of forms is embraced by another kind of discourse which analyses it and tries to discover what kind of animal it is. There is nothing homogeneous about this discourse, positioned as it is in disciplines and preoccupations, the proponents of which are often not aware of each other's existence. I have tried to select as major contributions those works which I have seen as offering unique insights – Lejeune, the literary theorist; Bruner, the socio-cultural psychologist; Bauman, the ethnographer; Samuel and Thompson, the oral historians. My selection was based not only on what were for me powerful studies in their own right but also were representative of quite different routes into the field. It goes without saying I might have chosen others. My selection is autobiographical in the sense that it registers the high points in my reading, mostly over the last three or four years.

CHAPTER FIVE

AUTOBIOGRAPHICAL MEMORY

Autobiography is the rendering of memory into discourse. Memories densely populate our minds; it is the act of attempting to communicate them which turns them into autobiographical texts. Anyone who writes a life story or moments from it is likely to reflect on his or her memory processes, why, for example, some details are so fuzzy and elusive and others brilliantly illuminated; why, as Proust insisted, there are such differences between memories which come unbidden and those we consciously summon up. We are beset with doubts about dates, names, and the events themselves. We wonder why the past sometimes comes tinged or even suffused with emotions and at other times drained of them and we sometimes discover that our 'recollections' are sometimes plain wrong. The reflective autobiographer is always confronted by the question, 'How does memory work?' or, more precisely, 'How does autobiographical memory work? How is it triggered by an object, a song, a photo, a smell, a phrase? What exactly is going on?' Less likely but always possible is that we may ask ourselves about the memories we share with others – family, the community, the nation, different, sometimes conflicting, versions.

Academic psychology has had great difficulty in getting to grips with such matters and in treating memory in such a way as to encompass autobiographical acts. It must surely be significant, and, to say the least, baffling that an authoritative and weighty tome, *The Oxford Companion to the Mind* (1987), has entries under Memory i.e. Memory: Biological Basis (p.456) and Memory: Experimental Approaches (p.460) and an entry under

Remembering (p.679) but is positively poverty-stricken in respect of auto-biography. However, the first entry starts promisingly enough,

> For materialist theories of the mind, it is axiomatic that there must be brain representations of memory. This may not be intuitively obvious when we consider our own individual memories, for we can clearly rehearse in our minds the histories of past experience (the memories of a childhood birthday party, the image of an absent friend's face, the opening notes of a Beethoven symphony or the taste of a roast dinner) without these rehearsals affecting our external behaviours in any obvious way. (p.456)

The whole piece is properly concerned with how the processes of learning and recall are registered by the properties of the brain system. Nevertheless. to say 'without affecting our behaviour in any obvious way' ignores that familiar and important phenomenon that our behaviours *may* include the transformation of past experiences into verbal representations of them. Quite simply, we tell them. The entry is written by Steven Rose, whose book *The Making of Memory* I have already cited and in which he shows himself to have a very much broader view of autobiographical memory. He clearly did not consider that to be an important preoccupation under the rubric, 'Biological Basis'. All the same, he permits himself towards the end of his entry to comment,

> All this may seem a long way from Marcel Proust's evocation of youthful memory, *A La Recherche du Temps Perdu* with its sense imagery. (p.460)

Which is reasonable for his specific purposes, but what is a matter for legitimate concern is that an encyclopaedic work, ten years in the making, has no room for the Proust phenomenon which in more modest form is to be found in the psycholinguistic activities of everyone. It would be a strange mind which was not alive with autobiographical memory. Steven Rose himself more than makes this good in his own book which, as I hope to show, takes a much more complex stance.

Putting that to one side for a moment, I want to look at work on memory which makes a direct connection with that of oral historians. They, as we have seen, have tried to disinter history by the relatively straightforward act of asking people to talk at length about their pasts. This resolute exhumation can come from a single individual. Often, however, it comes from the members of particular groups which share a common past – war veterans, miners, women factory workers, fisherfolk, domestic servants, senior citizens, etc. Here we enter shared memory. There is something refreshingly everyday about this experience. For there are particular occasions which we all know will almost inevitably dip into a shared past. These are those gatherings like weddings, funerals, reunions, commemorations or more informal, convivial moments, in pubs, in sitting-rooms, on park benches. Such moments establish and strengthen bonds and can become part of the process by which identities are discovered, defined, fashioned and changed. Frequently it is a twosome which savours a particular event and produces a kind of collaborative telling which involves reciprocal editing through promptings, alternative versions and interpretations. This too is autobio-graphical memory at work. Jacques Brés (1992) has a fine example. He analyses in detail the transcript of an account given by a miner and his wife. They have both participated in a sit-in at a mine in the Cevennes which was threatened with immediate closure. They tell their story in tandem, a story of a hectic and somewhat violent moment. It had been the agreed intention to take le patron by force down to the bottom of the mine (a carnivalesque inversion, observes Brés). The miner's wife insists that the women in contrast to the men would have gone through with it to the bitter end and, indeed, that it would have been especially appropriate for the women to carry him off to the bottom of the pit. The husband blusters and proposes that there are other correct unionist ways of going about things. A sexual inversion is at the heart of this interchange, says Brés. The wife says, '...les femmes on aurait été plus méchantes que les hommes'.

We are not left undisturbed to get on with this business of constructing our memories together, a business which is as accepted and perhaps as unnoticed as breaking bread together. There are potent forces which take us by the arm and quite insistently intrude their own intentions on our collective memories, instructing us how and what we should remember and which are promoted or sanctioned by the state itself like Remembrance Sunday or commemorat-ing D Day. There are group memories which chime with or resist the flags and bugles or which are more complex interanimations of the two, highly charged with ambivalence and contradiction. Alistair Thomson (1990) in 'The Anzac Legend' lays bare the complexities of this double articulation.

> Some men threw away their medals; one used his as fishing sinkers. Others stayed at home on Anzac Day. Even now they switch off Anzac movies because 'it was not what I experienced in the war...'

> Recently my interest has shifted back to the diggers who were not involved in radical politics and who did not have an articulate oppositional memory. Their experience of hardship in the war and interwar years often contradicted Anzac Day oratory. Yet their memories had been scrambled and entangled by the legend. For sixty years they had been members of the RSL and attended Anzac

Day parades... Memories were also reshaped by present-day situations and emotions. Lonely old men living in council bed-sits were eager to recall the cameraderie of the army or the adventures of the war. I could not simply use memory as a pure record to challenge public myths (p.77)

There is a quite different sense in which we can talk of memory being social, as being different from that version of memory which used to figure in typical psychology textbooks and still lingers in many of them. That was when thousands of piddling investigations were carried out on the memorising of nonsense syllables and the central preoccupations were with short-term and long-term memory and with some useful distinctions between recognition and recall, and remembering how and remembering what. There was a remarkable lack of concern with memory as meaning-making, that is the organisation of our pasts as our richest resource for making sense of our lived worlds. I have a powerful recollection of the disappointments of reading what I might call the official version of memory. Where, I asked myself, with growing frustration, is the rememberer with a headful of recollections of last year or twenty or sixty years or more ago? And where were the tales told outside laboratories everywhere by everyone?

Yet in 1883 Sir Francis Galton initiated the scientific study of autobiographical memory, but the dominant procedures of psychology ensured that his novel ideas and findings were not taken up until very recently. As long ago as 1952 the philosopher, Suzanne Langer, in a pioneering work called *Feeling and Form* proposed a comprehensive theory of art and felt that in order to do so she needed to give some attention to memory.

There is a normal and familiar condition which shapes experience into a distinct mode, under which it can be apprehended and valued; that is memory. Past experience, as we remember it, takes a form and character ... Memory is the great organiser of consciousness. (p.262)

That was to abandon at one stroke all those tired and time-honoured metaphors of memory as a storehouse, a wax tablet, a super recording instrument, faithfully registering experience dispassionately, like the pen on a seismograph. From Langer's viewpoint, memory is a process, by means of which the meanings of then become the meanings of now, the feelings of then become the feelings of now. Memory is not a thing but an activity, not so much what we have as what we do. Suzanne Langer again,

To remember an event is to experience it again but not in the same way as the first time. Memory is a special kind of experience because it is composed of selected impressions, whereas actual experience is a welter of sights, sounds, physical strains, expectations and minute undeveloped reactions. Memory *sifts* all material and represents it in the form of distinguishable events. (p.263)

It is this sifting process which transforms memory into meaning because it teases out a pattern from the sheer muddle of events, which is why the paradigmatic form of fiction always simulates the working of memory, why it is 'virtual memory'. In some cases it mimics autobiography or conflates virtual memory and actual memory to produce what these days is called unproblematically autobiographical fiction.

The story of the reinsertion of autobiography into the psychology of memory and the rediscovery of Galton and Bartlett marks an important point in the general process of autobiography coming in from the cold and, as so often happens, the recovery of ideas left behind as the prevailing concepts, which proscribed them as improperly scientific, dissolved. Alan Baddeley (1989 in Butler T, *Memory*) writing of the work of Ebbinghaus whom he calls 'the father of research on human memory' says,

> The Ebbinghaus tradition played an important role in the development of the psychology of memory but it has the weakness that it tends to concentrate too heavily on simplified and apparently soluble problems and to neglect the richness of memory in the world at large. (p.45)

This is somewhat disingenuous since it offers no explanation of the origins of the 'weakness' i.e. the well-known behaviourist stance and its social, political and economic origins. It was Ebbinghaus who carried out a set of experiments which were designed to lay bare the fundamental laws of human memory and in doing so left us the dubious legacy of experiments with nonsense syllables and the like, a legacy enthusiastically taken up by the empiricist and behaviourist psychologists who followed. Baddeley goes on to discuss one psychologist who did attempt to come to terms with different kinds of memory and to include in his scheme autobiographical memory, though that is not what he called it. Tulving (1983) distinguishes two aspects of memory which in a commonsense kind of way many non-psychologists do: episodic memory and semantic memory. Episodic memory is the kind of memory which gives rise to all autobiographical acts i.e. the recall of personal experiences, of past events; semantic memory is concerned with the data we need to operate in the everyday world, knowing the cost of bread, how many months there are in the year, the way to the nearest station, etc. However, that commonsense and academic distinction begins to dissolve rapidly when we notice that behind every semantic memory there stands an array of episodic memories. Moreover, every episodic memory is buttressed by semantic memory. As so often happens with sharply defined dualisms, the two components interact.

The history of what he calls 'the beginnings of systematic empirical research on autobiographical memory' is set out in a paper called 'Autobiographical Memory: a historical prologue' by John Robinson (1986). In it he links, perhaps surprisingly, the pioneer work of Galton and Freud. Unlike Ebbinghaus, who insisted on studies and experiments on memories uncontaminated by meaning in the pursuit of 'scientific psychology', they were both advocates of the direct study of personal recollections. Galton investigated his own memories and the language used to express them. He was moving towards a classification of recollections but moved on in his restless way to other interests. Nevertheless, as Robinson comments, he was only a short step away from the study of life history and personality.

The practices and the folklore of psychoanalysis have entered popular consciousness and we are no longer inclined to think that words like *extrovert, introvert, inferiority complex, repression* etc. are esoteric technical terms. There is in addition a more diffuse awareness that psychoanalysis has something to do with the telling of, and the revision of, life-histories. Popular consciousness has got it right and sometimes includes the knowledge that these ideas have a founding father – Sigmund Freud. He used memory as the major tool in understanding neurosis and thus the elicitation of life stories of his patients became a basic procedure and those autobiographical memories were the materials to be rendered fully intelligible by the analyst's skilled interpretation.

Galton left a legacy in psychology which established measurement and statistics as a means of studying human individual differences. He moved on from an early interest in autobiographical memory, using his favourite methods to investigate topic after topic. He also contributed the method of using questionnaires to study personal memories and at the very least he brought real memories, albeit very constrained, into psychological studies. Freud's clinical methods, on the other hand, installed autobiographical memory at the heart of psychology and a vast literature of case studies and their interpretation has accumulated and is accumulating to this very day. Any autobiographical act can be interpreted in psychoanalytical fashion. Oliver Sacks contrasts ' arrays of facts without design or connection' (1973) with Freud's case histories which are of course life-histories.

> ... the matchless case-histories of Freud. Freud ...shows with absolute clarity that the on-going nature of neurotic illness and its treatment cannot be displayed except by biography. (p.206)

It is sometimes forgotten that Freud put great emphasis on the role of emotion in memory in both remembering and forgetting. For him, recollections without affect were not recollections at all since emotions are essential for the creation of memories, shaping them, giving them organisation, placing their significance as events unfold. Others have stressed the ways in which emotion is intrinsic to the process of recalling the past but they have been less inclined to consider that this is the only way in which memory is something more than episodic. There are also the colourings of values, attitudes, beliefs and reflections, all of which are inter-related. An ideological stance is always taken up.

I want to turn now from early attempts to bring autobiographical memory into psychology to its resuscitation after a long sleep.

> There is one peculiarity in the history of autobiographical memory..: although much original research was performed in the late 1800s and early 1900s, there is a gap in the research record between the 1900s and the early 1970s and in which only a handful of studies were reported. This is what Cohen (1986) refers to as the 'hundred years of silence' (Conway, 1990, p.16)

In order to illustrate how the silence has been broken I shall need to draw on studies which come from different kinds of sources but which seem nevertheless to suggest that a common impulse unites them in their pursuit of a new understanding of memory. That impulse is a determination to restore autobiographical memory not only as a legitimate research tool but more profoundly as an essential means of understanding the human mind, thus unlocking a whole new archive.

To scrutinise the current situation, the state of the art, as the cliche has it, it helps to leave the playing field marked out by psychologists for themselves (I shall return to it) and take a look at other arenas in which the game is played out.

Philosophers have been busy explaining memory since Greek times at least and, for all I know, non-Europeans have concerned themselves with it for as long or longer. In her short and lively book, *Memory*, (1987), Mary Warnock, as we might expect from someone who is, amongst other things, a philosopher, entitles her opening chapter 'Philosophical Accounts of Memory' and conducts us through the ideas of Hobbes, Hume, Mill, Descartes, Russell, Ryle and others. I do not propose to recapitulate that chapter here but rather want to draw attention to her own views, for she addresses autobiographical memory as a kind of culmination to her book in the final chapter, 'The Story of a Life'. What sets her book apart from so much other work is that, while she readily acknowledges the physical aspects of memory she is above all concerned with consciousness and why we value our memories. She sees as one end of the memory continuum those memories which not only come charged with emotion but are also highly prized. Like Suzanne Langer, her chief interest in memory is ultimately its role 'in the life of the imagination, in art and, above all, in our own self-esteem.'

> Memory cannot be understood as long as we persist in thinking of the mental ghost in the physical machine, neither can the peculiar delight and insight that we derive from recollection... An autobiography is the story of a life and such a story can be regarded in two ways. On the one hand, it is the record of the comings and goings of a continuously existing animal, a live creature, who, being human, can assert and grasp his own identity from childhood until the time when he writes. But on the other hand, a story has a theme, a plot and a hero. It is told to the world at large and can be understood by them. A good story has been worked on so that it conveys a truth. It speaks this truth to the world in general, not just to its author. And so the memory of an individual, encapsulated in autobiography, has a general and universal meaning. (p.viii)

Memory seen in this way clearly cannot be delivered by simple-minded little 'objective' tests. However, Mary Warnock has eyes and ears only for how memory is turned into art and is therefore deaf and blind to all expressions of autobiographical memory which would not meet her criteria. But I do not want to belittle her book, for it is in many ways a fine contribution to the rehabilitation of autobiographical memory and the study of autobiography. It contains careful distinctions and useful discussions of such matters as memory and personal identity, the causal connection between memory and the past, the past as the subject of reflection and therefore subject to change. Moreover, it makes no reference to mainstream psychological studies, though it does look briefly at psychoanalytic theory in order to reject the idea that it alone can show us what we are in the historical perspective of our lives. Suzanne Langer, thirty years earlier, was more direct on this subject.

> ... for memory has many aspects which psychologists have not discovered but of which the poet, who constructs its image, is aware. But the poet is not a psychologist; his knowledge is not explicit but implicit. (*op.cit.* p.267)

In spite of the book's virtues, I find it has serious limitations. Let me try to put them briefly. In the passage on autobiography cited above she writes of 'the peculiar delight that we can derive from recollection' and this with her is a recurrent theme. But there are recollections saturated with cruelty, horror and every kind if misfortune. I think of Primo Levi's books which give a calm but chilling account of his memories of the death camps or of an old lady's unpublished autobiography which I read recently. She remembers being evacuated as a child during the Second World War and being ruthlessly and sadistically persecuted by the head of her hostel. Primo Levi, with something approaching despair, speaks of his need to testify to the world. We also need to exorcise our demons or simply, as we say, 'to come to terms' with harrowing events, to confront past failure and lesser injustices and sadnesses. Some autobiographical discourse is a kind of mourning or keening. All of which is so obvious that it remains to ask why someone of Mary Warnock's bright intellect is lured into such euphoria about recollections of the past. I believe that this is because she is wedded to that familiar set of Eurocentric beliefs about High Art and its league tables. So she can say, speaking of James Joyce's *Portrait of the Artist as a Young Man*, 'probably the greatest masterpiece about childhood ever written' (p.122), which is one of those casual arrogances which implies a rich acquaintance with the whole of world literature. And she uses that hazardous word 'universal' to refer to a very specific cultural practice. There are lengthy appraisals of Wordsworth and Proust so that the canonical proprieties are duly observed. This does not mean that her views about these writers are necessarily wrong; her pursuit of their theories of memory as playing a central role in the creative act is, indeed, helpful. What it does mean, however, is that an implicit exclusion order operating in her text ensures that hers is a very narrow and non-comprehensive view of autobiographical memory. In Chapter Two I set out the wide range of autobiographical acts from Proust-like books to brief, spontaneous spoken utterances. Of almost all of the latter Mary Warnock has nothing whatever to say and thus we have only at best the beginnings of a discussion of autobiographical memory.

A final comment on the paragraph above. We are told that a story has 'a theme, a plot, and a hero'. These are the very battered terms from traditional literary criticism and certainly much of Mary Warnock's discussion could well have been plucked from any work of literary criticism untouched by developments in literary theory. She seems to have no acquaintance with Roland Barthes (*SZ*, 1975), Gérard Genette (*Narrative Discourse*, 1980), and Gerald Prince (*Narratology*, 1982) and others. I have in mind such things as the system of codes proposed by Barthes, the functions of the narrator in Genette and narrative grammar in Prince.

It could all have been so different. In the midst of a lengthy discussion of self-exploration which includes a very productive consideration of diaries and how they differ from autobiographies (i.e. a different relationship to memory) she turns to Sartre:

> Towards the end of his life he developed a theory of history... that it consists of a dialectical clash between different economic classes, he nevertheless held that an account of such a class conflict cannot intelligibly be wholly materialist. It needs to be 'interiorized' before it can be fully understood. The writer, in his view, has a duty to present the dialectical process of history from the standpoint of individual people who, formed within a particular socio-economic context, lived their own lives with particular and individual interests and insights. (p.114)

Sartre is concerned here to outline what he believes to be the duty of a *writer* rather than anyone else who might be engaged in the production of autobiographical discourse; but he is touching on a central issue, the relationship between individuals and their class allegiances when speaking of their pasts and there is therefore no reason why we should limit the relevance of his ideas to people who have been given the privileged status of 'writer' nor why, in principle, anyone might not offer 'particular and individual interests and insights' as indeed many have done without benefit of that special status. Warnock is willing to accept Sartre's marxisant account of one important aspect of autobiography which she says is

> ...to uncover as far as possible the presumptions and presuppositions within which a subject lived. Such presuppositions may be revealed in 'reliving' the life of the subject, as it seemed to him at the time. This is the philosophical justification for the writing of lives. (p.115)

Why should philosophy stop short at the writing of lives? This glaring limitation of sensibility stops Warnock at the very point in her text when she might have taken a leap forward in her ideas of self-exploration and memory. What a pity she denied herself some great possibilities and perceptions. She cites two autobiographies both from, as she says, 'privileged male English persons, both Etonians, though of different sorts' (L.E. Jones and Henry Green) and says that their books, respectively *A Victorian Boyhood* (1935) and *Pack my Bag* (1940), had the intention to explain what it meant to live in a class-dominated society. If only she had taken that notion and run with it! Or at least knocked on the door of the oral historians who could have told her about 'the recovery of voices from below' (Alistair Thomson, p.175 *Life Histories and Learning*, 1994) and showed her how she might have discovered uses of memory which don't enter her text.

I turned to Mary Warnock precisely because she came from outside the enchanted circle of memory psychologists and I think that excursion is worthwhile. I now want to repeat that manoeuvre by turning to someone who has already put in an appearance, Steven Rose (*The Making of Memory*, 1992).

Rose is, amongst other things, a distinguished researcher working at the leading edge of neuroscience who might easily have written a captivating book which confined itself to his own engagement with memory – neurobiological research and scholarly theoretical explorations connected with it – but at the very outset he sets his face against this strategy and instead promises an account of his laboratory practice set 'into the richer and more complex context which the present day philosophy, politics and sociology of science have revealed as framing scientific theory and experiment'. Moreover, he draws on 'literary criticism, psychoanalysis, neuropsychology and cognitive neuroscience ... and more besides'. And he is as good as his word though even this ambitious programme does not do justice to the heteroglossia and genre play of this work. I am, for example, intrigued by the fact that there are, as I commented before, several autobiographical excursions of some length (a day in his lab, attending a high-powered international conference, the process of composing and getting accepted an academic paper). These chapters are clearly meant to buttress the themes of his text, giving it the support of highly personalised testimony. But my strong feeling is that they are doing much more than this. They declare to the reader that these are displays of the sheer complexity of human memory. He is, as it were, doing memory under our very eyes.

His own experimental work, carefully and accessibly described in the book, is with the memory of day-old chicks but he knows that that leaves a vast problem in the study of memory. He is able to show that the chicks, after once pecking at an evil tasting substance on a bead, actively avoid it thereafter and he has been able to show very precise changes in their brains which register this functioning of their memory, autobiographical memory, we might say. However, as anyone can see, this tiny single act of memory of a day-old chick, beautifully and relatively uncomplicated from an experimental point of view, tells us nothing or very little about the staggeringly complex processes of remembering and forgetting in human beings. Rose, of course, knows this very well

> Day by day in the lab I explore the biology of memory in experiments with young chicks; in the evening I go to a world richly inhabited by my own personal memories. (p.6/7)

He is very ready to admit that as yet the neuroscientist cannot show how our most intimate and elaborate memories are registered in the brain by connections between nerve cells and the electrical flux between them, the synthesis or breakdown of certain proteins.

I have to accept the limits of neuroscience, to concede that it has so far been left to the other half of our fragmented culture, the terrain traditionally inhabited by poets and novelists, to try to explore the subjective meanings of memory. (p.7)

It is also, he insists, not just the subjective meanings of memory which have to be reckoned with but also that we are much more than treasure-chests of purely personal memories. We are also social beings and therefore memory 'bursts the confines of the individual, the personal, and has become collective'.

There is for me a nice irony in the fact that it takes a neuroscientist working with his day-old chicks to confront very boldly the working of human memory in its most complex forms. He is prepared to say that his chicks, remembering, and therefore avoiding, the nasty taste on the bead, and the consequent changes in its brain, can reveal some truths about human memory. He rehearses for us the methodological, epistomological and ontological objections to making this connection – that lab methods cannot replicate 'natural' learning, that there are fundamental differences between chick knowledge and human knowledge, that the examination of brain molecules tells us nothing about meaning and intentionality. In rejecting these criticisms, he acknowledges that he appears to live in two different worlds, in the lab and in the uncontrolled working of his own memory out-side it. The post-modernist tells him that must be inevitable since we have multiple personalities and therefore our world in incurably fractured. Rose replies,

To look with different epistemologies is not to concede that the world is irretrievably fractured, merely that in our present state of knowledge that is the best we can do. (p.310)

Nevertheless, he maintains that his many years of work with the chicks and the theoretical speculations to which it has propelled him have taught him some things about human memory – about all memory, human and animal. To summarise, when an animal learns, specific cells in its central nervous system change their properties and these changes can be measured morpho-logically (the structure of neurons and synaptic connections), dynamically (changes in the blood flow and oxygen uptake of neurons), biochemically (the synthesis of new proteins). All these processes are *necessary* for memory to occur but it cannot yet be said whether they are *sufficient*. But he can say that the brain is not, as some very plausibly would have it, an information storing and processing device. On the contrary, memories are dynamic and dispersed, located in different ways in different parts of the brain. We remember a name by deploying a range of different strategies because that name has been classified by us in different ways. the 'simple' chick operates in the same way. It has to remember the bead and if it cannot remember its colour, it remembers its shape. Memory only begins with learning: it is recall which fully transforms it into memory and that, as we all know, is the difficult bit. His studies and those of his colleagues have shown him that,

> Memory is not some passive inscription of data on the wax tablet or silicon chips of the brain, but an active process. Furthermore, this points to something the psychoanalysts have long emphasised: that forgetting can be more than the erasure of stored information as in wiping a disk clean. It is also an active process. (p.320)

So memory is not to be found in a clearly mapped location in the brain to be labelled like those old phrenological diagrams but is a property of the whole brain. More, it is a property of the whole organism. And it is at this point that Rose's book comes closest to very direct relevance to my preoccupation with autobiographical discourse. Rose's intense awareness of the power of human memory, an awareness which pervades the whole book, leads him finally, after having insisted on qualities which we share with other animals, to set out ways in which human memory has its own distinctive properties. Firstly, there is the immense significance of language. We do not only have memories incorporated physically within our bodies but we can speak of them, eventually, perhaps, in very sustained and highly elaborate ways which can evoke complicated responses in others. To be able to speak of memories is one of the means we have of teaching each other. It is 'procedural' memory which is dominant in animals; they remember how to do things. It is 'declarative' memory which is dominant in the human animal; they remember that such-and-such was the case. Declarative memory, I would say, is what makes all autobiographical acts possible.

Finally, Rose reminds us that we not only have an array of complex storage systems which give us access to our own pasts and the pasts of countless others but we are also inducted into collective memory. Dominant forces in our society guide our memories into certain interpretations of the past but other groups struggle to assert their own collective memories – socialists, feminists, black movements, members of ethnic minorities and many others. There is an awakened interest in collective memory, a concept which does not merit even a passing mention in earlier studies both of memory and of autobiography. I shall return to it shortly.

Rose is clearly motivated by an optimistic, almost utopian, view of the future study of memory, a future in which biological and social viewpoints can be triumphantly unified without reducing one to the other. As in his favoured metaphor, the Rosetta Stone, it is a matter of translating from one code to another.

If autobiographical memory was excommunicated from the true church of behaviourist psychology along with the anathema of meaning and mind, the times are changing and the very phrase, autobiographical memory, is now legitimated. Two recent books (Rubin, 1994 and Conway, 1990) have just that title. In *Theoretical Aspects of Memory* (Morris and Gruneberg, 1994) the editors pose the question, 'How do you capture the richness of the real world of remembering...?', thus signalling a major switch of attention. A whole chapter by Winograd (p.273-295) has a title which would, not very long ago, have been considered quaint – 'Naturalistic Approaches to the Study of Memory'. However, it turns out that most of the chapter is about studies of forgetting in general and amnesia in particular. There is, it is true, a section on autobiographical memory which is not based on laboratory experiments and describes two studies. The first, 'a heroic diary study', is by Willem Wagenaar, who for six years made a same-day diary entry for every day. Every event was logged under the rubric of *who, what, where and when.* In trying to discover which of these questions was the most potent in attempting to retrieve memories, he found 'when distinctiveness or cue-loading was controlled for, it turned out that differences in cue potency were largely eliminated'. Or, in other words, none of the questions is more power-ful than any other in triggering recollection of the past. Then, there is Brewer's study of college students who recorded their activities, feelings and thoughts every time their bleepers went off and then had to recall them some time later. Their recall was most effective when the original experience was most distinctive. All this, and other work described by Winograd makes it clear that 'naturalistic' is being given a very special and limited gloss. It does not mean what a lay person might be led to expect, that is, the study of autobiographical memory as it occurs without being managed in an intrusive fashion. Wagenaar's six-year diary is constructed on principles which are intended to make it amenable to carefully constructed recall procedures. Brewer's students must undergo recall interrogation. The laboratory psycho-logist's methods die hard. Which is not to say structured recall procedures cannot provide some insights into genuinely self-motivated autobiographical memories. However, millions of diaries have been written with no intention of providing data for formal psychological analysis. It does not seem impossible that these could be used as the basis for a qualitative study of memory. Karl Miller, in his autobiography *Rebecca's Vest* (1993), adopts an unusual procedure in many passages of his book. His present-day text walks alongside a diary he kept from his adolescence and with which he maintains a conversation.

> Literature was my friend, so was the diary I began to keep in which this self at its most unrestrained was written down. It was far from identical, I would guess, with the human being visible to those around me, and it is now comic and painful to me in the rewriting; even at the time I could see the joke. (p.13)

> Looked at, as anticipated, in the future, the workings of the adolescent mind seem a good deal more representative than strange. It is the diary of a self-seen outcast, and is often wretchedly self-engrossed. It reviews the books I read. It contains troubles and complaints and confessions, poems and stories and girls, earnest bookish friendships with older males. It hurriedly recalls a series of crises, elations and longeurs. (p.26)

The diary and the reflections on it when Miller is in his early sixties is 'naturalistic' memory at work, visions and revisions, which are a world away from Wagenaar's artfully professional diary and Brewer's students' bleepers which insist that, motivated or not, they must do their stint for the prof.

Clearly the pressure in the world of psychology to embrace autobiography is mounting. Brewer and Wagenaar published their work in 1986. In the same year David Rubin edited a collection of papers, *Autobiographical Memory* (1986), which registers a variety of attempts by psychologists to show that autobiography can and should be an appropriate field of study for them. How far they are prepared to risk abandoning their commitment to traditional laboratory methods of studying memory is very varied. The editor himself in his introduction is at pains to stress the ways in which his contributors break new ground: the use of 'phenomenological' reports, the study by the psychologist of his/her own processes of recall, the study of what 'subjects' have to say about their own processes of recall, the examination of how memories distort, change and are lost over time. Finally, in an unexpected shift of perspective, he acknowledges that literature and philosophy are good sources of insights into autobiographical memory. Yet we should not be beguiled too easily; there is work reported here which in both its language and practices reveals a yearning for the good old days, in spite of the fact that one contributor, Robinson, says that psychologists knew 'precious little about the denizens of that natural habitat, the mind'.

What, for example, are we to make of this?

> Crovitz and Shiffman (1974) obtained 1745 dated memories by asking 98 undergraduates to record autobiographical memories evoked by each of twenty high-imagery, high-meaningfulness, high-frequency nouns.

Or of similar work by the same authors about which it is said

> The subjects who were tested individually were instructed to provide a specific autobiographical memory for each stimulus word. (Rubin,p.203)

There is no point in elaborating how distant these procedures are from the ways in which people generate autobiographical memories, nor the arbitrary features of the memory. Why nouns, for example, and not verbs or adjectives? Many memories are, of course, not triggered by words at all but by things, places, music, old photos, particular foods and much else.

If this were all the book had to offer I would not be discussing it. It contains much which justifies Rubin's claims. Let me take just one instance, Margaret Linton's 'ways of searching and the contents of memory' (p.50-67), because the very questions she poses speak with a new voice and set out a new agenda.

> The questions relevant to a serious study of the mind include: what memories survive, thrive, and populate the domain? Whither do they come and where go, and what forms do they take during their tenure? Answers to these questions, I believe, have the greatest possibility for providing links to the total individual and the widely disparate areas of psychology that together map the totality of the individual: developmental, personal, social, biological, and cross-cultural. (p.51)

Linton works in her own very distinctive style, not only studying the contents of her own memory in diverse ways for fourteen years but also trying different ways of accessing them. Yet she disarmingly admits that what worked for others did not necessarily work for her. Her resources included 'free recall', 'memory watch', and 'thoughts that come unbidden'. the latter are for her 'delicate memory fragments that occur year after year' and that prove to be highly significant. She has her own method for luring these fragments into consciousness and it is a method which comes much closer to the ways in which we let our minds slip into memory mode. In her simple but effective system she selects a theme and, rather than using a disciplined search, she 'floats about' in her memories and soon the unbidden memories surface. She discovers that these memories coincide very little with those elicited by standard recall procedures. Over the fourteen years she conducted many studies of her own memory and one of them, reported fully in Rubin's book was conducted over six years. I cannot do it full justice here but suffice it to say that, after a minimally structured warm-up activity (an interesting idea), she then, using free recall, accumulates all the events she can from the preceding year. From this work she feels able to propose a structure of memories which I reproduce below

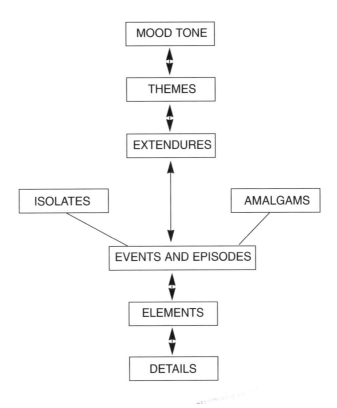

Hierarchical outline of memory categories. From M Linton, 'Ways of searching and the contents of memory' (Rubin, 1986, p.58)

Let me gloss very briefly the interrelated items in this structure, noting that Linton says 'the simple labels are intended to represent a complex over-lapping fabric'.

- *Mood Tone.* The simplest examples are negative and positive moods but these can be supplemented and refined (stress and tension, euphoria, etc.). This category cuts across all others.

- *Themes* (and sub-themes). Coherent directions or unifying aspects of life. They may run throughout great stretches of one's life, e.g., inter-actions with parents, but may not be easily summed up in a brief phrase.

- *Extendures*. Sets of memories: smaller and more time-limited than *themes* and bound by common context, e.g. when I worked at Fords.

- *Events and Episodes*. Self-contained sets of actions and happenings which have independent coherence. Though discrete they may be linked explicitly or implicitly to causes and consequences. They are embedded in extendures.

- *Isolates*. If the events have a solitary coherence they appear to exist independently of unifying aspects of one's life.

- *Amalgams*. Episodes which are logically unrelated to others but which occur with them in recall. They are unstable and after a long lapse of time the events are remembered independently.

- *Elements*. Features and components of events/episodes. They specify who, what, where, etc. and are the details which fill out memories. I would say these establish in many different ways the texture of memories.

- *Details*. Nuances of colour, sound, texture, exact location, etc. They are often implicit.

I have lingered over Linton's hierarchical structure because it has some important implications for autobiography, that is, the transfer of autobiographical memory to autobiographical text, a process to which Linton makes no reference at all. In fact, there seems to be an assumption that the two are identical. The structure she proposes may be seen as a conceptual architecture constructed post factum by careful scrutiny of a set of protocols. But is it also a structure operating in the deep process of autobiographical composition rather as Chomskyans argue that their grammar is delivered by a language acquisition device in the human mind? That seems unlikely. Autobiographical acts can enter by any one of the structural elements. Nevertheless, the hierarchical scheme may be useful as a kind of template to place over autobiographical acts. What would this yield, to take just one possibility, if one used it to compare women's and men's autobiographies?

I would need to add at least one other category to Linton's set, a notable absentee from so much psychological analysis. Where has ideology got to? It is just as pervasive as mood, perhaps more so. It penetrates every autobiographical act, either exhibiting itself on the surface of its discourse or ticking away in the sub-text. Narratologists have never been in doubt about this, as the following passage in Gérard Genette (*Narrative Discourse*, 1980) shows. He begins by considering the emotive function in a narrative text.

> ... this is [the function] accounting for the part the narrator as such takes in the story he tells, the relationship he maintains with it – an affective relationship, but equally a moral or an intellectual one. It may take the form simply of attestation as when the narrator indicates the source of his information or the degree of precision of his own memories, or the feelings which one or another episode awakens in him. We have here something which could be called *testimonial function* or function of *attestation*. But the narrator's interventions, direct or indirect, with regard to the story can also take the didactic form of an authorised commentary on the action. This is an assertion of what could be called the narrator's *ideological function*. (p.256)

More directly, Terry Eagleton, in his book *Ideology* (1991), shows how ideology penetrates all discourse. Linton's hierarchical model loses the ideological component which pervades all levels

> It may help to view ideology less as a particular set of discourses, than as a particular set of effects within discourses. Bourgeois ideology includes this particular discourse on property, that way of talking about the soul, this treatise on jurisprudence and the kind of utterances one overhears in pubs where the landlord wears a military tie. What is 'bourgeois' about this mixed bunch of idioms is less the kind of languages they are than the effects they produce... These effects are discursive, not purely formal, features of language... (p.194)

But I am perhaps being hypercritical and failing to do justice to Linton's work and her long-term attention to what she calls 'real-world events' and 'real-world memory'. Her use of the dissection of the contents of her own autobiographical memory laid bare some interesting discoveries. She finds that when freely recalling old memories she used four strategies, each one yielding different contents: they were, simple chronological order, reverse chronological order, categorical summaries (or dominant themes) often with embedded extendures, and graphical and time-line expressions. The latter are simple diagrammatic representations of her past. How far do these strategies represent the repertoire we all use when deliberately trying to recall the past? For it must be remembered that it is not only psychologists who cast about for a magic hook which will draw towards them a rich haul of autobiographical memories. All kinds of interrogators do it, and so do friends and others who have a natural curiosity about our pasts. (Where did you grow up? What was it like? What did your parents do? etc.) Oral historians do it: Paul Thompson (1988) has a schedule of questions thematically subdivided and running over ten closely printed pages (p.296-306). But the most persistent interrogator is oneself. What, I ask myself, was the name of the Underground station I walked out of sixty-three years ago? Was it really sixty-three or sixty-four or sixty-two? How did my mother persuade me to undertake this daunting visit to a lady of another class with a posh voice? Had she invited me? How did I know the way? What did we have for tea? What did I say about her strange paintings which she spread out for me on the floor? Who expected what outcome from this embarrassing encounter which still haunts me?

I suspect that my strategies are very different from Linton's but she sets us on a very productive task. For a group of would-be autobiographical rememberers could add to her list and we might discover what are the commonest and most effective strategies for those making a very conscious effort to remember. It would be helpful to know what strategies are used by those engaged in writing lengthy autobiographies. I have recently read 105 unpublished autobiographies written by people almost all of whom were between the ages of mid-sixties and mid-seventies. They were all novitiates submitting manuscripts to the British Libraries National Life Story Collection competition called Life Story Awards. The scripts were fifty thousand to seventy thousand words long and every one used a chronological strategy although it must be said that it does not follow that the textual strategy corresponded to the search strategy. Linton found that strategies operated on a law of diminishing returns as the events receded, which points to the use of a learned written-discourse strategy in these autobiographies rather than a recall strategy. Remarking on changes over time, Linton observes that the contents of memories become more structured in middle-age and that there are deletions and changes of emphasis. New features appear which show a different assessment of an event.

> For example, meeting a shy scholar five years earlier takes on a new importance when I begin to date and decide to marry him. The earlier meeting now rewritten or recategorised takes on the character of a landmark or beacon in previously unmarked terrain. (p.64)

That comment adds to a growing consensus that our inner autobiographies are always in a dynamic state and thus undergoing constant revision.

Linton is modest about her unique work. She cites Salaman (1970) who studies memory in old age and who maintained that it was only then that the meaning of childhood was resolved and she herself adds, 'Even a study of a dozen years is relatively brief in the context of a lifetime'.

In the history of ideas it is by no means uncommon for innovative thinking to lie quiescent like a hibernating bear and to be roused after a great lapse of time into vibrant new life. The work of Gramsci, for instance, which burst into the discourse of new-look Marxists after almost half a century of neglect in Britain comes to mind. And this is how it was with the work of Frederick Bartlett, whose *Remembering: A Study in Experimental and Social Psychology* (1932) broke new ground on memory and then was ignored by all but a few scholars until the Eighties. But then Bartlett was complicit in the long sleep of his early ideas, for, as Mary Douglas (1980) wryly remarks

> The author of the best book on remembering forgot his own first convictions. He became absorbed in the institutional framework of Cambridge University psychology, and restricted to the conditions of the experimental laboratory. (p.25)

Given the appearance in the Eighties of a new and serious preoccupation with autobiographical memory, it was inevitable that Bartlett's early work should be dusted down, freshly scrutinised and used as a launching pad for new kinds of exploration. It makes sense therefore at this point to take a look at his creative investigations and what he concluded from them.

Bartlett was determined to study memory in ways which were as close as possible to the ways it functions when people actually do their remembering for life purposes and then express it in words. This means that he restored to the study of memory *the significance of the context in which remembering is done*. Where and when we remember affects how we remember. From what socio-cultural location do we speak? The original events and everything which surrounded them are now perceived by the rememberer in the micro- and macro-world in which he/she is now speaking. and which determined the form and content of the articulated memory.

Bartlett's work, now highly valued, is often represented by summaries of his 'The War of the Ghosts' experiment, which is a landmark in the study of memory (see, for example, Fentess and Wickham, 1992, p.32-36). It is a parlour game adroitly lifted to the level of a locus classicus. In one form the game consisted of his asking a group of people to retell a story following his instructions. Only one person was given the story who then told it to one other and in this way it travelled round the whole group. As every party-goer knows, the final version is very different from the first. In another form of the experiment one person retold the story at various intervals of time. What adds special significance to the retellings is that Bartlett had chosen his story with particular care: it was a Native American folk story which followed the conventions of such narratives, conventions very different from those in the European tradition, so much so that it seemed to Bartlett's storytellers to be permeated by ambiguities and discontinuities to such a degree as to make it baffling. The outcome was that the retellers 'obliged' the story to make sense, that is, they changed it in different ways but always so as to give it *their* kind of intelligibility. They reculturalised the story, making it cross the boundary between the Native American narrative world and the British one.

Maintaining his naturalistic stance Bartlett asked his collaborators to discuss their ways of remembering and in the process discovered that some of them used as a mnemonic the very vivid images of the original. However, he held to the view that such actual traces of the past become woven into reconstructions of memory, for this is what stands at the heart of his contribution – that memory functions by interpreting the past in order to give it meaning. Moreover, that interpretation and meaning, conscious and unconscious, emerged from the culture of the person retelling the past.

If the import of Bartlett's work were restricted to a demonstration of how people remember stories, its interest would be limited, perhaps, to folklorists, ethnographers and narratologists, but it has relevance for students of autobiography, too. Remembering a story you have been told is, of course, a kind of autobiographical memory. For example, I first encountered the Yiddish story of Bontshe Schweig (Bontshe the Meek) when my grandfather told it to me. Only much later did I discover that it was a classic Yiddish short story. It remains for me an essential part of the way my grandfather figures in my autobiographical memory as a teller of stories both fictional and autobiographical. The stories we remember do not float in mid-air; they exist firmly anchored in the context of part of our lives. Somewhere in the labyrinth of their memories Bartlett's subjects would not only have a version of 'The War of the Ghosts' but also of the intriguing events surrounding their acquisition of it.

Bartlett's emphasis on the reconstructive nature of memory adds to the views coming from other commentators who have looked at autobiographical discourse and found it an inventive reconstruction. Perhaps that reconstruction reaches its most challenging form in autobiographical fiction. However, his work which he saw as a social-psychological study, is criticised by Middleton and Edwards in *Collective Remembering* (1990) for not being whole-heartedly social. They had replicated his serial reproduction experiment with 'The War of the Ghosts' in which each storyteller, they say, passes on his version to the next in line in a kind of one-way traffic. What this eliminates is the possibility of conversational interaction and therefore of witnessing the social creation of memory.

There are no conversations: the 'subjects' have no opportunity to engage with each other communicatively. It occurred to us that, however messy the data might get, there might be an advantage in allowing the participants to talk to each other, and to create together, a joint version of remembered events. This might get us closer to the social creation of memory, which Bartlett himself sought. (p.24/5)

The social act of remembering I shall be returning to shortly. For the moment, note that the above citation not only reinserts the social and the collective into autobiographical memory where they had been lying low since the Twenties but also brings into view what is virtually absent from recent studies of autobiographical memory, its occurrence and meaning in conversation, which in general has been passed over. This is hardly surprising when we see how much energy is poured into experiments which, in spite of differences in design, share an almost obsessive preoccupation with having participants (usually students, of course) make records which yield the number of memories they have logged or the dating of particular memories, (see Conway, 1990, Chapter 3). Conway in his introductory text which is, for me, the best and most comprehensive account of the state of the art seen from a cognitive psychologist's point of view, comments at the outset of his book,

Autobiographical memory constitutes one of the areas where cognitive psychologists have no choice but to confront aspects of human cognition which are often set aside in mainstream cognitive research. (p.xvii)

and later,

Unfortunately, however, the concepts of 'emotion' and the 'self' are not sufficiently well-developed in psychology... One further problem is that there are no generally agreed models of either emotion or the self. In fact, both these areas ... [are] currently undergoing something of a research revival. (p.89/90)

And about time too! For it is something to marvel at that there could be a credible psychology which by-passed emotion and the self.

Conway, like Middleton and Edwards (*op.cit*) does give some attention, albeit very brief, to the possibility that 'autobiographical memory is taught within a culture in the form of explicit instructions provided in, say, mother/child interactions' (p.102). If memory is culture-specific, then we must wonder how it comes about that the analysis of autobiography scarcely acknowledges the existence of autobiographical discourse in non-'Western' cultures. It has needed the vigorous intrusion of feminists, 'other' ethnicities and a rare scholar like Michael Fischer (1994) to turn our gaze away from the confident allocation of the beginnings of true autobiography which places them quite unconditionally in Europe. Fischer's programme attempts to install an entirely new agenda.

> I have been making a plea for the cross-cultural, the comparative, the critique of the categories we use and for cross-disciplinary conversation on uses of life-histories to rebuild social theory, to rebuild the technical polity, to rebuild theories of psychology and to refashion the world we live in. That seems to me a not unambitious project for the study of autobiography to undertake. (p.126)

Behind his plea is a complex, even elusive, view of memory of which we catch no more than a glimpse or two in other writers. This is memory structured somewhat like geological strata, each with its own characteristics and fractures but 'collaged together in consciousness and in unconscious manoeuverings' (p.80) and therefore posing a hermeneutical challenge to anyone attempting to dissect and anatomise it.

To read Fischer is to experience a kind of embarrassment as his horizon is so wide as to render our own views parochial. All the same, the stirrings of the 'research revival' which Conway speaks of are giving rise to some new preoccupations. There are two recurrent themes which are worth dwelling on – flashbulb/significant memories and involuntary memories – the very names of which seem to propose a willingness to investigate the kind of memories with which we are all very familiar and hitherto have looked for in vain in the literature. Anyone can offer you memories which in the mind are as bright as sharp as a film even after huge intervals of time, while others are fuzzy and elusive. Are the very vivid memories in a special class of their own? Brown and Kulik (1977) certainly thought so, so much so, in fact, that they invented the term 'flashbulb memories' for them. It comes as something of a surprise that their research concentrated upon memories in which people heard of a dramatically important event (typically the assassination of John Kennedy). These are memories logged within circumstances of exceptional national importance. The choice may be convenient for the researcher but for many the circumstances of the death of a close relative may be much more momentous than that of a national or international figure. The flashbulb term was adopted because it is as though a memory of an event which has caught someone off guard and is, as we say, sensational lights up the contextual details, however trivial they may be. Brown and Kulik suggested that these autobiographical memories constituted a special category because they were encoded in a different way owing to their special biological meaning i.e. a response to a particular threat which generates a special awareness and a need to file away the record. Moreover, they noted that flashbulb memories frequently illustrated such aspects of the moment as the who, what, when, where and why.

Seductive though the flashbulb metaphor is, it has been dismantled thoroughly by other scholars who have been able to show that the perfectly remembered moment in time is often wrongly remembered, often endowed with significance after the event, or even before it. Further, the structure given to the remembered event is derived not from a unique encoding but conformity to well-known conventions of narration which even unsophisticated narrators deploy and is likely to have been through many repetitions. A much more modest view of flashbulb memories has now been established. While it is readily acknowledged and supported by copious evidence that there exists a class of memories which are peculiarly vivid, such memories, however, are not uniquely recorded. What makes them different, as we might guess, is the high level of emotion which saturated the original experience and its meaning in the life of the rememberer. In spite of the frequent mis-remembering demonstrably contained in many of them they prove to be peculiarly resistant to change; they achieve a canonical form which seems to render them proof against amnesiac loss.

Conway (*op.cit.*), pursuing the decline of memory in the elderly, turns to Salaman's book, *A Collection of Moments: a Study of Involuntary Memories* (1970). The respectful and lengthy attention he gives to this book constitutes an intriguing intellectual event. The research psychologist places before us the testimony of someone who is doing no more than inspecting and analysing with healthy intellectual curiosity, her own memories and those of some famous writers. Conway quotes substantial passages from her work and he listens respectfully to what many would dismiss as anecdotage from a lay source. My appetite whetted by Conway's citations I could do no less than turn to Salaman's book.

Salaman was a research physicist who worked with the celebrated scientist, Rutherford; but she was also a novelist and autobiographer. Her sensitivity to autobiographical memory must, I believe, be seen as related to the fact that she is an inter-cultural, multi-lingual woman, one of those many people who embody in one person two or more cultures, several languages and a changing, adjusting identity and for whom memory does not only reach back into the past but into another place where it speaks another language and operates with other codes. Memory for them must travel past frontier posts, literal and psychological. Although memory for them does not enter a totally alien world, it is rather the extreme form of all memory. For the past, as L.P. Hartley told us, is a foreign country. Salaman says,

> It was years before I realised that my homesickness in Berlin had been for the
> past, that people who have never left their country have similar experience: we
> are all exiles from our past. (p.16)

Nevertheless, hybrids like her are propelled more irresistibly towards their
lost lands. She spent childhood and adolescence in Russia in a well-to-do
Jewish family, left in 1919, studied physics and mathematics in Berlin and,
on Einstein's advice, went on to study under Rutherford in Cambridge.

Her book proved to be compelling for it assembled coherently an unusual
interweaving of materials which constitute her resources for pursuing the
theme of involuntary memories. The chief nodes of her book are her own
substantial autobiographical moments. They are buttressed by citations from
the work of writers of autobiographies, some of them with massive reputa-
tions like Goethe, Tolstoy and Proust and others far less well-known like
William Hutton and Harriet Martineau. Around these materials she con-
structs her speculations and reflections and I must give some inkling of her
methods and ideas.

Let me begin with Salaman's discussion of the way experiences came into
her mind after fifty years and, once there, how they drew towards her a
constellation of connected memories. She goes on to say that our understanding of memory would be deeper if people gave, when they were able
to do so, the history of involuntary memories. This would be particularly
true of writers who are for the most part too busy getting on with the job of
writing their memories to linger over how they got there and how they disinterred them. That is why she is at pains to gather together those occasions
when a few writers like Proust and Dostoevsky make their comments on the
working of their memory. However,

> ... often a writer does not himself remember when one of his early memories
> came back involuntarily, and we, his readers, cannot tell whether he is recording
> a memory a few minutes old, or is writing the memory of a memory a few years
> later. Sometimes it happens that the revival of a memory is itself fixed in sensa-
> tions, space and time. (p.111)

She has already shown us this happening to De Quincey. He has a vivid and
joyous memory of looking from a window at a country town market when
he was three years old. He then in adulthood remembers this moment of
intense pleasure when wretchedly he is running away from school at the age
of seventeen. Salaman herself in her fifties remembers remembering, at the
age of thirteen, stealing a piece of soap when she was five years old. She
offers us her earliest memory as an example of this memory-of-a-memory

phenomenon. I must quote it at some length, not only because of the interest in the points she is making but also to reveal her characteristic use of her own memories.

> I was playing one fine morning outside our house, the one we left when I was eight; Mother was talking to a friend when suddenly I rushed and told her excitedly that I remembered going with her in the diligence. There may have been something about a journey in a diligence in what she had been saying, or the diligence may have just appeared (it was the hour when it usually arrived from Kiev drawn by many horses – always a fascinating sight) or both may have happened simultaneously. I began to tell Mother that she was wearing her rotonde (a cape lined with fur) and that I was inside it. She said: 'But you can't remember. You were too young'. Her friend must have suggested that I was mixing up that journey with some other because I remember Mother telling me that the only time she had taken me by diligence to Kiev was on the occasion of her brother's wedding. I gave her more details but I am certain that I did not tell her the heart of my memory; I could not have, even if I had wanted to.
>
> The diligence used to start on its return journey to Kiev at about four, but on a short winter day it was dark when it passed our house. The moment I had remembered was this: we had settled in the dimly lit diligence in the left corner by the door, but it had not yet moved. I am on my Mother's lap, inside her rotonde. Her large smooth black fur collar was standing up round her head; on her head she had a black lace scarf. As she saw me looking at her, a smile of happiness lit up her broad fair lovely face and she gave that smile to me. (p.111/112)

There is the heart of Salaman's strategy. Having led us into the complexities of these multiple involuntary memories, she implicitly invites us to examine our own. But the detail of this highly treasured memory also invites us to look into much more than the single point she appears to be making – the way others negotiate and question our memories. Her book is full of them and they often tell us more than her comments do, perceptive though they often are. She does grapple with them, egged on by her keen sense that very little is known about involuntary memories. Trying to find an image for the particular characteristics of involuntary memories, especially of childhood, she wrote in *The Fertile Plain*, an autobiography which she wrote after the failure of much earlier attempts, 'My memories of childhood are like scenes lit up by sheets of summer lightning as one speeds in a train'.

This image, which recalls the flashbulb metaphor, she notes is very close to Harriet Martineau's , who wrote that her memories, '...were revived in an inexplicable way as by a flash of lightning over a far horizon'. Involuntary memories are those which come without warning and bring back a past suffused with emotion. They have a particular quality which gives a sensation of once again living in that moment, whether it be joyous or distressful. As an autobiographer, writing at a period in life when maturity generates many new involuntary memories, Salaman is confident that autobiography cannot be constructed from conscious memories alone but that room must be made for what has surfaced from the unconscious mind while the conscious mind diligently takes pains in doing its own work. Failure to make this accommodation leaves an autobiography constructed from 'rationalising and invented sentiments' alone and therefore impoverished.

She goes on to make discriminations which are suggestive rather than fully argued. A feature of involuntary memories is what she calls the difference between 'the background' and the central event in the memory. The terms are not really helpful. What she is discussing is what I would call the setting or precise location of the memory and the core of the moment. One of her examples, as always, makes the distinction very clear.

> One day, while working on some early memories, and living in one of the 1905 Revolution, when I was five, I was terribly taken aback. I was looking out of the window when I was five, with my eyes on two women running past, just underneath, each frightened in her own way. They had neither hats nor kerchiefs and their hair was bobbed. 'The Revolutionaries', Mother said, close behind me: I turned my head to her. To my amazement I realised that the room I was looking at was the sitting-room to which we moved when I was thirteen. (p.32)

Which puts a different gloss on flashbulb memories as they were first proposed and when the assumption was that what made them unique was their total reliability. For Salaman there is what she calls an 'island' and this is inviolable, whereas the rest is expendable. On the other hand the sitting-room, post-thirteen years of age, she admits as a totally reliable memory. What is left unresolved is why the relocation of the 1905 event takes place. Salaman makes the proposal that we need to remember the setting of the core moment but, if we are removed from our environment in early childhood, we have to 'borrow a background' for our early memories. Perhaps or perhaps not: but what Salaman has helpfully done, and she has other examples, is to draw attention to a neglected aspect of involuntary memories recalled in old age. The scene-shifting could well have a significance in its own right.

As against this mise-en-scene (the past moment relived in the present) Salaman has memories which she calls 'fragments' which seem to float in the mind, devoid of setting, not fixed in time or space or even sensations. Her hypothesis is that although they recapture powerful feelings, they have lost the sense of shock or, as a Freudian would say, have been repressed.

Ultimately, Salaman's book is a kind of celebration of involuntary memories which, even when they are painful or poignant or tragic, can in a certain sense be cherished. Why should this be? She feels that they yield meanings of great importance and that these meanings help us to live. The older we get, the more they contribute to an appraisal of an entire life. The book is also a plea for us to examine closely the history of our involuntary memories for there remains much about them which is still not clearly understood and her own book does not pretend to be more than a meticulous reconnaissance. It is, I need hardly say at this point, yet another outstanding instance of a contribution to the study of autobiographical memory from outside the world of appointed experts.

Let me enter here a note which I value partly because it sheds light on how this book is getting itself written. I was, having written the last few sentences, impatient to turn to very recent developments in the study of memory which I was very much in tune with. A day or two elapsed before I did so during which I received a gift of Oliver Sacks's *An Anthropologist on Mars* (1995). It had some important things to say on autobiographical memory including a special insight into what I had just been writing about Salaman's description of fragments or floating memories. Sacks is writing about an extraordinary autistic woman called Temple Grandin who had become an expert on animal behaviour and a teacher at the University of Colorado. He is impelled to visit her not only because of her rare achievements as an autistic person but also because she had written an autobiography, *Emergence: Labelled Autistic* (Grandin, 1986). How, he wondered, could an autistic person write an autobiography? It was a contradiction in terms. The outcome of his visit I shall leave to his own characteristic case-study narrative but I select one moment in it when Temple Grandin tells him of the time when a slaughterhouse manager spied on her in order to watch how she calmed excited animals. Sacks writes,

> I was struck by the vividness of the re-experience, the memory, for her – it seemed to play itself in her mind with extraordinary detail – and by its unwavering quality. It was as if the original scene, its perception (with all its attendant feelings) was reproduced with virtually no modification. This quality of memory seemed to me both prodigious in its detail and pathological in its fixity. (p.269)

Temple herself says her mind is like a quick-access computer; she has to play the whole scene and cannot access separate parts of it. To this phenomenon, which she so clearly explained, Sacks adds a fascinating footnote in which he comments that her memories are not reconstructed, as Bartlett had argued, and, moreover, does not fit in with the most recent views of this matter. He instances Damasio's *Descartes' Error* (1994).

> Images are *not* stored as facsimile pictures of things, or events, or words, or sentences. The brain does not file Polaroid pictures of people, objects, landscapes; nor does it store audiotapes of music and speech; it does not store films of scenes in our lives...In brief, there seems to be no permanently held pictures of anything, even miniaturised, no microfiches or microfilms, no hard copies. (cited in Sacks, p.269)

What is Temple doing then? Just deceiving herself that she has perfect recall, something we all do from time to time. Perhaps Bruner is right when he says that sometimes there may be failure of integration of perceptual systems with higher integrative ones, and with concepts of self, so that *relatively* unprocessed, uninterpreted, unrevised images persist.

In another chapter called 'The Landscape of His Dreams' Sacks elaborates ideas about memory provoked by a painter, Franco Magnani, who spends decades painting hundreds of pictures from memory of the native village in Italy he had known in childhood. By the time Sacks meets him Franco has achieved recognition in the USA where his works were displayed in an exhibition called 'A Memory Artist'.

> ... he indeed possessed a prodigious memory – a memory that would seemingly reproduce with almost photographic accuracy every building, every street, every stone of Pontito ... It was as if Magnani held in his head an infinitely detailed, three-dimensional model of his village, which he could turn around and examine or explore mentally, and then reproduce with fidelity. (p.143)

In 1965 at the age of thirty-one he settled in San Francisco where he had a strange illness during which he began to have vivid dreams of his beloved Pontito. Having scarcely painted before, in twenty or so years he painted thousands of pictures, every one of which was a view of Pontito. You may get a good idea of his work from Sacks's book for there are illustrations in colour of Franco's paintings placed side by side with same-view photographs of Pontito. Sacks's story of Franco is not only utterly compelling by virtue of what it narrates but also touches the imagination because it is told with infinite wisdom and empathy. Sacks meditates on the subject of autobiographical memory provoked by his experiences of meeting Franco and his paintings.

He is moved to observe that Franco's amazing visual autobiographical productivity is the work of an exile. As I have suggested, this cross-over from one kind of life to another gives a potent thrust to recollection which is a particularly poignant form of mutability, separation and loss. Discontinuity and nostalgia, suggests Sacks, are at their most profound when the expatriate or exile loses the very site of childhood, though like Salaman he acknowledges that we are all exiles from our past.

We have already seen how much the recollection of the past undergoes a constant re-editing which alters, forgets, adds, elaborates afresh in what Bartlett called an imaginative reconstruction. Sacks, however, is disposed to speculate on whether there are not unusual forms of which this is not true. He instances not only Luria's celebrated 'mnemonist', (*The Mind of a Mnemonist*, 1967), but also rote memories of long epic poems in oral cultures and the formidable memories of 'idiots savants' and the compulsive replaying of traumatic memories, all of which he sees as 'a fixation or fossilisation at work' which differ from the dynamic, constantly revised memory. He never completely resolves the riddle of the perfectly reproductive memory as against the creative one, but tentatively suggests that any view of autobiographical memory must include both concepts. Franco's pictures are 'minutely accurate in the tiniest details' but are also 'serene and idyllic' and highly edited to leave a picture of a kind of paradise. They are a myth of happy childhood. There is no question that both the autistic Temple and the compulsive Franco are rare and remarkable people but it is something of a surprise that so diligent and eagle-eyed a writer as Sacks does not give greater attention to his own words. Temple, he says, replays a scene 'with virtually no modification'; Bruner speaks of images which are 'relatively unrevised. This is scarcely 'fixation' and 'fossilisation', however closely it approaches them. What all this suggests is that even in memories of such reproductive and prodigious accuracy as those which Sacks reports, there is a reconstructive process at work, albeit minimal. So much is not changed, however, that it seems right to argue that we are observing a different phenomenon from the proven reconstructions of flashbulb memories.

Autobiographical memory, then, is not a single kind of monolithic process which delivers equally a monolithic kind of text. It grows out of different kinds of images which in their turn, when they are verbalised, are shaped by a diversity of textual resources and social contexts.

* * * *

Up to this point this chapter has been concerned to look at the ideas of scholars who, however powerful their insights, have taken memory to be a psychological phenomenon which functions within the individual. From time to time another viewpoint can be glimpsed in my account, notably Bartlett's attempt to put the social into any discussion of remembering and to make room for the role played by culture and context. I now want to return to that theme for very recent work not only proposes a social view of memory but takes that notion much further than Bartlett ever did.

There are those who set in sharp opposition the private and the public, the self and the other, the individual and the communal, and for whom memory is perhaps the greatest and most powerful instance of the functioning of the private individual self. To use a word like individual, let alone the more overtly ideological word individualism, is to pluck one of the most resonant chords in Western aesthetics, ethics, economics and politics, chords which can be heard loudly sounding in the dominant appraisals of autobiography, as, for instance, in the extraordinary claim that it was invented in Europe and in its true form is derived from the Romantics. To challenge this view is 'to be engaged in a struggle with a single dominant text: the centrality and sovereignty of the individual and the problems to which it gives rise' (Shotter and Gergen,1989, p.xi). In fact this struggle is well under way and memory itself is now seen as something different from the view powerfully represented in both individual psychology and in most of the foremost students of autobiography over a long period. There are now others who counterpose vigorously to that view the concepts of social memory and collective memory (see, for example, Middleton and Edwards, 1990 and Fentress and Wickham, 1992). Some feminists in particular, scenting a patriarchal component in the dominant view, have also challenged it (see Stanley, 1994). There is a sparse but highly valuable legacy here.

Innovators, however iconoclastic, look to their forebears and it is in just this spirit that the work of Maurice Halbwachs has only recently surfaced. *Collective Memory* (1992) is assembled from two publications in French of 1941 and a posthumous volume of 1952. He was the pre-eminent pioneer of the notion of collective memory. For him this was not a special kind of memory but rather all memory which arises from our most telling ex-perience in social groups – the family, the neighbourhood, our working lives and a host of other formally or informally constituted institutions. Auto-biographical memory for Halbwachs always arises from our interactions with others with whom we share a group membership. The remembering 'I' remembers by virtue of interactions with 'you', 's/he', and 'they' who are in some sense always fellow members of a group. Stated baldly in this way without Halbwachs's supporting text, it can be perceived as a daring and total reversal of the prevailing view. But he went much further than this and showed how all societies are involved in building an elaborate superstructure of commemoration. There is an imperative which comes from the dominant culture, sometimes operating with overt compulsion but more often by incorporation which says to its members, 'remember this'. There are rituals, statues, inscriptions, ceremonies, centenaries, symbols, icons, traditions (some recently invented!) which foreground selected events, especially wars and battles, and halo-ed individuals. There is no need to elaborate except to add that commemoration can be contested and alternative icons and ceremonies be installed, the Tolpuddle Martyrs, for instance; commemoration can reach into the micro-structure of our lives – families' annual visits, wedding anniversaries, etc. In other words there is often a social struggle to gain ascendency over our memories and those who feel the pull of two different cultures, ethnic, religious, linguistic, national, class-based, will experience the dilemmas and often the pain of this battle fought out within their social consciousness.

To attach 'collective' to memory requires us to scrutinise more closely its meanings. It is easy to understand the ways in which there is a public, closely-observable collection of activities which we can properly label collective. Yet can we properly allot them to autobiographical memory? There is always the danger that public memory-making can become so routinist that it scarcely impinges on some individual's memories. For others it may be momentous and move from autobiographical memory into autobiographical text because in one way or another they represent peak experiences, as I shall try to show in a moment. The intensely personal and the publicly acknowledged may merge to make them indelibly recorded – a funeral, a prestigious award. There is nevertheless a much deeper and more direct way in which we should see autobiographical memory as social, even if it is somewhat elusive by virtue of its being overlaid by individualist concepts and the fact that the most vivid memories are so rich in fine detail.

It was in the family first of all where Halbwachs saw social memory being constructed. Beside the few home-based formalities, religious holy days and anniversaries, there is always an informal process at work in which there are not only shared rememberings but highly memorable shared events. Nor are they necessarily separate from the official and quasi-official. A family involved in one way or another in the second World War will represent it to each other in a very different manner from the approved version. Members of families collaborate in teaching each other what is memorable. Children are taught to remember and what is to be valued in their remembering and they overhear memories being talked about. 'Do you remember when...?' is common currency in every family. A memory becomes collective because it emerges from the constant negotiation of conversation.

There is more to it than that. Memories must be saturated with social meanings as soon as they are turned into texts, spoken or written. They may have been formulated already in inner-speech but when they are externalised they must draw on memories of existing texts. These resources can be seen at every linguistic level and they are all a social creation. Every text is a complex intertwining of social meanings encoded in language. This can be seen in the central device of autobiography – narrative, with its own strategies, tactics and conventions, many of which are available to everybody. Autobiography can and does draw on other social linguistic legacies: any discursive model may be followed. Bakhtin (1981) shows how in the novel one genre can be set alongside another and be given a particular tone. This kind of generic insertion takes on a new meaning by virtue of being played off against another, usually the mainstream text. In autobiography, too, there is often generic diversity when the writer or the speaker shifts the mode of discourse to philosophise, analyse, draw on relevant expertise or offer quotation. All text, as Bakhtin says, is dialogic and this, too, makes it social. Halbwachs saw memory as being structured by language which makes possible teaching and the sharing of experience. Some autobiographers may be highly aware that their tellings of life-stories are intensely social acts but, whether they are so or not, they cannot exempt themselves from the social worlds inscribed in their texts. This does not mean that a kind of autobiographical determinism totally controls the writer who becomes no more than a channel through which one or other social voice is speaking or a mere pen being inexorably pushed by social forces. We all incorporate within ourselves many voices, loud and soft. Each one of us becomes a unique assemblage in a constant dynamic state, the meeting place, the intersection point of innumerable forces. Like every individual in the social world, the autobiographer is not a free soul rising above it but, as Marx said, his social being determines his consciousness. He or she is not, nevertheless, a zombie scribe for there are degrees of choice and intensely personal experiences which cannot easily or totally be attributed to social origins. Moreover, we can say that the degree of socialness is highly variable.

I have a vivid memory (now written as a story 'Memoir for Beatrice Hastings', unpub.) of my very first sortie in somewhat bizarre circumstances into the world of the upper middle-class to which I have already briefly referred. I was invited or sent to visit a most unlikely new friend of my mother in her flat in Belsize Park in North London. In her person, the furnishings and what transpired on that occasion, it turned out to be for me overwhelming, embarrassing and disastrous. I was eleven or twelve, I can't say for certain. Something good and special was, I imagine, supposed to emerge from this encounter. At one point on that winter's evening, after crumpets and tea, the woman in question showed me some of her large abstract paintings and I knew with utter certainty that I was expected to make some intelligent and sensitive response and I knew with the same certainty that I had absolutely nothing to say. When I left I was miserable with a sense of failure. Now it is not difficult to see that occasion as saturated with social meanings – a social class encounter, a Jewish/gentile encounter, a generational boy-and-fiftyish-woman encounter, a gender encounter, a low-culture/high-culture encounter. All this came to be realised in fine details – the carpeted room, the pools of light from shaded lamps, the walls hung with pictures, the tea tray and B.H. herself with her upper-class speech, her straight, clipped grey hair, long blood-red ear-rings and loose clothes in shades of brown. There is a social template we can place over all this which would reveal that this occasion matches to perfection all of those millions of other collisions with which it shares so much and which make it inescapably social. But in the end, though that template would tell us so much, it can only do so by covering up many features which make the occasion unique to me. Every fraught, baffling meeting of this kind has its specificities which are not trivial. Only someone absolutely bent on a comprehensive social tidy-up would brush away the fact that in the sub-text is my mother's capacity for making unlikely friendships or the little mystery of why I remember the street name painted on a wall, flaking black and white. We have need of a new term. My memory of that moment is both individual/social and social/ individual and we have as yet no word for that particular inter-animation.

I wrote one story a few years ago called, 'Comrade Rosie Rosen' (Rosen, 1992) which, I think, shows several aspects of social memory at work. the last section of the story tells of the time when I was sent to school on Empire Day without a Union Jack, an unheard-of provocative and outrageous act engineered by my communist mother when I was eight years old. The story registers three different forces at work. First is the very loud noise of official, national, imperial, military remembering embodied in a nationwide ritual, sanctioned, promoted, embellished by the State, reinforced in patterned rituals in which The Flag is made the central icon. The schools were both allocated and took on willingly the role allotted to them. And each individual child was incorporated into the fête-like construction of the day by being called upon to declare an act of allegiance, the bringing and brandishing of a flag and dressing in best clothes. Everyone was being enjoined to remember both the day and a certain version of the history of Empire. Against this there is my mother's mode of countering this commemorative strategy. In one way it is anti-memory, in another it is counter-memory, a contestation in which I am given a particular role. The third component of the memory is a struggle between being faithful to my mother's powerful ideas which I believed in totally and having to endure a kind of martyrdom – the only child without a flag. In the end I succumb to a teacher's kind gesture. She buys me a halfpenny pasteboard flag. This is for me both a massive relief and an appalling betrayal. The autobiographical story, then, recalls a public commemorative act which recruits children to the idea of Empire and attempts to implant the day, its icons and its rituals at the very core of their social memories. My mother, on the other hand, is challenging for the same memory space. In fact she had almost totally encamped in it, especially as she could promote a rival symbolic day, May Day, which also occurs in the story. But this struggle to construct social memory is not as simple as that, at least not within me. I attempted to play all this out in the story.

> On this fine summer's morning I turned grumpily into Myrdle Street, passing the other children flaunting their finery and flags at each other. Not me. I was in my usual old jersey and scuffed shoes and no flag. My mother was not going to have me tainted with the iniquity of Empire and at least one person was going to crack the enamelled surface of unanimity – me. Carefully she had lectured me on what the Empire really meant. She had lots of pamphlets on the subject with appalling pictures in them, of floggings, shootings and hangings presided over by men in pith helmets. They haunt me to this post-holocaust day. As ever, I only partly understood what she was saying but I approved of all of it. It was my mother saying all this and she knew. She knew the truth about Empire as she knew about everything else... which was all very well but she had made it quite clear that there was going to be no flag for me and no poshing-up. It was one thing to be dazzled by her inside knowledge but quite another to be selected as the representative of her principles, defying the British Empire all by myself. (p.19/20)

Elsewhere in the story I wrote,

> ...I knew she had to be right. The trouble was, I was dazzled by the Lord Mayor's Show and that golden coach. As for soldiers, I wouldn't have dared to admit to her that I tingled when they marched by with their shining bands. (p.17)

For many, collective memory is shot through with conflicts, contradictions ambiguities and doubts. Wars, battles and skirmishes are fought out in their heads and may emerge into the light of day through their autobiographical acts.

CHAPTER 6

FROM THE MARGINS?
FEMINISM AND AUTOBIOGRAPHY

Feminists have for some time been conducting their own long march through the institutions, to adopt that heady aspiration of the Sixties. That expedition must of necessity include the extensive territory of discursive institutions without which the fabric of contemporary society is inconceivable and within which, installed uncomfortably, is autobiography. Certainly feminists have turned a disenchanted eye on its established forms and its revered works. They have advanced their own analyses and championed 'femino-centric' works which they believe have slowly created an alternative tradition. And this is no straightforward business of articulating a facile antithesis to the views of authoritative males. As Sheila Rowbotham (1973) pointed out, the task is to overcome 'a paralysis of consciousness' and this has to be 'the result of great labour'. Even now that labour is far from complete. Many propositions have to be advanced tentatively and some, as I attempt to show, are dubious and not subjected to the same critical scrutiny as is directed at those that they attempt to replace. As always, part of the painful process involves the attempt to construct a new lexicon; sure enough, feminist writing on autobiography is accumulating one – gynesis, autogynography, femino-centric, phallologocentric, androcentric discourse, cultural ventriloquism, alterity. Let us leave aside for the moment whether these terms enrich and sharpen analysis. They insert themselves because, like all radicalisms, feminism needs its own touchstones and signposts and, when it emerges from the academy, it must have the authentic ring of learned neologisms.

There is now a well-established feminist literature on autobiography, not only numerous papers and articles but also substantial works like Estelle Jelinek's editing of *Women's Autobiography: Essays in Criticism* (1980), Sidonie Smith's *A Poetics of Women's Autobiography: Marginality and the Fictions of Self-Representations* (1987), Shari Benstock's collection, *The Private Self: Theory and Practice of Women's Autobiography* (1988), Liz Stanley's *The Auto/biographical I* (1992). From this rapidly expanding literature there emerges a set of themes and propositions which surface again and again. Let me list them:

- A critique of both male autobiography and male discourse about it which shows them to be preoccupied with self and incurably tainted by individualism; the autobiographies are predominantly stories written by that familiar lambasted figure, the Western, white, middle-class male

- An act of recovery and re-reading which disinters from the past feminist autobiographical writing which has either been buried by silence and neglect or which remained unknown because it was never published

- When women's work does get published it struggles, not always totally successfully, to free itself from the constraints of the role allocated to women and the established and legitimised forms of autobiographical discourse

- As women break free from these constraints, unlike men, they orient themselves to the other and others ('alterity'); their mode is interpersonal rather than intrapersonal

- Women autobiographers display qualities which they share with other oppressed and marginalised groups (ethnic and religious minorities, Blacks, Jews, homosexuals)

- Women adopt less circumscribed forms to tell their life-stories – diaries, journals, letters

- Women play with established conventional forms and experiment with language, operating from the boundaries of discourse.

Before I elaborate on these diverse but interconnected themes I must digress to draw attention to a curious paradox in almost all feminist writing on autobiography. Sidonie Smith, whose book (*op.cit.*) is a major serious attempt to set right the bias in twentieth century autobiographical criticism, illuminates her thesis that 'woman speaks to her culture from the margins', where, in spite of the limitations, she can be 'polyvocal and heretical'.

> From women's autobiographies erupt, however suppressed they might be, rebellion, confusion, ambivalence, the uncertainties of desire. The inventiveness and originality of women's autobiographies in the history of the genre and the source of their fate at the hands of traditionally-minded critics (those arbiters of the symbolic order and its ideology of gender) lie in that very attempt to reconcile sometimes irreconcilable readings of the self, to sustain and subvert comfortable fictions. (p.176)

This 'coda' as she calls it could well serve as a compressed manifesto for feminist views of women's autobiography. However, if we turn back to the outset of her book we find that she tells us (the condemnation can be found in other feminist writers)

> ...the majority of autobiography critics still persist in either erasing women's story, relegating it to the margins of critical discourse, or, when they treat women's autobiographies seriously, uncritically conflating the dynamics of male and female selfhood and textuality. Too many contemporary historians remain oblivious to the naiveté and culpability of their own critical assumptions and presumptions. (p.15)

Yet it is Sidonie Smith herself who confines her attention to 'formal autobiography as it emerges in the West', turning her back not only on letters, journals and diaries which other feminists have emphatically told us are often the preferred forms for feminist autobiographers but also on all oral autobiographical activity. The unblinking and quite properly censorious inspection of male 'naiveté and culpability of their own critical assumptions' does not extend to this neglect of women's oral telling of life stories, a practice which is often dialogic and collaborative, displaying the very qualities which, it is often asserted, are characteristic of women's autobiography. The assumption among many feminists is that autobiography is quintessentially a written mode. Shari Benstock (1988) places autobiography at the crossroads of writing and selfhood and relegates to a footnote this extraordinary assertion,

> ...without **graphe** autobiography would not exist – that is, it is only known through writing. (p.11)

It has been a major contention of this book that autobiographical activity not only includes many oral forms but that in those forms we can discover the roots of all autobiographical activity. The failure to acknowledge this and give it proper attention is not only a paradox of feminist accusations of the culpable silence of others but also nothing short of ironic when we encounter such phrases as '*speaking* at the margins of discourse' and 'female *voice*' (my emphasis HR), semi-metaphors which should have pointed in an obvious direction.

When we are swept along by the novel propositions and investigations which make us look afresh at the autobiographical and critical discourse which they generate, we have to stay alert to assertions which are uttered with incontrovertible certainty and remain unexamined. There are too many of them, as we shall see. Nevertheless they may represent the consequences of the painful struggle to articulate a new set of ideas. That scarcely justifies Sidonie Smith's scriptist and verbal bias.

> ...yet memory is ultimately a story about, and thus a discourse on, original ex-
> perience, so that recovering the past is... an interpretation of earlier experience
> that can never be divorced from the filterings of subsequent experience or
> *articulated outside the structures of language and storytelling.* [my emphasis
> HR] (p.45)

Bear in mind that Sidonie Smith is here speaking of written language and storytelling. *Never* should be used with caution and in this context it betrays an ignorance of non-verbal forms of autobiography. Think of the sequence of Rembrandt self-portraits or Hogarth, of whom Paulson says that his paintings 'drew upon and authorised his own experience' (Flokenflik, p.189). There is the whole world of photographic albums, collages and personal assemblages of memorabilia.

Giving due attention to women's oral autobiographical acts would both strengthen and extend the feminist propositions. For instance, Paul Thompson (*op.cit.*) gives us –

> Isabelle Bertaux-Wiame observes how among immigrants to Paris from the
> French countryside, 'the men consider the life they have lived as their own', as
> a series of acts, with well-defined goals; and in telling their story they use the
> active 'I', assuming themselves as the subject of their actions through their very
> forms of speech. Women, by contrast, talk of their lives typically in terms of
> relationships, including parts of other life-stories as their own; and very often
> they speak of 'we' or 'one' (*on* in French) symbolising the relationship which
> underlines that part of their life: 'we' as 'my parents and us' or as 'my husband
> and me' or as 'me and my children'. (p.157)

And this is precisely what feminists mean by alterity in written autobio-graphy. However, there is much more to it than this. Women's spoken autobiographical acts reveal features of their own.I can best give some notion of what rich possibilities are being overlooked by examining a series of studies by Peggy Miller and her colleagues (Miller and Moore, 1988; Miller et al , 1990; Miller, 1994) on personal experience stories from caregivers (usually mothers) and two-year-old girls. The work is not presented as in any way a feminist exercise; it is rather a sustained exploration and empirical investigation of the places where narrative and self intersect in ordinary talk. Her contention is that 'narrative can be said to play a privileged role in the process of self-construction'. In one study she made recordings and field notes in South Baltimore of an urban community of working-class families. These revealed 'certain categories of narrative material':

- caregivers' stories told about children in their presence

- caregivers' intervention into the children's storytelling

- children's appropriations of stories other than their own. Peggy Miller (1994) tells us that she virtually stumbled upon the significance of personal experience stories when she was doing research on early language socialisation. What emerged from the talk of the women and infant girls?

It soon became clear that stories of personal experience were a major form of adult talk occurring profusely in everyday conversation. I was impressed, as I listened, not only by the ubiquity of these stories but by the vigour and skill with which they were told. Men and women alike were accomplished practitioners, capable at times of inspired performances. (p.161)

Stories around the child occurred in 38 of the 40 samples at an overall average rate at 8.5 per hour. (*op.cit.*)

Many of these stories are about the child's own experience, typically addressed to another in her presence. Peggy Miller (1990) believes that by making the daughter the central figure in the story the mother makes the child an actor in her own right, whose experiences are worth telling. At the same time the stories provide models for the child of how to interpret her experiences.

...the stories are like a series of snapshots of the child protagonist in action: they contain specific images of the child and, by implication, of the parent, images that recur across stories and across children. Mothers recounted their children's achievements – getting weaned, attempting to sew, burping the baby, drawing a circle, remembering to stay on the sidewalk. They recounted mishaps. An active and spirited child fell off her bike or burned her arm and they themselves responded coolly and competently. They described acts of mischief in which a disobedient child broke an ashtray or bed, pinched her mother, wrote on the wall, or dumped salt, pepper and peanut butter into the pancake batter. In these stories the child was portrayed as 'bad' but also as quick, enterprising, and funny, the mother as exasperated but amused. (p.297)

Peggy Miller (1988) catches the earliest moments of girls' autobiographical activity and the mother's role in shaping them. Feminists often draw attention to the special significance of mother-daughter relationships (see Friedan, 1963 and Chodorow, 1977) and the way these emerge in women's autobiographies but sadly they show no awareness of the day-by-day construction of this relationship in the personal experience stories told to and by young girls and its specific features. Furthermore, women care-givers not only socialise their charges but in the process they socialise themselves.

When care-givers habitually tell and retell personal stories they are constantly reminding themselves of the experiences that are meaningful to them and relevant to their child-bearing beliefs and practices. (p.26)

I hope that this glimpse of Peggy Miller's is sufficient to indicate a much more profound and diverse autobiographical process at work than can be captured by analyses which attend only to written autobiography, the more especially as her work is based on interaction in working-class families, for whom the expression of personal experience is normally an overwhelmingly common practice within conversational interaction. Here is one personal experience story collected by her. It is told by a young mother about the occasion when she and friends had to work late on the assembly line and faced walking home in the dark. The story is one of a series which revolves round the hazards of urban streets.

So the next night we work over again till 6. And I said to Molly 'Well, Molly, it looks like it's just you and me again'. Hazel said, 'Well, I'm walkin' too. My husband can't come and get me so we're all gonna go together.' She said, 'I'll tell you what, Mar,' she said, 'beings I'm an old lady I'll stand there and fight 'em off and you young ones can all scream' [*laughs*] 'I got news for you, Hazel, I'll scream and I'm gonna be runnin' at the same time. You can just take care of yourself" [*laughs*] (*op.cit.*, p.4)

Peggy Miller tells us that in the working-class community in South Baltimore, to which these women belong, everyday conversation is studded with stories of this kind. Feminist writers on autobiography dwell at great length on relatively few women writers. Their work cannot be complete until they give the same attention and respect to the vast world of women's oral stories and test out their principles and theories on this very different material. The experience could be a formative one. It might lead them to ask whether personal experience stories by women are oppressively controlled by men or whether, as I have concluded from the work of Miller and others, women have, as it were, enclaves in which, removed from the typical surveillance of the written word, they operate with uninhibited oral autonomy.

Women, like men, speak, literally speak, their lives, often to one another and, when they do, they are likely to speak them in their own ways for they have their own kinds of life-stories to tell. They speak them from a different place. I have an audio-tape which I treasure and which is one such story. It is not easy to write about because the quality of the woman's spoken language is difficult to capture in written words and also because I find it profoundly moving. The speaker calls herself 'a Cree Indian' and she is speaking to one of her tutors, a woman. She is Sylvia Lee Oldpan from Alberta.

> My name is Sylvia Lee Oldpan. I live in Obima [?], Alberta. I am a widow and I have eleven children and nine grandchildren. Six of my children still live with me. Going to University is not easy, especially when I have to leave, especially when I have to leave my children behind but they know that I am working hard so that we can have a better life... when I'm finished... My grandmother and my mother did not have the opportunities that have opened up for me. My grandmother did not speak English. She went to a mission school where she learned to cook, sew and learned to read the pre-syllabics. She did not learn to speak English there... My mother, on the other hand, never went to school but she had to stay at home and take care of her little brothers. She talks about the horses, cows, chickens, geese and turkeys that they had. It took a lot of work to look after all these animals. Perhaps that is why she was not allowed to go to school. She was fifteen when she married my father, she kept house and raised her children. She always told me she was going to make sure that all of us were going to school and we did, too. But it was not the kind of school I would like to send my children to. I went to a convent school where there were rules and morals. The emphasis was on religion and making us good little housewives.

In another taping session Sylvia Oldpan tells how she doesn't like to talk about her schooldays 'because there were so many things that hurt me', whereas at home she 'ran about the farm free'. She wasn't allowed to speak Cree and was told to abandon all her Cree ways; she singles out one concrete instance, 'My hair was long when I went and they just snipped it off'.

> Many things we had to do penance for because our pagan parents were at it again, doing the Sundance and holding religious ceremonies that were a disgrace to our people.

She gradually goes with the system and becomes ashamed of her parents and her culture. Eventually, however, she rejects the indoctrination and discovers 'I am a Cree Indian and proud of it'. She teaches her children the same pride. She reached the point where she decided to work hard 'for the benefit of myself and my people'. But that came much later, after she had travelled a hard road from leaving school at Grade 5 level. She went back to the farm, then took a job in Banff and then got married.

> I raised my children and stayed home for twenty years, raising my children and I stayed home for twenty years. It never entered my head to go off and do something on my own. This is what I had been taught – to stay at home and raise a family. After all, I was a woman. I wasn't a man. I couldn't go out. So there was a lot of things I wanted to do but I couldn't do that. So I stayed home and there was never anything exciting. I suppose it was exciting raising a family but that was something I had to do. I love my children. It's just that it never occurred to me to do anything on my own... and, er, well, things got a bit rough at home and I went out on my own finally.

That was when her youngest was nearly four years old. With the help of her mother as babysitter, she got a job as a teacher aide in a kindergarten. This was clearly a turning point for her, though she is not one to put things in that way. After two and a half years of working in the kindergarten, she is asked to 'teach culture' (her own) at the Hall of Culture where her lack of teacher education makes her feel frustrated and to some extent incompetent, but, as she says, 'I kept going'. Eventually someone who must have been talent-spotting in a very principled way sent her on a special programme in Montana. What follows in her storytelling makes clear the main reason why I have selected it. This passage begins with the only comment she makes on the all-important Montana experience.

> It was really something – my own native people. They had certificates to teach. They had degrees. This is what I wanted and I came home full of plans. They had been talking about having a cultural college affiliated to the University of Calgary. I made application to enter the University. It wasn't easy. They weren't going to accept me. Here I was after all in my forties; throwing away money on an old lady like me. But I persisted. Finally I was accepted. I had a taste of university work. I had gone to a course at the University of Alberta in the summer of '74. It wasn't easy for me. I found it hard but I had made up my mind. This is what I was going to do. I was going to be a teacher and I was going to get a degree and when I had been home I had really everything I could lay my hands on. I had listened to the radio and I had TV and had kept up with current news. So when I started at college they told me I had the equivalent of Grade 9. But Mr. Bob X, the Director of the College, told me it was not going to be easy

for me and I told him I knew it was not going to be easy but this is what I wanted to do. So I started. I asked for a leave of absence. They wouldn't give it to me. So I resigned as teacher-aide and I went to university full-time. I've done three years now. One more year and I'll get my degree. It's, it's just wonderful. I didn't think that I would ever in my life – I would go to university. This is the marvellous feeling that I have. I've accomplished so much that I thought I would never do. It's marvellous.

Here, if ever there was, is a woman's story told from the margins, just as feminists say, from what Sidonie Smith calls no-man's-land. Yet it is also from no-writer's-land. Woven into it are what are by now classic feminist themes – the education of girls to fit them for the roles allocated by men, the life of childrearing and chores, being immured in the home and ultimately the determination against all the odds to break away and get a real education. But Sylvia Oldpan is a Cree and English is her second language. A crucial part of her testimony is that it is spoken out of a double oppression, that of her people and that of a woman within the Cree culture. These themes, of course, can and do find their way into written autobiography, usually after an academic formation which teaches how to deploy the resources of written language in general and, if need be, of autobiography in particular. Here, however, is someone drawing on the resources of the spoken language to deliver a lengthy monologue, but she is using those resources in her own special way which any listener would notice at once.

Her voice is low and the volume stays uniform throughout as does the slow rate of speech. The language is what is usually called spoken standard but on the whole it deploys neither the full range of complexities usually used by the educated in 'careful' speech, nor those used in spontaneous speech by relaxed speakers amongst intimates. The rhetorical devices which story-tellers customarily use are just not there – no dramatic pauses, sudden rises and falls in volume, drawn out vowel-sounds, no meta-narrative turns towards the listener, no non-verbal orchestration of sounds. There is no artful use of voice quality nor are there incursions into the speech flow which would signal to us an emotional sub-text. She does not even include that essential resource of the oral storyteller, the use of dialogue. Super-ficially she might be telling someone else's story which did not deeply involve her. There is an almost total absence of specific events except for when she tells us of the occasion at school when her long hair was snipped and when Mr Bob X told her it was not going to be easy. These two moments are presented minimally, one short utterance for each, no more. Either might have made a separate story. In a word, her story is unadorned and, we might even say, bare. The apparatus of seduction which so cajoles listeners is scarcely put to use. All this should be a recipe for boredom in all but the most generous of audiences. Yet it commands rapt attention throughout. Firstly, we hear a speaker who, given the life she is putting before us is speaking with massive restraint, a kind of decorum which seems to rule out all histrionics. I do not know whether this comes from her own culture or not. I may be listening to the idiolectal features of a stoic but the power of her telling lies for me in the staggering contrast between this cool, un-demonstrative voice and the momentous life-events she is narrating. Secondly, we can easily hear a sub-text of pain, frustration, sustained battle. Feminists tell us that women have recourse to alternative forms when they go into autobiographical mode, that they find their own ways of telling their life-stories. Certain written forms become their part of the escape route from man-made discourse. Sylvia Oldpan has her way, too. She is light-years away from the boastful, paradigmatic male and his self-vaunting tales. Perhaps she is closer to the language of women's consciousness-raising groups but I am disqualified from making that analogy. I want instead to look more closely at some other features of her story. The first is that she has her own way of making salient certain aspects of her experience, that is the use of a kind of refrain. I choose two from the full text. The first is about her entry into the world of formal study.

- sometimes it's hard for me to cope with my problems

- going to university was not easy

- it wasn't easy

- I found it hard

- Mr. Bob X told me it was not going to be easy for me

- I told him I knew it was not going to be very easy

And the other side of the coin:

- but I kept on going

- this is what I wanted

- I had made up my mind

- this is what I was going to do

- this is what I wanted to do

146

These repetitions are an extreme form of what happens in all spontaneous speech and some poetry and give to the particular utterances an amplified resonance.

The story is not only quintessentially a woman's story of oppressive schooling, twenty years of running a home and bringing up eleven children, and the long incredible haul towards a degree. It is also the story of a Cree regaining her ethnic identity in the teeth of efforts to erase it. 'I know how it is to work for the benefit of myself and my people'. Not many university students think of themselves as working for their people but on the other hand she never makes it explicit that she is thinking of herself as working for other women like her. Yet she shows quite clearly an intense awareness of unquestioning acceptance of the allotted woman's role and the need to break out of it. I have already commented on the low-key voice quality of Sylvia Oldpan. One effect of this spoken style is to give amplified significance to anything, phonological or lexical, which departs from it. Thus the hair-snipping incident leaps at us from the tape, giving it a resounding symbolic force, the amputation of female Cree-ness. In the same way her concluding words, untypically overt in the expression of joy at her achievement, sing to us because they verbalise what has been sounding louder and louder in her sub-text.

> But here I am. This is the marvellous feeling I have. I've accomplished so much that I thought I would never do. It's marvellous.

Here, in fact, is an example of the commonest form of women's autobiographical activity. Common, but also unique.

Not all feminists ignore the oral. Liz Stanley (1992), for example, in sharp contrast to Shari Benstock and Sidonie Smith, comments that to locate autobiography in written text

> ...excludes recognition that most autobiography is not produced through 'graph' at all but through talk, through spoken versions of self and others, in which biography and autobiography are intertwined. (p.93)

And this is more than a mere piety, left behind almost as soon as it is uttered, for her own practice has included at least one oral project.

> In a project entitled 'Our Mothers' Voices', I and a number of other working-class by birth feminist sociologists focussed on our mothers' pasts and the intertwining of these with our own and with the dead weight of academic work on class ... I tape-recorded my mother on a number of occasions from 1984 to 1989, concerning 'her' autobiography, which was in fact the history not only of

her family/friends but also of the complexities of working-class Portsmouth in the inter-war period, producing some fifty hours of talk. (p.87n)

After that excursion into the world of womens' speaking voices, noting how their talk is so frequently autobiographical, I must return to the list of themes and propositions which I listed above and in commenting on them I shall follow the same order.

- *Male preoccupation with the self: individualism and the white, Western middle-class male*

It is axiomatic among feminists, though they are not alone in this, that the history of autobiography criticism is the history of male control by means of which a model emerges which defines 'true' autobiography and rejects any autobiography which does not conform to its prescribed structures and language. It is men who declare prescriptive criteria, elevating the intro-spective self and its separateness. This domination, which includes the assumption of the right to appraise womens' autobiography and to allocate it to its proper place, reveals itself in how autobiography comes to be written by men and by women who succumb to their rule book. That special rarified world of autobiographical poetics is seen by feminists as what has been called an androcentric enterprise. Typical is –

> Clearly all the model types are male models, a fact which suggests once again the degree to which Western discourse has conflated 'male' norms and 'human' or universal norms .... Even the rebel whose text projects a hostile society against which he struggles to define himself, if he is male, takes himself seriously because he and his public assume his significance within the dominant order. (Smith *op.cit.* p.9)

It is an achievement of feminists that they have documented with such pre-cision how men have ruled the autobiographical roost and that they have challenged even the most revered of contemporary theorists like Gusdorf (1980), exposing his dogmatic assertion that 'autobiography is only possible in Western society' which alone accommodates the unique, private indivi-dual. However, I have to question the way in which some feminists move easily into assertions, offered as self-evident, but which are at least question-able. What kind of work has gone into the study of the 'rebel' autobiography which entitles Smith to her dismissive last sentence? It is true that there are male autobiographers who 'take themselves seriously' but their public is not necessarily in the dominant order. They address themselves to other rebels and potential rebels.

There is for example the little-known autobiography *Out of the Old Earth* by Harold Heslop (1994). Heslop was a lifelong socialist and political activist, a self-taught miner who died at the age of eighty five in 1986. He finished his autobiography in 1971 after having written novels, plays, short stories and monographs. It was not published until fifteen years after his death. His editor, Andy Croft, comments that Heslop is only a minor character in his life-story.

> Of his own childhood he tells us little, of his hopes and ambitions as a young man even less, and of his wife and children, almost nothing at all. Harry hardly mentions his seven published books ... (p.7)

It is not so much that Hislop 'takes himself seriously' (ultimately a silly phrase in this context) as that he takes the world seriously and, in particular, what it means in that world to be a miner. Feminists searching for models of 'alterity' must surely know that women do not have a monopoly of this orientation to the other, just as they must know that 'cultural ventriloquism' must mean that there is no shortage of women's autobiography in which 'the (male) autobiographical self as solitary consciousness, and as explorer and coloniser of dark continents' (L. Marcus, *op.cit.* p.220) is the model being followed.

Sneering dismissiveness becomes even more reprehensible when we consider that Sidonie Smith, too, takes herself seriously because she can assume a certain audience of mostly white, middle-class university-educated women and men. In any case the anxiety to reveal the culpability of male dominance leaves some feminists writing as though no male autobiography ever gave them pleasure or insights, whether it was inside or outside the canon.

Fortunately, not all feminists are lured into this comfortable dogmatism. It takes an agnostic one like Liz Stanley to consider the much repeated phrase 'the male autobiographical canon' (a very useful one in some contexts, I believe) and pose some very awkward questions.

> A feminist autobiographical canon is in the process of formation. Paradoxically, in view of its proponents' sometimes harsh criticism of the guardians of the often-explicitly male autobiographical canon, it has many of the same modes of operation and standards of critical judgement and produces a similarly small, select and largely agreed-upon group of 'good' autobiographies, written predominantly by women who are deemed to be 'good writers'. (Stanley, *op.cit.* p.90)

And Stanley's sounding of a sceptical note can be found in others. Laura Marcus (*op.cit.*) observes that there is a strong tendency for feminists to urge that all generic frontiers must be stormed. Since the male model is at bottom a fraud and generates a discourse in which women have no real place, it should be by-passed and female inventiveness left to create an alternative discourse. There already exists autobiographical writing by women which registers the possibilities of this alternative (for instance, Maxine Hong Kingston's *The Woman Warrior*, 1977, and Carolyn Steedman's *Landscape for a Good Woman*, 1986). Laura Marcus, eagerly urging that boundaries are contestable and that literary criticism, labouring to erect them around auto-biography comes to a dead end, nevertheless is more sceptical and cautious. She reminds us that autobiography has never been monolithic in spite of all attempts to make it so and that its 'pervasive hybridity' lends itself to the exploration of new identities. There might be, she suggests, some life in the old dog yet.

> Before we celebrate the bonfire of controls, we might wish to think further about the possibilities for transformation and innovation of certain of the structures we have inherited. (*op.cit.* p.281)

When the autobiographical mandarins held their noses and ordered all kinds of texts off the premises, that did not mean such texts had ceased to exist. It is too easily forgotten that hundreds, possibly thousands, of autobiographies, both published and unpublished, were produced by working-class men and women from the nineteenth century onwards. W. Matthews's bibliography, *British Autobiographies, Bibliography of British Autobiographies Published or Written before 1951* (1955) lists 6,500 published British autobiographies and over 2000 diaries. David Vincent (1975), too, has studied dozens of working-class autobiographies from the period 1800 to 1850. When feminists speak of autobiography as androcentric enterprise, they do not appear to have considered material of this kind when they do their labelling. I believe that, if they did, they would have to change their formulations or, at the very least, make clear that they are not talking about men and autobiography but rather certain men and certain autobiographies.

Let us see how this might happen simply by looking at the material edited by John Burnet in *Useful Toil* (1974) and *Destiny Obscure* (1982). The first consists of extracts from 'autobiographies of working people from the 1820s to the 1920s' and the other 'autobiographies of childhood, education and family from the 1820s to the 1920s' In contrast to Virginia Woolf (1960), who dismissed autobiographies by working women because they 'lack detachment and imaginative breadth' and have 'no view of life as a whole and no attempt to enter into the lives of other people', Burnet finds that 'the first and most obvious characteristic of working-class autobiographies and diaries is the general high quality of the writing itself'. (*Useful Toil* p.13). But more relevant to my theme is that Burnet, after steeping himself in this material, concludes that it is quite distinct from mainstream autobiography.

> Evidently there existed a working-class literary form, which was quite distinct from 'polite' literature. What its origins were, how it was transmitted and how widely it diverged from vernacular speech can only be guessed at. Occasionally it is partly derivative as in the mannered style of John Robinson, the butler, or William Lanceley, the house-steward, where these upper servants reflect the language as well as the attitudes of their employers; in the diary of John O'Neill his avid reading of the daily press is clearly a major stylistic influence, while Lucy Luck has to some extent modelled hers on the penny novelettes she must have read. For others, the Bible, the Prayer Book and the English hymnal were major influences on thought, imagery and vocabulary .... But obviously derivative writing is exceptional. Most of the authors use a form which is their own, which has been cultivated but which bears so close a resemblance to writings from quite different regions and occupations as to suggest common roots. (*Useful Toil* p.13)

This scarcely constitutes 'a metaphysics of selfhood' nor have the texts been written by people 'whose lives have been culturally endorsed'. On the contrary, with the spread of literacy in the last quarter of the nineteenth century, the writing of life-stories was not unusual amongst working people who had no claim to fame, not even as radical leaders nor as conspicuously reformed characters. In Burnet's words, 'the writing of autobiography was evidently a widespread and popular form of self-expression'. Among these non-eminent people is Kate Taylor who wrote her unpublished life-story at the age of eighty-two (1973). She left school at thirteen and until the age of seventy nine was in domestic service.

> Mother taught us all to sew but as there were fewer of us at home and she had more time she taught me to knit and crochet as well. At school the Head Master's wife was in charge of the needlework class. She would never allow me to do anything worthwhile. Oddments of wool to knit, unknit and reknit – the same with needlework, just odds and ends to stitch together, unpick and restitch. One afternoon, after taking the same little piece of calico sewn, unsewn and resewn for the sixth time, I just threw it on her desk, jumped from the seat, through the door, jumped the playground wall and was away home. I had just explained to mother when two of the bigger boys arrived to take me back. I flatly refused to go back. Of course, Father had to be told and he just said 'Take your punishment – it's the penalty for being a pauper'. The Head Master kept me standing in front of the class for an hour before caning me again, six severe strokes on each hand, and as I faced him he gave me a severe cut on the back

of each hand saying 'Cry, damn you, cry'. I merely smiled, knowing I'd beaten him. He enjoyed inflicting pain, but I hadn't given him the satisfaction of knowing he'd caused me pain. (*Destiny Obscure* p.292)

These are not the words of a woman participating in the highly conscious contemporary project to create a new form of autobiographical discourse but of one who, a few years before her death, said, 'I am still a rebel, an outsider and a loner...' The point is a very simple one. Autobiographers like her did not have to wriggle desperately out of the grip of the dominant male model. That model was no part of their discursive world, a world which nevertheless was not lacking in ways in which people could talk about their pasts. That women could do so, and can do so, should not be in any doubt. There are, for instance, two substantial volumes by Elizabeth Roberts, *A Woman's Place* (1984) and *Women and Families* (1995), both subtitled *Oral History of Working-Class Women 1890-1940*. The subtitle is somewhat deceptive since the books turn out to consist of Roberts's text constructed around generous quotations from oral recordings which figure on almost every page but there is no complete and faithful transcription of any contributor. Nevertheless, it's very clear that Roberts had no difficulty in obtaining all her material.

• *The recovery of women's autobiography*

Feminists have set out to show in a very robust manner that women's autobiographical voices have in the past been silenced or ignored or dismissed. On the other hand, where women have managed to break through the barriers, every effort was made to shepherd them into safe terrain – the life of motherhood, domesticity, dutiful wifedom, exemplary piety or posthumous righteousness. Why were men so exercised by incursions from women outside the constricting enclave whose frontiers they had defined? At its simplest level. the answer lies in the fact that autobiography places the writer in full public view, licensed, perhaps, to express all kinds of dangerous sentiments or, at the very least, to bid for a position of authorial equality. The woman autobiographer assumes the right to represent directly who she is, what she has done, how she has lived and what happened to her, through her own voice and not through the voices of men. But this is to commit trespass, to enter the forbidden zone, or so runs the argument of many feminists. When a woman attempts to become an autobiographer,

....she is not man coming to centre stage: and therein lies the crux of her matter. She does not enter from the wings so much as she enters from that space beyond the wings of the patriarchal order and its textualizations. Hers is an

> extremely precarious entrance, then; hers, a potentially precarious performance
> before an audience whom she expects to read her as a woman. Her very choice
> to interpret her life and reveal her experience in public signals her transgression
> of cultural expectations. (Smith p.42, *op.cit.*)

and

> .... the contributions of women to the genre have traditionally been perceived as
> forms of contamination, illegitimacies, threats to the purity of the canon of auto-
> biography itself; and their works, defined as anomalous, are set aside in
> separate chapters at the ends of chapters. They are silenced. (*op.cit.* p.43)

So then, a rescue operation has to be mounted, re-reading those women's
autobiographies which did somehow achieve publication as precarious performances, or diligently searching in the shadows for neglected texts and
manuscripts in order to set them in daylight. Moreover, since women must
speak from the margins of discourse, an analysis must be developed which
lays bare the effects of this on how women write autobiography, caught as
they are between the patriarchal narrative and their own. Virginia Woolf,
writing of forgotten women autobiographers, refers to one as 'some stranded
ghost .... who has been waiting, appealing, forgotten in the growing gloom'
and Jane Marcus (1988) picking up this image, speaks of the missionary zeal
involved in publishing the out-of-print works and shuffling about in the
dusty limbo of unread books

> The obscure feminist, black, Chicana, or lesbian critic looking for her people, left
> out of literature and history, shining lights in out-of-the-way libraries and second-
> hand bookshops, does feel like a missionary. As we have rescued our own
> stranded ghosts, read them, reprinted them, and urged others to read them, we
> have played the life-giving role...[Woolf's] Dantesque portrait of a literary limbo
> containing all the lost souls of women and other obscure autobiographers
> throughout history endows their readers, their discoverers with powers of
> resurrection. (p.119)

As the first sentence above demonstrates, there are others engaged in similar
resurrections. Meanwhile, what successes have been registered by this
feminist one? Let me begin with Liz Stanley (1992) who edited Hannah
Cullwick's diaries for publication (1984). Stanley, in her discussion of that
work, is centrally concerned with the kaleidoscopic process of writing a biography and its closeness to autobiography, a viewpoint which I disagree
with. My concern here is only to show that the feminist Stanley is instru-
mental in amplifying a woman's voice from the past and a most unlikely
voice at that. She first came across Hannah Cullwick's diaries in a re-

maindered copy of Derek Hudson's *Munby: Man of Two Worlds* (1972), 'the best thirty pence I have ever spent'. Surprised that no one had worked on the diaries in spite of the rarity of a female working-class voice of that period (1833-1909), what seizes her is that Hannah, born in a little market town and working her way through the typical drudge jobs of a working-class girl, at the age of twenty-one met the well-to-do writer, Arthur Munby, and entered into a secret relationship which lasted fifty-four years. Stanley's study places side by side both Munby's and Hannah's diaries as well as other documentary material. The extraordinary relationship has attracted the attention of others, including some feminists who disagree with Stanley's reading, but nothing can take away from the fact that it is Stanley who got down to the job of editing and publishing the Cullwick diaries (*The Diaries of Hannah Cullwick*, 1984).

The strength of Sidonie Smith's work is that it asks us to look again at women autobiographers whose work was in some sense known, but not in our day salient, and re-appraise them. She turns to *The Book of Margery Kempe*, written in 1436, the first known women's autobiography in English. This extraordinary work did not even see the light of day until 1934 when it was discovered by Hope Emily Allen in the archives of the Butler-Bowden family, since when feminists have given it close attention. There is something of an irony in Smith's analysis of what is usually described as a spiritual autobiography, an entirely acceptable enterprise for women. Kempe was the mother of fourteen children who ultimately abandoned the married life and its sexuality when she received the message that she would be acceptable to Christ by becoming chaste. She then went on her travels, establishing herself as a powerful public figure of piety. Smith, as an admirer of Kempe, says of her work,

> ... always there is the voice of Kempe's narrative, intimate, close to the surface of the text, self-effusive rather than self-effacing. Always in the foreground, never in the background, she seems to use the occasion of narrative (as she used it in life), to talk about the subject of most interest to her – her own special importance. (p.82)

For Smith, Kempe's voice is both supportive of the patriarchal order and disruptive of it. Yet there is a contradiction here. Kempe's focus on 'her own special importance' is decidedly in the patriarchal mode which so often feminists have told us is typically obsessed with self in contrast to women's concern for alterity. Whatever else Kempe may have to recommend her, it is certainly not alterity. Strangely, Smith has nothing to say about this.

The feminist programme of recovery of women's autobiographies includes the disinterment of long-buried works, the reappraisal and rehabilitation of patronised and undervalued works and respectful attention to those which, though perhaps given serious, even rapturous, attention in their own day, have gradually receded from view. Jane Marcus, in her essay (1988), 'Invincible mediocrity: the private selves of public women' chooses a set of women autobiographers who fall into the last category and who, as she says, follow a trajectory which is 'the opposite of the one which feminist historians have chosen to study, the move from private to public'. (p.124 *op.cit.*) They are, as she tells us, white, privileged, turn-of-the-century women, all of whom have made their distinctive mark as the first women of high achievement in their fields and only then turned to personal discourse. It is an unusual coterie, names which very rarely crop up in feminist restoration activity. They were,

> ... not obscure in their own day. That is why they raise interesting questions for a theory of women's autobiography. They were famous women in the public eye. They left their signature on public discourse. But they anticipated obscurity because of their gender and they wrote their memoirs as a hedge against a certain deflation in their reputations. They were not writers but made themselves into writers in a bid for eternity. Their memoirs were all very successful when they were published but are now out of print, shuffling about in the dusty limbo of unread books... (p.120/21)

So we have conjured up before us Elizabeth Robins (*Ibsen and the Actress*, 1928), an actress and a suffragette, Dame Ethel Smyth (*Impressions that Remained*, 1919 repub.1981), a prolific composer whose two volume autobiography was highly praised in her own day, Sophie Kovalevsky (*A Russian Childhood*, 1978), an important Russian mathematician, Jane Ellen Harrison (*Reminiscenses of a Student Life*, 1925), a classical anthropologist and Marie Bashkirtseff (*Journal*, trans. Mary Serrano, 1928) a Russian painter. What all these eminent women share is that 'they anticipate the coming of the resurrecting reader and speak directly to her and they write consciously in the female tradition of the memoir' (p.122). Each of these women autobiographers who step into the light is seen, in spite of massive differences, as establishing a special relationship between the female writer and her woman reader. Marcus's analyses reveal how feminism, as it turns to autobiographical restitution of the repressed narratives of women, is caught in a web of difficult problems.

Does recovery mean the rehabilitation of any autobiographical works by women? In principle it is easy to say yes. However, once you begin to construct a counter-canon, you also begin to posit criteria of acceptability which, if only by implication, reconsign certain works to oblivion, if they display the very qualities which you have railed against in men's autobiography. One way of dealing with this embarrassment is to label it ventriloquism; this is the process by which these women have unfortunately let the male voice speak through their helpless mouths. This is very like those who were intoxicated by Gramsci and were inclined to dismiss those who disagreed with them as being victims of what he called 'false consciousness'. Jane Marcus finds herself caught up in this dilemma when she is discussing the work of Marie Bashkirtseff. Some feminists, it would appear, are so uncomfortable with her autobiography that they are glad to push it out of sight.

> It has not been celebrated or reprinted by contemporary feminist scholarship precisely because her supposed vanity and selfishness challenge our romantic notions about virtue. Whenever I wish to make generalisations or propose a theory of women's autobiography based on writing through the other in a patriarchal world, I am faced with the stark egotism of Marie Bashkirtseff: 'I am my own heroine'; 'I love myself'. (Marcus p.122)

Poor Marcus. Having once selected Bashkirtseff as one candidate from the club of ghosts in limbo, fit to be called back to life, she does not really know what to do with her. Should she join other feminists in a witch-hunt of the unworthy or insist that she is a fit person to enter the feminist pantheon? We never find out the answer, and this poignant indecision reminds us that bold generalisations cannot meet all cases. Marcus's final judgement is that the journal is 'a classic in the male tradition' and 'an extreme form of the romantic ideology of individualism (p.124). She contrasts it with Kovalevsky's *A Russian Childhood* which 'writes the self as a cultural history of her people'. Yet she lingers lovingly over the journal and judges it to be 'the great lyric outpouring of the striving woman artist' (p.137). She even finds it necessary to tell us that Bashkirtseff was one of the first apostles of feminism. This leaves some feminists to indulge in the guilty pleasures of reading works by women which have an uncomfortable resemblance to those by self-indulgent, self-dramatising males.

- *The struggle against legitimised roles and forms of discourse*

The great contribution of feminism has been painstakingly to lay bare all the manifold ways in which women's lives have been defined, installed and patrolled by men. It goes without saying that this has always included the policing of women's speech, the control of their voices. Thus we have two complementary processes at work in which women autobiographers are caught up, the ways in which their lives were defined and the forms of discourse through which they could legitimately speak. Women had to be daughters, mothers and wives and accordingly had to locate themselves in relation to their fathers, children and husbands and to display the quintessential virtues of wifely rectitude and maternal devotion. The other legitimate role was that of the intensely pious woman who wrote a spiritual life. Sidonie Smith considers that traditionally there were only four life scripts which were possible for a woman – wife, nun, queen and witch. In the nineteenth century there was, with a few exceptions, a perfect match between the domestication of women and the domestication of their autobiographies. It follows, then, that the huge effort to struggle for full human roles for women was accompanied by the difficult attempt to change the ways in which women made their entries into and exits from every form of discourse. This inevitably included autobiography, which must include what women's autobiographies have been, now are and might be.

Yet there are oversimplifications. Feminists may feel that they are rescuing lost women autobiographers but very few acknowledge, as Linda Peterson does (in Folkenflik *op.cit.*), that many seminal women's autobiographies would be lost to history were it not for the efforts of Victorian editors (all male, let it be said). She instances the Quaker *Friends' Library* (1837-1850) which included twenty autobiographical accounts by women, all in the traditional spiritual mode, and displaying no differences from the men's accounts in their style or thematic concerns; 'domestic memoirs' published by antiquarian societies (1829-75) including texts by women; Hunt and Clarke's *Autobiography* series (1826-1823) which at first excluded women but by the seventh volume contained *Memoirs of Mrs. Robinson*, an actress and the mistress of the Prince of Wales and *A Narrative of the Life of Mrs. Charlotte Charke*, a transvestite actress. Linda Peterson's historical research puts a different gloss on the feminist history of women's autobiography which emphasises the male marginalising of women writers. Furthermore, the notion of ventriloquism takes some hard knocks from Peterson who is so sacrilegious as to suggest that gender is not the hermeneutic key to women's autobiographies.

For many feminist critics what ultimately happened to women autobiographers was that either they were obliged to conform to male prescriptions (which included a special domestic memoir niche for women) or they were despatched to outer darkness. A few, the argument runs, struggling in their bondage, were able to begin to take the long road to a true women's autobiography, the first achievements of which we are now seeing. Though this argument is a powerful and persuasive one, it is somewhat too neat and tidy, omitting as it does a serious discussion of whether the Augustine/Rousseau model was not a perfectly comfortable one for some women autobiographers who followed it to great effect. While there may be something we can with confidence call women's autobiography, we can also say that alongside it there exists an autobiographical tradition flexible enough in its discourse and essentially modest in its literary pretensions to accommodate anyone. Where feminists stand on their strongest ground is in their powerful critique of dominant autobiographical theory which is derived from a scrutiny of very few male authors. The subtext to that work is that there are no crucial differences between the life experiences of men and women and, in any case, that women's autobiographies are of no major significance because of the nature of the female mind.

Is there, then, such a thing as distinctive women's autobiography, autobiography with a difference, which is a new kind of creation constructed by women for women? As I have already noted, if the answer to this is yes, as feminist critics assert, then the other side of the coin is that women who write in the dominant male fashion are, as Liz Stanley (p.88) notes, dismissed as 'unwomanly', grandly brushing aside people like Simone de Beauvoir and Gertrude Stein. Clearly, there is not, nor should we expect, unanimity amongst feminists as to what constitutes the specifics of truly feminist writing, but I find it unsatisfactory that they very rarely ask whether the characteristics they single out could not be applied to many autobiographies by men. Women in general and feminists in particular do not share a common social space. Even academic feminists, a relatively homogeneous group arrive on the campus by very different routes and are caught up in importantly different experiences. Small wonder, then, that in both their autobiographies and their autobiographical criticism we can hear different and even opposed views.

In search of that elusive discourse, feminist autobiography, Liz Stanley, never seduced by grand claims and pieties, is cautious.

> The question of a distinct genre of women's autobiography is related to but not synonymous with the question of whether a distinct *feminist* auto/biography exists. Certainly there are biographies and autobiographies by feminists. [She lists seven examples] However, is the fact that a text is feminist *authored* or about a feminist *subject* sufficient to define it as feminist autobiography? Is the *form* or *structure* of what is written as feminist auto/biography, not just the sub-

ject who forms the bones of its content, actually different from any other auto/
biography? My response is that it is, or rather could be, different. (p.247)

Some feminist claims of difference are frequently repeated in the critical
literature and extended to all, or most, or many women's autobiographies
rather than solely to feminist ones. Thus it is often asserted unproblematically that men's autobiography follows a chronological trajectory, a clear
pathway through time, whereas women's autobiographies are texts which
have no neat pattern of that kind; the path is a broken one and there are diver-
sions from it. Men's autobiographies are said to be integrations of the public
and private whereas women's are rooted in the specificities and intimacies
of private life. Women's life-stories are often described as being above all
thematically focused on the lives of others as against men's notorious
egotism. It is, to say the least, surprising that these views can be advanced
in spite of the fact that many men's autobiographies could be described in
these terms and women's life-stories, like women themselves, encompass a
huge diversity. Other feminists, dazzled both by deconstructionism and post-
modernism (see, for example, Stanton, 1984) refuse to relate women's life-
stories to their actual lives but give attention only to external features of the
texts themselves since 'referentiality' is suspect. Moreover, they all too
readily assent to the death warrants served on the author and the self. These
are crippling limitations to place on the analysis of women's autobiography,
denying as they do the materiality of the social world, women's particular
experience in it, the material presence of women writers, and assuming that
because the self is problematic it does not exist. These are very complex
issues. I find Liz Stanley (op.cit.; see her chapters 'The Presumptive
Feminist' p.87-123 and 'Is there a Feminist Auto/biography?' p.240-256)
conducts a thorough interrogation of many feminist critiques. It is a good
place to begin to explore fully what she calls the polyphony of feminist
voices on the subject. A healthy scepticism pervades the explication of her
own feminist standpoint, which includes an inspection of the ideas of other
feminists about the differences between men and women as autobiographers.

> A feminist interest in autobiography provides an analysis as well as substantive
> purchase on both these difference arguments [i.e. the differences within
> women's experience and the putative differences between men and women]
> and by doing so perhaps enables us to surmount their apparent mutual
> exclusiveness. A concern with the details of particular lives – even if these are
> read in highly representational terms – points up difference in the first sense. It
> stops in their dubious tracks 'women this' and 'women that' categorical state-
> ments by showing the importance of time, place, gender, community, education,
> religious and political conviction, sexual preference, race and ethnicity, class

and of the indomitable uniqueness of people who share social structural similarities. (p.242)

Autobiography is therefore a uniquely located form of discourse for resolving the argument about difference. Moreover, there is another important difference, the difference of feminists from other women.

> Regardless of what feminist grand theories may suggest, feminist *experience* is of different and disagreeing interpretations of the world, founded upon the often profoundly different material and experiential positions of differently socially located groups of women. Feminism is actually feminismS, internally highly differentiated in experiential and analytic terms encompassing both unities and multiple divisions. (p.243)

For Stanley feminist autobiography is for the most part a programmatic project which goes beyond a consideration of autobiographies written by feminists and picks up from Kate Millet's *Flying* (1974) and *Sita* (1977), 'part diary, part free-form writing, part stream of consciousness', and Steedman's *Landscape for a Good Woman* (1986) who, she claims, de-centre self which becomes an interactional process as well as a product. She concludes that the three essential features in feminist autobiography are the taking up of postures which do not put the 'I' in the sustained glare of the spotlight, the underlying assumption that truth is dependent on very particular circumstances, and the rejection of realism (i.e. fidelity of representation). To these she adds the discursive practices of feminists, and the specific textual ideology of their work. The difficulty is, as Stanley admits, that none of these features is a monopoly of feminist autobiographers. To go on to say that together they constitute defining characteristics explains why Stanley's prescription is not only a project for tomorrow but perhaps incurably Utopian.

Women have achieved a degree of success in throwing off the autobiographical role allocated to them by men but have been far less successful in inventing a new form of autobiographical discourse, at least no more successful than men who for one reason or another struggle to discard the old models. But then many forms of discourse have a longevity which makes them highly resistant to subversion.

- *Alterity: women's characteristic mode is inter-personal rather than personal*

It would seem that for feminists there is a prevailing or predominant man. He emerges from his work like a character from a mediaeval mummers' play. His discourse is utterly and irredeemably obsessed with self. He is positively pre-Copernican in his sense that all the galaxies and the sun itself revolve round him. Against this there is autobiographical woman who with exemplary self-effacement directs us to others, to the collective community, particularly the community of women. Thus the monstrous preening and strutting of men is counterposed to a sensitive modesty turned away from egocentricity towards an understanding of other people who are allowed to occupy centre stage. A caricature, of course, of the feminist stand on alterity, but at times it cries out for just such a caricature. The first bold expression of this idea comes from Mary Mason in 'The Other Voice: Autobiographies of Women Writers' (Olney, *op.cit.*) in which we find,

> ... the self-discovery of female identity seems to acknowledge the real presence and recognition of another consciousness, and the disclosure of female self is linked to the identification of some 'other', that is, of an 'other' who is not the self. (p.210)

The idea of alterity is echoed in Brodzki and Shenk (1988 Brodzki B. and Shenk C. *Life-Lines: Theorising Women's Autobiography*)

> Being *between two covers* with somebody else replaces singularity with alterity in a way that is dramatically female. (p.11)

But why? Is it that women are just better people than men and more readily care for others and understand them and that, consequently, they write auto-biography with an orientation towards others whereas men cannot see their world and its inhabitants in this way and their flow of empathies is a miser-able stream? I take this with a pinch of salt. Which autobiographies does Mary Mason, and those who follow her eagerly, have in mind? All the male and female writers? Most of them? The most significant?

I have deeper reservations than these. Firstly, it is quite impossible to write an autobiography which does not include interaction with and reflection upon the lives of others. My own short collection of autobiographical stories (Rosen, 1983) is peopled with others – my mother and her indomitable socialism; my teachers, some gentle and some ferocious; my fellow pupils, caught in the scary no-man's land between their Jewish culture and the Anglo-Saxon gentile one. When I think about that period of my life it is alive with other people and, if I linger over self, it is another self for, as feminists tell us, the self is not a stable essentialist entity. Mary Mason is clearly aware of this problem but brushes it aside.

> ... the egoistic secular archetype that Rousseau handed down to his Romantic brethren in his *Confessions*, shifting the dramatic presentation to an unfolding

self-discovery, are little more than aspects of the author's evolving consciousness, finds no echo in women's writing about their lives. (p.210)

There is no point in lingering over the absurd dogmatism in this extract
except to say that any reader would find no difficulty in pointing to echoes
of Rousseau-ism in women's autobiographies (see, for example, Maria
Bashkirtseff's *Journal, op.cit.*, or Doris Lessing's *Under my Skin*, 1995) nor
to alterity in men's (see, for example, Gorky's *Fragments from my Diary* or
Herzen's *Memoirs*). However, this does not rule out the possibility that an
important truth is hidden in the thickets of alterity. I find myself much more
drawn to the proposition if it is phrased much more cautiously. Thus – given
women's experience and actions in the world, they are somewhat more likely
than men to write or speak about their lives in ways which find room for the
lives of those they have interacted with once they have thrown off completely the constraints of the canon. Liz Stanley is once again the sceptic: she
gives many instances of autobiographies by men and by women which turn
Mason's ideas on their heads (p.132/3 *op.cit.*). The question which remains
is exactly why a feminist like Mason does not take the simple step of reading
enough autobiographies to lead her to doubt one of her chief propositions.
This is a sad case of self-inflicted blindness which helps neither feminists
nor students of autobiography. There is, too, a looseness in the way in which
the Other is conceived. It can mean one other or several others, or a collec-
tivity like all other women, the sisterhood, or members of another marginalised or oppressed group.

This is so much more than a quantitative matter. Simone de Beauvoir's *The
Prime of Life* (1965) is densely populated with others, but for all their
variety they turn out to be overwhelmingly the denizens of Left Bank Paris
and everything within it is brought to bear on her pervasive preoccupations
with selfhood. Contrast that with *The History of Mary Prince* (1831, and
Pandora, 1987) which, while it relates the suffering and humiliations of a
black woman slave in the Caribbean, unambiguously and explicitly relates
them to the fate of all slaves.

> Since I have been here I have often wondered how English people can go out
> into the West Indies and act in such a beastly manner. But when they go to the
> West Indies, they forget all feeling of shame, I think, since they can see and do
> such things. They tie up slaves like hogs – moor them up like cattle and they lick
> them so as hogs or cattle or horses never were flogged – and yet they come
> home, and say, and make some good people believe that slaves don't want to
> go out of slavery. But they put a cloak about the truth. It is not so. All slaves want
> to be free – to be free is very sweet. (p.83/4)

To conflate this way of the telling of the story of a woman's life with those which in many different ways concern themselves with others is to crassly ignore the differences between them and the ways in which class, ethnicity and other factors shape a different kind of narrative. Furthermore, there are quite different ways of orienting a text towards others. These others may emerge from heterogeneous encounters or they may emerge as members of a group to whom one has a special commitment; one's life cannot be conceived outside that membership. Any account of orientation to the other must also include an awareness that the collective other may well change during a life or that there may be a tension between others in one's past and others acquired later, typically in the life of an immigrant.

The attempt has been made to develop a sound theoretical base for alterity. Susan Friedman (in Benstock *op.cit.* p.34 et ff) turns to Nancy Chodorow for a psychoanalytic explanation. The male child, we are told, is obliged to reject his mother and in the process develops an 'impermeable sense of self'. This gives him his entree into the world of patriarchal dominance. The girl-child, on the other hand, retains her relationship with her mother and thus her sense of self grows in an unbroken relationship with another. The deep feminine relationship with others, which is supposed to be a major feature of women's autobiographies, is all seen as growing out of this primal bonding. This puts an intolerable strain on one's credulity and once again would call for some sort of explanation of all those women's autobiographies which show no basic difference from men's. Can they all be accounted for through ruptures in the mother-daughter bonding?

If women's alterity is a coded way of naming women's essential altruism then it doesn't bear serious consideration. If it is a way of eluding the narratives of certain male autobiographers, enthroned in the male critical canon, it remains more of a project than an established achievement, an aspiration for discursive emancipation.

• *Women's autobiographical writing shares qualities with those of other marginalized groups*

Nothing defiles the white margins of the page, whose sole function is to be non-text, a kind of graphic wordless silence. In principle, that is. In practice there have always been violators of the margins of printed books: the scribblers of comments, objectors, emenders, unlicensed editors, the lovers of question marks and exclamations, the pedantic and the sacrilegious. For them, the margins are turned into a playground of reader-response. Is it this (and much else) which lies behind the recurrent feminist use of the margin metaphor to encapsulate women's position as autobiographers? Such writers are banished to the silent white spaces and thus their voices are effectively gagged or muffled.

> ... she [i.e. the woman autobiographer] remains marginalized in that she finds herself resident on the margins of discourse, always removed from the centre of power within the culture she inhabits. Man whether a member of the dominant culture or of an oppressed culture maintains the right to name 'his' woman. In her doubled, perhaps tripled, marginality, then, the autobiographer negotiates four sets of stories, all nonetheless written about her rather than by her. Moreover, her non-presence, her unrepresentability, presses even more imperiously yet elusively on her; and her position as a speaker before an audience becomes even more precarious. (Smith, p.51, *op.cit.*)

Metaphors deployed in argument are powerful instruments and 'margins', 'marginalised' and 'marginality' strike home with force for those who know the history of women's autobiography. Nonetheless, once this metaphor becomes immovably installed in the theory of women's autobiography, it carries implications which need to be inspected and questioned, especially when it gets carried into doubtful extensions. It gives an unmistakable suggestion that women as autobiographers have been utterly reduced to nothingness at the edge of the page: this, as we have seen, is not an absolute truth. What is true is that women remained for a long time as intruders and interlopers in the world of autobiography, acceptable only within male-decreed limits, this being one realisation among others of exclusion from 'the centres of power'. However, just as trespassers in the margins inscribe their own graffiti, so women in the past have spoken from the metaphorical margin and today increasingly they take over the main body of the text. Indeed, Sidonie Smith suggests there are positive advantages in operating outside the authorised texts, speaking from the underground, as it were.

> ... woman speaks to the culture from the margins. While margins have their limitations, they also have their advantages of visions. They are polyvocal, more distant from the centres of power and conventions of selfhood. They are heretical. Perhaps that is why I have found women's autobiographies to be both eccentric and alive, whatever their limitations. There is a theatricality about them, but of the regional stage. Characterised by dysphoria, by the restlessness and anxieties of self-authorship, women's stories frustrate expectations and thoroughly enchant the reader because they are vital, unconventional. From them erupt, however suppressed they may be, rebellion, confusion, ambivalence, the uncertainties of desire. (Smith *op.cit.* p.176)

Of course, Sidonie Smith must know that many women's autobiographies are not even faintly like this, those of public figures, for example. Margaret

Thatcher's autobiographical, *The Downing Street Years* (1993) is deter-
minedly monovocal, utterly conventional and most certainly does not
frustrate expectations. But then, academics, especially when they deploy the
old tarnished rhetoric of 'appreciation' ('vital, unconventional') behave as
though such works are beneath consideration, even though they claim to be
talking of women's autobiography in general. It is not only high establishment figures who should be included but also autobiographical writings
which slip through the academic critical net. There is, for example, *Soul
Providers* (McNeil, 1994) which is a collection of autobiographical writings
by single parents who are, for the most part, highly educated and articulate
women. I get no sense that they are in any way 'eccentric' or that they are
'characterised by the restlessness and anxieties of self-authorship' nor is the
language in any way different from that which we can find in similar
writings written by men. Mostly, the story runs like this.

> Joe is my life, my partner, my friend, my touchstone to reality. He is also (as a
> besides) the most beautiful boy in the world and I have always looked after Joe
> since that strangely sunny Saturday... in November 1985. I held him, looked at
> him and wished him all the happiness in the world ... all in that split second when
> the midwife handed him over to me. Suddenly my life made sense. Sounds
> idyllic? Well, maybe it was. Now seven years on things don't always seem so
> clear... (p.154)

Or in somewhat different vein:

> I was not prepared for the intensity of feelings I experienced in the first few days
> after her birth. The love I felt for her was so powerful it felt like a kind of manic
> happiness. It was both very specific – it was this baby I loved, this human being
> with the golden fuzz on her head – and something universal. As if it was a
> glimpse of how we could care for one another. (p.94)

I can now say that the first of these extracts is by a male single parent, Keith
Hawkins (there are two male contributors to the collection) and the second
by a woman, Anna Keigh. Glib claims for the uniqueness of women's autobiography should, at the very least, be modified to take into account writings
in which men and women share (without ventriloquism!) an available discourse. The power of Soul Providers comes not from a strange marginalised
discourse but from marginalized lives or, to put it more optimistically, from
accounts of refusals to be marginalized.

It has to be said yet again that feminist literary critics themselves do some
marginalising, through silence, of women whose autobiographies are constructed orally. Women's autobiographical talk is not so easily swept into the

margins. It impregnates their conversations and their lives. The scrupulous oral historian, Elizabeth Tonkin, (1992) turns our attention to the fact that the rhetorics of orality are virtually unknown to many literary scholars whose apparatus is based solely on the study of written texts. Her study of Yoruba women's oral stories with their 'oblique and complex placings of persons and of time', their subtle deployment of every possibility of the speaking moment leads her to conclude that, so far from being voices struggling from the margins to be heard, exactly the contrary is true.

> The means and effects of these rhetorics [i.e. the means used to render stories plausible and convincing HR] exploit the features of orality, which are so often forgotten by literates and resistant to their analytical assumptions. Women animate words, as they bring life into the world; the past is purposefully deployed so as to change the future and people are honoured and individualised by specifying the names and the past of these names. No wonder, then, that the language structures in which they speak can carry such oblique and complex placings of persons and of time ... (p.65)

It is only a small step from elaborating the marginalization of women auto-biographers to claiming kinship with all others who in various ways are also marginalized in society. The solidarity of shared invisibility. We may take Susan Friedman as representative of this gesture of recruitment.

> The model of separate and unique selfhood that is highlighted in his [i.e. Gusdorf's] work and shared by many other critics establishes a critical bias that leads to the (mis)reading and marginalization of autobiographical texts by women and minorities in the process of canon formation. (in Benstock, p.34)

and

> When women are members of minorities they are in a situation of double jeopardy – defining not only the category WOMAN but also by the category BLACK, JEW, or whatever other group the dominant culture has isolated from the main stream. (p.47)

The minorities invited to join women in the margins are ethnic, sexual, religious. The embrace takes in blacks, Chicanos, Jews, lesbians, gays, muslims – the list is endless, though in practice most attention is given to black autobiographers, especially if they are women. What is the commonality of these disparate groups? That they are equally and similarly oppressed? That they all share a sense of hybridity by occupying an outlandish territory between two worlds? That they are all marginalized in the same way and to the same extent? That the members of each group experience marginality in the same way despite differences of generation, class, exact location, education, group history, and much more? That they all resolve the pull of assimilation in the same ways? For the most part the comradely gestures of solidarity do not stand up to close inspection and what, in any case, is the point of these gestures? They seem to spring from the desire to convince us that women or feminists have a special empathetic understanding of autobiographies written by sharers of the margins. Or is it that other marginalised groups tend to produce autobiographies which in important ways are similar to those produced by women? The intricacies of the processes by which certain groups are thrust towards the edges reveal different forms and different degrees of violence and need to be examined with great care when a close affiliation is being proposed. Suffice it to say that these intricacies are not discussed by feminists when they make that proposal. The stereotypical marginalized figure begins to dissolve when the precise actualities are registered in autobiographies. Henry Louis Gates in his autobiographical *Coloured People* (1994) writes of his family,

> [Grandmother] became a socialist in 1919 and was the first person in Cumberland to subscribe to W.E. Du Bois's *Crisis* magazine. She died a socialist. Her husband was a Lincoln Republican.

> In 1890 Maud Gates founded St Phillip's Episcopal Church in Cumberland: coloured priests from Haiti and Jamaica were enlisted to serve there. Maud's daughters' children did well: they all graduated from college, from Howard to Harvard. Three generations at Harvard, including Harvard Law School. Three generations of dentists and three of doctors. On her sons' side, however, the story is a different one. The seven sons all went to work in factories although my daddy attended school in New Jersey for a while. That was around the time he wanted to be a priest. He was the head acolyte within his generation, the seventh son, the golden boy on whose head grew Jesus Moss. His Aunt Pansy, who told me she wanted to adopt him, sent him up to Newark, New Jersey, where he attended a predominantly Jewish school. Everyone there thought he was Jewish, until he went to school on Rosh Hashanah. 'Heinie,' his teacher asked him, 'what are you doing in school today? It's Rosh Hashanah.' 'Rosh what?' Daddy replied. His uncle Fred had passed for Jewish, had even married a Jewish woman. He never contacted the family again. (p.72/3)

I am not, of course, attempting to demonstrate with this passage an exemplary triumph of social mobility but rather to illustrate that it does not conform to the monochrome picture which well-intentioned commentators have of oppressed black people. This is the same Gates who in another guise tells us that black feminists 'have never been obsessed with arriving at any singular self-image ... or policing the boundaries between us and them'.

Homi Baba (1994) will have none of the easy task of binding together oppressed minorities and women in one indiscriminate sweep.

> We find ourselves at the moment of transit where space and time cross to produce complex figures of difference and identity, past and present, inside outside, inclusion exclusion ... What is theoretically innovative and politically crucial is the need to think beyond narratives of originary and initial subjectivities and to focus on those moments or processes that are produced in the articulation of cultural differences. (p.1)

He goes on to argue: 'the representation of difference must not be hastily read as the reflection of the pre-given ethnic and cultural traits set in the fixed tablets of tradition'. (p.2).

To sum up, feminist critics have insisted on the marginality of women's autobiographies but that marginality has never been total and, further, it is possible to be more or less marginalized and for some not to be marginalized at all. The claim becomes more plausible only by ignoring women's spoken autobiographical acts. However, the kinds of marginality which have been engineered by men in the past, and which, for the record, it has been important to document and assess, no longer has its former power and that is to some extent a positive consequence of feminist politics.

- *Women's use of different forms – diaries, journals, letters*

Literature, as a social institution, has its bastards, its misbegotten children born outside the legitimacy of what Bakhtin called The Fathers. Autobiography, as we have seen, is in many ways the most embarrassing of them and there are others like diaries and letters, although a few of these have had their birth certificates amended – Pepys's diary and Lord Chesterfield's letters, for example. Against this I have powerful and even fond recollections of an Oxford University Press series: each volume was a selection from the work of a canonical writer, beautifully printed and bound (Oxford blue and gold lettering on the covers!). That was more than half a century ago when I was a Sixth Former. The editors saw it as an obligation always to include a selection from the writers' letters and sometimes diaries. It was my first experience of eavesdropping on the daily lives and thoughts of previously embalmed literary greats. I was never sure, nor I believe were my teachers, whether this material was included as 'background' or because it was judged to be literary in its own right. This and subsequent experience lead me yet again to have reservations about feminist repeated efforts to persuade us not only that letters and diaries have a special allure for women but are in many cases a preferred outlet for their autobiographical activity. It is true that, being private and intimate, they are often the only kinds of writing which some women have produced. It is when the proposition is extended and asserts not only that women take to these forms like ducks to water but also use them in unique ways quite different from men's that I begin to demur. That there are some women of whom this is true I do not doubt. But then it is also true of some men.

The diaries of women writers are ransacked, just as men's are, as a rich source of biographical information or quite simply as a source of social and historical facts, but the feminists turn to them above all as autobiographical texts by women who have refused the demand of writing a monumental 'life'. The alternative becomes in this view a welcome defiance of literary imperatives. Though they never say so explicitly, it is clear that the enthusiasts are usually talking only about certain kinds of diaries and letters, in practice always ones written by women who were also novelists or poets and whose diaries and letters have sooner or later been published.

However adventurous diarists or letter-writers may be, they are not resorting to forms which are totally unregulated by custom and convention. There is no escaping the force of intertextuality which operates just as much here as everywhere else (all those epistolary novels and fictional diaries!). Letter-writing became a very self-conscious activity from the eighteenth century onwards when manuals were published giving detailed advice and instructions. That said, these forms undoubtedly left writers much more free from the usual constraints and they could, if they wished, be more colloquial, more discontinuous, more centrifugal, more playful than a meant-for-publication literary text usually permits.

The celebration of women's propensity for diary and letter-writing leaves some insistent questions to be answered. The most obvious of them is that, since men, too, take to these forms, why should women be said to have special claims to them? I have to confess to contradictory responses to what feels like the usurpation of spaces which for me are open to all. It feels as threatening as a take-over bid to the about to be taken over. On the other hand I have what amounts to no more than an intuition that women are more likely to be drawn into diary writing and perhaps letter writing, too. But when they do, do they use them in a different way? Nancy Walker (1988) thinks so, believing that in men's writings of this kind the private and public in their lives are mutually supporting or defining but that for women they are often opposed. Discussing the letters of Emily Dickinson, the diary of Alice James and the letters and diaries of Virginia Woolf, she writes,

> Most obviously these are the letters and diaries of women, and even though these women do not share a common generation or nationality their most personal writing nevertheless reveals common concerns and devices that set it apart from similar writing by men. Traditionally the published letters or journals have been intended as records of 'great lives' and their autobiographies have served as guides or cautionary tales. (p.272)

The hazard of this kind of bold proposition is glaring, namely the selection of her chosen women favourites and the juxtaposition of them to her chosen demon men, writers of 'great lives'. If she had chosen Gilbert White rather than her own example, Benjamin Franklin, she could not so easily have slipped into special pleading. As for 'devices that set it apart', Walker's lengthy paper fails to identify them at any discursive level. Yet there are un-doubtedly women who do experiment, like Madeleine Grumet (1990). With-out making any feminist claims she does let us see her at work on her journal(s), making entries in which she sees 'that struggle and its resolve to develop ourselves in ways that transcend the identities that others have constructed for us' (p.324). She also gives us a glimpse of a rare experi-mental activity. This is how she describes her pre-journal diaristic habits.

> I have read that Virginia Woolf left jottings everywhere. At times I have toyed with that possibility, for there are few other attributes of hers that I can appro-priate to my own identity other than her writing habits. But this scatter method has never worked. I lose the jottings, I crumple them up and throw them away in a clean sweep of tidying or use their backs and margins for telephone numbers which get tucked into secret places where they won't be lost and from which they can never be recovered. The only scatter notes I've ever saved were the little pieces of paper recording the timing of my contractions when I went into labour. And even now I don't know whether I saved these jottings because I wanted to remember how it felt to be pacing round the quiet house at two or three in the morning, wondering whether these spasms would dwindle ... or bring about birth – or whether, upon finding them on my return from the hospital propped up on the mantel, on the dining room table, or on the kitchen counter near the phone, I saved them because their scatter seemed worthy of Virginia's labour as well as mine. (p.322)

Madeleine Grumet's writing reminds us that diary-like activity can take many forms (notebooks, scrap books, personal miscellanies, etc.) and it is only proper that the scatter-method should have had as its inspiration Virginia Woolf who, wrested from the male establishment, has become the patron saint of feminist critics because she is the best possible example of the innovative use of diaries and letters. They are irresistibly drawn to her massive archive (six volumes of letters and five of diaries!) which she came to regard as accumulating source material for the autobiography which, in the event, she never wrote and which stand alongside all her other numerous sorties into autobiographical experiment, such as *A Sketch of the Past* (1978) and *Moments of Being* (1978). Here is the pre-eminent feminist autobiographer who uses her diaries and letter meta-autobiographically, well aware of the risks of triviality, formlessness and heterogeneity. She wrote in a review of Olive Schreiner's letters that they were 'a jumble and muddle of odds and ends'. In one of her diary entries she sets down her own principles of diary making.

> There looms ahead of me the shadow of some kind of form which a diary might attain to. I might in the course of time learn what it is one can make of this loose, drifting material of life; finding another use for it than the use I put it to, so much more consciously and scrupulously in fiction. What sort of diaries should I like mine to be? Something loose knit and yet not slovenly, so elastic that it will embrace anything, solemn, slight or beautiful that comes to my mind. (entry 20 April, 1919, 1977-85)

In another entry (Jan 20, 1919) she refers in her diary to her 'haphazard gallop' and in a later one to 'all this scribble'. In spite of this self-deprecatory tone the diaries do confirm that she succeeded in making them 'loose knit but not slovenly' and that feminists are right to see them as uniquely exploratory and as a proving ground for her ideas about writing. However, it is one thing to set out with reverence Woolf's achievement, which no-one can seriously dispute, and quite another to see her as representative of a phalanx of women diarists and letter writers. Furthermore, feminist critics have not really searched through men's diaries to test whether or not some have been as innovative as Virginia Woolf.

I have just re-read Franz Kafka's diaries (*The Diaries of Franz Kafka*, 1914-1923, Secker and Warburg, 1948, 1949) and they show him beyond a doubt using the diary form to fulfil his essential needs as a writer. It is my guess that many writers, both men and women, have on their desks at this moment diary-notebooks which would read very much like those of Woolf and Kafka and that they plunder their own ephemera eagerly for their published works. The Kafka diaries are an extraordinary assemblage of writings, aphorisms, long versions of dreams, outlines of stories, sometimes in several versions, whole stories, floating fragments of stories, accounts of plays seen and books read, passages of dialogue possibly meant for plays, agonisings over his personal relationships, mini essays, copies of some of his letters. Always there is pessimistic critique of his own writing. Like Virginia Woolf he stops from time to time to look at the diary itself.

One advantage in keeping a diary is that you become aware with reassuring clarity of the changes which you constantly suffer and which in a general way are naturally believed, surmised, and admitted by you, but which you'll unconsciously deny when it comes to the point of gaining hope or peace from such an admission. In the diary you'll find proof that in situations which today would seem unbearable, you looked around and wrote down observations, that this right hand moved then as it does today, when we may be wiser because we are able to look back on our former condition and for that very reason have got to admit the courage of our earlier striving in which we persisted even in sheer ignorance. (entry 23, Dec 1911)

They are two of a kind, Virginia Woolf and Franz Kafka. Not the same kind of writer, of course, but the same kind of diarist.

- *Women play with established autobiographical forms and experiment with their discourse*

The centre cannot hold, as Yeats told us a long time ago, and post-modernists say a fervent yes to that. All texts, they tell us, are many-voiced and resound with voices which contradict each other. The self which was formerly held to be at the inviolate centre of autobiography is now presented as a dislocated and fractured thing emerging in texts which are criss-crossed by multiple selves. Reality or 'out there' is a grand illusion, for like the self it exists solely as a creation of texts. No words, no reality. Autobiography begins to take on a different substance in the light of this intellectual attempt to destabilise it. The post-modernist iconoclastic rhetoric needs full debate which I shall not pursue. I turn to it not because it is sternly revisionist in its analysis of autobiographical discourse but because it turns an admiring gaze on those autobiographical works which quite deliberately assume a generic ambiguity, violently disrupt chronology, consciously blur past and present and fact and fiction and private and public, and in many other ways challenge the reader to work out what they are up to. In this context it is easy to see why feminists welcome these forms of resistance to the booming monologue of established forms and recruit them for women.

If we search the shelves for volumes which confirm this readiness of women writers to change the recognisable features of most autobiography, we shall find them without difficulty because the feminists have taught us to be on the look-out for the doyenne, Gertrude Stein, and the newcomers Kate Millet, Maxine Hong Kingston, Maya Angelou, Christa Wolf and other discursive rebels. I choose one not often cited, Carmen Martin Gaite, not only because her book, *The Back Room* (1983) places question marks over both gender and genre but also because she is an active theorist of autobiography. Her book was given its formal status as a novel but she herself has called it an autobiography. That at once gives a hint of its unembarrassed slipping to and fro across the generic frontiers. The sense of autobiography we take to the book is soon disturbed when a man in black arrives and engages the writer in lengthy nocturnal conversation which is about her life, politics and literature. Critics were quick to seize upon its utterly disrupted chronology and its adroit evasion of a shapely closure. The man in black, we come to see, is a kind of alter ego, though he is presented to us as a literary critic. By means of this dialogue, Martin Gaite calls into question both autobiography and fiction as we know them and shows how dangerously they insinuate themselves into our thinking and resist all efforts to shake them off entirely.

Once again and for the last time in this chapter I ask why feminists do not acknowledge that some men also seek to find ways in which to create anew the role of autobiography? What kind of censorship leads most of them to make an un-person of Proust, no less? And then there is Michel Leiris, the anthropologist, whose autobiographical writings started with *Manhood* (1939) and continued throughout his life through four more volumes (*Biffures*, 1948; *Fourbis*, 1955; *Fibrilles*, 1966; *Frêle Bruit*, 1976 – collectively given the overall title *La Regle du Jeu*). I want to do no more than indicate just how deviant is his lifetime's attempt to build a monumental autobiography. I borrow Germaine Brée's description (1980) of his heterogeneous and idiosyncratic ways of working.

> ... Leiris applies the research methods of the anthropologist to his own life. He has constituted an archive (an extensive one it would seem) of index files wherein he accumulated the data upon which he works – the record of dreams, of fantasies, encounters, love affairs, moods, word games, poems, observations, fragments of analysis. He also kept a diary; and he refers to loose sheets of paper on which he notes more sustained thematic developments. (p.197)

From all this emerged what Brée calls 'anti-autobiographic autobiography'. It would have been possible for feminists to give serious attention to this massive effort, even if in the end they might decide, 'No, not that way'.

By now it must be clear how I see the feminist long march through autobiographical institutions. Despite my grumbling reservations I hope that what has emerged from this chapter is that both autobiography and autobiographical studies would be infinitely poorer without the contributions made by feminists. It is not possible to ignore their challenge.

CHAPTER 7

AUTOBIOGRAPHY NOW

...the life stories of Britain's 1,000 oldest people will be among the 72 projects of the millennium celebrations... Story of a Lifetime is an attempt to compile an oral history of the nation. The 1,000 oldest people in the country will be asked to give recollections of their lifetimes. These will be on an electronic archive, accessible to the Greenwich celebration, starting on January 1, 2000. (*The Guardian,* Nov 1996)

Autobiography (in this case in its oral form) has indeed come a long way when it is given such a prominent role in a great official and public activity such as the millennium celebration. We can only guess at the fascinating history of the decision to construct this unique archive and at the fine detail of the procedures which will be involved. Certainly, the official embrace will at the very least run the risk of producing a tamed and domesticated selection. However, the promoters will be able, if they wish, to draw on a solid body of recent work to help them in carrying out their scheme and have possibly already done so. In the United States *The Art and Science of Reminiscing* (Haight and Webster, 1995) and in the United Kingdom *Reminiscence Reviewed* (Bornat, 1995) each register in their characteristically different ways that old people telling the stories of their lives are no longer dismissed as being engaged in trivial or even harmful garrulity but rather in a self-transforming therapy and, beyond that, putting material before all of us which adds significantly to our social understanding.

In this final chapter I start with this current development because even now it is possible for students of autobiography either to ignore totally, or to marginalise not only certain written forms but also oral life stories. Yet Joanna Bornat (*op.cit.*) writes of the period of the mid-1970s onwards as one which 'saw an enthusiastic almost evangelistic commitment to 'reminiscence therapy' or 'reminiscence work''. Life review and reminiscence take many forms and, although they may be of special interest when old people engage in them, we all throughout our lives participate in these activities. Our life-reviews undergo ceaseless revisions, elaborations, deletions and expansions. However, now that they have become a focus of interest and research, we have to see them as belonging somewhere on a continuum from the spontaneous to the elicited. Spontaneous reminiscence is the root from which all autobiography grows, while elicited reminiscence reminds us that inevitably the attempt is made by researchers to shape the outcome with a catechism of questions or a schedule of topics or even handbooks for composing autobiography. (See, for example, Rybarczyk in Haight and Webster, *op.cit.* p.209 which uses the term 'interview' and supplies five 'basic rules' for conducting it.) We have now reached the point where all kinds of practitioners use reminiscence on a scale which three decades ago was unthinkable and which at its worst we might call the industrialisation of the life stories of the elderly.

As ever, the great hazard, in spite of the work of Halbwachs (1992) and others, is the perception of the whole process as being yet another celebration of that holy icon of the West, the Individual. Buchanan and Middleton (1994), concerned about the many ways in which the term reminiscence is used, put their own anti-individualistic view in this way.

> ... we have tried to show that reminiscence work is a profoundly social phenomenon; what 'reminiscence' is taken to be, and what its benefits for older people are taken to be, are formulated and reformulated according to social-relational concern – the social position of older people, the care relationship and relations of expertise and equality. Reminiscence work is fundamentally concerned with the rights of older people to have a voice in their relations with others, and the issues we have discussed are essentially concerned with struggles to give or withold that right to a *voice*. Research approaches which reduce reminiscence to an individual psychological process, with individual psychological benefits, marginalise the sociality of the reminiscence enterprise. (p.73)

This is to insert the whole escalating reminiscence enterprise into the politics of discourse. In the current diversity of autobiographical activity, as it is conceived of in this book, there is a continuation and proliferation of those forms we have lived with for centuries. The eminent and the notorious and those in the public eye for any reason preen themselves, justify themselves, leak a few secrets and rely on the insatiable demand for scandals and revelations. The only change is the scale of publication and dissemination. I am not at this point concerned with them. This final chapter is not intended as a comprehensive survey. I want instead to choose those ventures which, like reminiscence work, open up new possibilities. Inevitably, those who have already reached literary eminence tend to complete their oeuvre with an autobiographical work or a high profile lengthy interview on television, a carefully constructed video, or even perhaps a performance on Desert Island Discs.

Needless to say, we all go on speaking to each other of our pasts in the well-established modes of everyday interchange, relatively untouched by the manoeuverings of the literary world, its discursive discontents and efforts to provoke the reader and even undermine the very concept of autobiography. The autobiographical voice is now amplified in all the mass media and the 'serious' Sunday papers fill their acres of hungry space with interviews, confessions and ephemeral trivia presented to us as a day's, a morning's, an hour's experience inflated by fashionable slang – the quotidian as emptiness masked by the spangles of metropolitan sophistication. In spite of the mountainous accumulation from the past there are still those who find new ways of working which may even be offering new models.

Alan Bennett's *Writing Home* (1994) is the work of an established playwright who has enjoyed huge success and it was received with nothing less than rapture in that informal institution we call the literary world. His publishers tell us that it 'might be subtitled 'Scenes from a Writer's Life'' and that it is an autobiographical volume – which is not strictly true. Bennett himself eludes those inflated phrases, writing,

> This book brings together the talks, diaries, and occasional journalism that I have written during the last twenty years or so. (p.ix)

Nevertheless, the first clutch of pieces 'Past and Present' anyone would recognise immediately as being what we have come to know as autobiography and there follows 'The Lady in a Van' which moves into the diary mode to record his relationship over fifteen years with an old lady whose battered old caravan ends up parked in his drive. The Dickensian story which emerges from the entries is certainly intriguing. However, I refer to it here because Bennett is using what used to be the most private, often clandestine

177

form of autobiographical writing and turning it into a fully public medium, so much so that it is an edited text.

> The account of Miss Shepherd condenses some of the many entries to do with her that are scattered through my diaries. (p.88)

'My Diaries', which constitute the next one hundred or so pages of the book, turn out to be a particular kind of construct which Bennett carefully describes for us at the outset (p.99). He has kept a sporadic diary since the early Seventies which turns out to be, strictly speaking, raw material. Most of these diaries were originally published in *The London Review of Books* where the extracts were run together and the gaps between eliminated. 'What had been a series of jottings became a continuous, if disjointed, narrative.' (p.97)

> The writing is untidy, too; immediacy in my case doesn't make for vivid reporting which I've not had any scruples about improving and editing, though I've never altered the tone and sentiments. (p.7)

Bennett's annotation of his practices would not lead us to expect how deeply unimportant many of the entries are and how soon they are likely to fade into nothingness. Some do seem more durable and full of more solid social observation.

Will this kind of publication – reminiscence, plus improved and edited diary entries – open up a new route into autobiographical discourse, making a space for everything from the inevitable childhood memories to the briefest of entries (three names from the Albanian football team!). The model here is the heterogeneous assemblage which includes lots of photographs, prefaces to plays, reviews and even 'Stocking Fillers' in any one of which the autobiographical voice may take over. This kind of collage matters mostly because it demonstrates, albeit in an undemonstrative way, that autobiography lives in heterogeneity in more ways than one.

I have commented earlier on ways in which autobiographical discourse can be woven into other kinds of text and vice versa. These juxtapositions can usually be handled quite comfortably by a reader or listener who has no vested interest in genre purities, for speakers also blend their discourses. However, there also exist disturbing ruptures in some texts, deliberate nonsequiturs, anti-narratives. In her study, 'Autobiography as intertext' (1990), Ann Jefferson sees this in Robbe-Grillet's *Le miroir qui revient* and *Angélique, ou l'enchantement*. I borrow her comment on these two works, which she says,

178

...comprise a sort of patchwork in which fiction is juxtaposed with childhood memory, critical comment with anecdote about Robbe-Grillet's recent past, a defence of pornographic fantasy with a eulogy of Barthes and an indignant, highly detailed narrative account of the prosecution of *Glissement progressif du plaisir* with general quasi-philosophical statements about the nature of art. (p.123)

We may be familiar with this defiance of most readers' expectations which lures them into baffling struggles with text, if we encountered it long ago in modernist poets or avant-garde film-makers who abandoned the sacred storyline or abruptly shifted from manifest fictions to newsreels and back again. Autobiographical innocence disappeared a long time ago in the excitements of textual modernism. Writers like Gertrude Stein, Virginia Woolf and Leiris, each in their own way disrupted the formulaic pattern of life stories and fractured their smooth surfaces. They were all strongly anchored in the intellectual world and eventually arrived at autobiography.

While every kind of well-established autobiographical discourse may continue to offer us the comfort of familiarity, other works now appear which very deliberately refuse the invitation of that tradition and attempt a new kind of newness. Certainly in Christine Brooke-Rose's *Remake* (1996) we encounter the post-modern autobiography, post-modern in the sense that it is explicitly knowing, repeatedly inviting us to consider what she is doing and constructing a text that oscillates between present and past. The author, an established novelist and an academic in the field of linguistics at the University of Paris, sets out in her seventies to write her life story. Her publishers are happy to call it 'an autobiographical novel', a singularly un-helpful label, partly because the fictionality of autobiography is inescapable but also because it is so un-novel like in most of its strategies. *Remake* is yet another case of hybridity and also of meta-autobiography. She watches herself at work and does so with all the academic resources of one who is steeped in linguistic and literary theory. Someone who is not familiar with Chomsky's exemplar sentences will miss entirely a lot of her verbal play.

She appears first in the text as 'the old lady' and later as Tess (herself in child-hood) and later still as one of the 'psychologically healthy Houyhnhnms'. Utterly unpredictably she shuttles to and fro in time and place (Belgium, Holland, France and England) and only at the end of the book can you arrive with certainty at a map of the years spent nomadically. But if we consider that autobiography has one unavoidable prerequisite, namely, that its raw material is memory of the past then we find Brooke-Rose subverting that expectation:

> The old lady sits at seventy-two, feeling sixty, fifty, forty in a burotic study over-looking the orchards and vineyards and wooded hills and lavender plateaux. There is a word-processor and printer, an electronic typewriter and Xerox machine.
>
> Why is the old lady trying to intercept all those interseptic messages?
>
> Old-age? self-indulgence? No, the old lady's publisher has asked for an autobiography. But the resistance is huge. The absorbing present creates interference... only the text matters, if the text survives at all. But the insistent request has needled the interception. (p.6)

As we can see the writer's locus in the present is her little house in Provence where we find her quarrelling with neighbours. Her sorties into the past prove to be anti-chronological, not simply to enable her to forage to and fro in time but also to represent her mind, memory and imagination at work. Musing disinters the relevant moment. Anything may set in motion her remake placed against social and political events which are remakes too, concocted 'by the century's parlour tricks, dogmaticks and polempic games' (p.16). She presses forward, always sceptical, disenchanted with the world which she can now monitor electronically.

> ...the old lady can't decide, imagine, invent, select the life-file to call up first, if at all, even if re-treated as something else, in-putting the data-bank of culture, attaching personal experience to collectivities, significant mutations at least as memory joggers. But is that how memory was lived? (p.16)

Her method, for all her doubts about where the pen can or cannot take her, leaves space for the unhurried story of her mother's death which might have found itself, almost, in an old-style autobiography. Her mother had retired to a convent where she spent forty years as a nun. 'The old lady' extricated this memory with the help of 'a bit of a diary kept at the time'. There are other stories.

The book concludes with a long meditation on memory, more what it is not rather than what it is. Even at the very end her doubts about her own auto-biographical project remain.

> As flybyable, flowable time has slowly then swiftly extinguished the separate fullnesses of time, only the present fullnesses of time remain, and the remake of a life becomes more and more impossible. (p.172)

And her last word is that 'a remake is never as good as the original'.

The European intellectual in the very moment of the autobiographical act invents, meditates, twists and turns, narrates and plays extraordinary games with words. She has deep suspicions about the medium in which she conducts her stormy love affair with the past. But it is through these suspicions she can demonstrate that there is, as ever, room for innovation in autobiography.

However, there are quite different innovations in autobiography as it is being practised now which do not operate through the pyrotechnics of surprise, transition and verbal experiment. There is, for example, Theo Richmond's *Konin* (1996). It would be a simple matter to describe *Konin* in a way which would make it seem at most marginally autobiographical. Konin, the place, was 'a small Polish town... on the western edge of the Tsarist empire' from which Richmond's parents came before the First World War. In 1939 its population was 12,100 of whom 2,700 were Jews, a mere 200 of whom survived the slaughter in the woods outside the town in 1941 and deportation. Richmond's book, looked at in a very general way, is an attempt to rebuild the town, to reconstruct it as an archeologist would, but not from stones and bones but from the testimony, much of it spoken, by the survivors of the holocaust and by those who had left Konin earlier, from archives, from the historical record. Konin is autobiographical in a new kind of way although there is no sense in its prose and its shifts of focus that it is an avant-garde text, for we are not dealing with an established and innovative literary figure like Robbe-Grillet but a journalist and script-writer who, in January 1987, took the decision to 'write a book of my own about the Jewish men and women of Konin, a book that would interweave past and present'. This book, his first, appeared in 1996. The quest, as he calls it, is a complex and exacting task and produced a work which is the story of his life or, more precisely, the relevant parts of it during the years it took him to complete. Within the over-arching autobiographical text which holds the diverse components within its grasp there are autobiographical materials which he obtains from others on his geographical-psychological travels, material hunted down all over the world (Britain, North America, Israel) personally elicited to make contributions to a work whose purpose is nothing less than the mental rebuilding of a Jewish community and the story of its destruction in the words of the living and, occasionally, the dead.

What I am suggesting is innovative in this autobiographical writing is the assemblage in speaking and writing by many voices and hands all subsumed to the obsessive quest itself, recorded autobiographically and interwoven with the findings of archival research. Yet none of this can convey the achievement of Richmond's brilliant text which does not lie in the display of his collected materials, which would after all have been a fascinating anthology very like *The Konin Memorial Book* which first impelled him to begin his journey, but rather the way in which all the personal testimony is braided together with his own experience of eliciting it.

In 1968, *The Konin Memorial Book* (*Kehilat-Konin be-trihata u ve-Hurbana*, Tel Aviv, 1968) arrived in the London home of Theo Richmond, a completely anglicised professional, whose parents had spent their childhood in Konin although they, too, were settled in their professional London lives. The memorial volume, all 800 pages of it, was a closed book for him because it was written in Yiddish, which he could not read though he could transliterate the Hebrew characters. It was a compilation made in Israel by surviving Koniners from all over the world and consisted of history, geography and memoirs. Almost twenty years later Richmond looks at the black-edged pages which listed some two thousand names of murdered Koniners and sees for the first time amongst them various members of his family under the Polish form of the family name, Ryczke, including his grandfather and grandmother, various uncles, aunts and others.

> I turned over the pages and knew that the decision had been made for me. I must write a book of my own ... that would interweave past and present... I would learn Yiddish to unlock the contents of the Memorial book. (p.3)

We are soon plunged into an account of his tracking down of Koniners: Uncle Asher, Joe Fox, 89 years old, Henry, a survivor of Matthausen Camp, Izzy, a survivor of Auschwitz, Hersch, Henriek in Luton – 'Auschwitz and Matthausen were his universities', 'squire's' son Henry Kaplan, Lewin and Irene.

By the time we reach the end of the English phase of his quest his complex method is clear. He is writing an autobiographical symphony. First there are times when his memories of childhood and growing up are relevant to a moment in the text such as his troubled awareness of the rise of fascism and, much more pervasive, is the story of the quest itself – his journeys, the stays in cheap hotels, the overwhelming hospitable meals but, above all, the texture of his encounters with those who offer him painful testimony and silences. The Koniners' stories are drawn on in different ways, as gifts in the face-to-face situation. They speak of Konin before 1939, the destruction of Jewish Konin and its inhabitants, the camps and their own incredible survival. Almost everyone he meets knew some member of his family.

But there are those whose autobiographical acts enter the book by a different route. He draws on written testimony from the Memorial book, of course, to add some essential detail, Some material comes from the published auto-biographies of Leopold Infeld who was as a very young man head of the Jewish Gymnasium in Konin. He later became a world-renowned scientist and collaborated with Einstein. He gives a very unflattering picture of Konin in *Quest: The Evolution of a Scientist* (1941). At 65 his view mellowed (*Sketches from the Past*, 1978). An instance of a quite different kind comes from the 'Protokol'. This turns out to be the very lengthy and chilling deposition by a Konin veterinary surgeon, a non-Jewish Pole, before a local court just after the war. As a Gestapo prisoner he was taken into a clearing in the woods near Konin and obliged not only to witness the slaughter of men, women and children beside open pits but also to collect their belong-ings. Richmond was able to visit the vet himself in Konin, a survivor of the camp when, in the concluding chapter, he gives the story of his 'return' after he has completed the reconstruction of the town in his mind and in his text.

The diversity of autobiographical strands of which I have given only the barest indication never becomes mere heterogeneity because of Richmond's own voice throughout, restrained, sceptical and non-romantic. Neither Konin nor the Koniners emerge in a golden haze of nostalgia. There they are, warts and all, as indeed he himself is. No one would consider this a post-modernist leap. Yet it breaks new ground in autobiographical writing and could be a prototype for other works.

It seems only proper that during the time when I am writing this last chapter I should be hyperaware of the life-stories of others entering my own life. Just a short while ago I received from an old friend, Dick Leith, a recent paper of his, 'Storytelling and a Scottish Traveller Folk Tale, 'The Green Man of Knowledge'' (unpub). Some while ago I was in the audience when he presented this paper at a conference of storytellers. I was mesmerised. He had managed by the most adroit interweaving to braid together not only a subtle analysis of the language of the spoken story (he is, after all, a sociolinguist) but also how he had lived with that story, encountering it first in a printed version as an MA student of dialect in 1971. That version was a transcript of Geordie Stewart, an Aberdeenshire traveller, telling the story. But it was not until 1990 that he heard a taped performance of Geordie's telling. And then, much later, a kind of denouement when he met the per-former himself. Of this experience over all those years Dick Leith writes,

The question I have come to consider over the last ten years or so is why I keep coming back to *The Green Man of Knowledge.* Although people have often asked why I am so attracted to this story – or more precisely this narration of it – I have only recently come to see the point of this question. This is one reason why I have chosen to present this paper within the frame of an autobiographical encounter. The question, what does this story mean to me? invites, however, the further question: what does this story mean? And how separate are the two questions? (p.6)

For him the story is not simply a resource for narratological scholarship but an important and inseparable part of his life-story. How long ago is it when it would have been considered improper for an academic, delivering a scholarly paper, to permit it to become entwined with his personal life?

In *The London Review of Books* (7 March, 1996) with its four-column pages of very small print you hear the thumping sounds of intellectual aerobics. I find a long review of a work called *Peter Yorke's Eighties.* The first half of the review says absolutely nothing about the book. Instead it takes us through Andrew O'Hagan's account of his Eighties from the point at which

... my family felt everything would be fine if I could get something with a shirt and tie. My three elder brothers wore nailbags, overalls and aprons – the respective black robes of time-served apprenticeship.

He tries to get a job as 'office aide to the local brute responsible for most of the fencing around the estate' but the boss is 'jeest lookin' furra wee lassie tae mak the tea'. He becomes a clerical assistant at the local Jobcentre.

My box was full of dud jobs ... I came to hate that box, with its fetid stock of cards, its excruciating pile of non-jobs.

All this in contrast to Peter Yorke's life which was full of happy consumerist days obsessed with stylism. Eventually O'Hagan turns to the book he is reviewing and his strategy becomes clear. His own autobiography con-stitutes a comment on the book.

Peter Yorke's Eighties happened elsewhere. Little bits of it were no doubt happening in the shopping mall over my head that morning, but most of it was well out of my reach, nothing to do with our world at all.

This kind of writing (my story to comment on yours) is a literate form of what happens in conversations where the exchange of autobiographical stories is a form of serious debate. Add to Leith and O'Hagan all those autobiographical messages which flow towards me and I could in a few days compile a little anthology. So could many, many other people and demonstrate how extensively and ineradicably they permeate our communicative world. They nestle inside the life-stories of others like Russian dolls. They are not embellishments of experience to be pinned on like brooches but an essential component of the texture of our days.

It is only by considering the totality of such narratives in individual lives that we can perceive their full significance rather than by, let us say, the virtuoso feats of raconteurs. Only then is it possible to understand that activity as a means by which we all achieve and retain a hold on our social world and invite others to accept or to deny or to modify it. For most people this will be by means of continual oral activity. Only one very recent published attempt, so far as I am aware, offers a sustained analysis of this phenomenon – the gradual construction of a life story which is constantly undergoing revision.

Charlotte Linde's *Life Stories: The Creation of Coherence* (1993) is a study undertaken in the sociolinguistic tradition, an enquiry into everyday speech practices. Many of its conclusions and much of its discussion are based on generously quoted research protocols which were the outcome of interviews in which 'middle-class American speakers' came to choose their professions. Linde is well aware that she is only dipping her toe into the deep water of their life-stories and that there are hazards in generalising from speech elicited by an investigator which would not be produced spontaneously.

When Linde writes of life-stories, she gives her own special meaning to this term: she limits it to oral activity.

> A life-story consists of all the stories and associated discourse units, such as explanations and chronicles and the connections between them, told by an individual during the course of his/her lifetime that satisfy the following two criteria:
>
> 1. The stories and associated discourse units contained in the life-story have as their primary evaluation a point about the speaker, not a general point about the way the world is.
>
> 2. The stories and associated discourse units have extended reportability; that is, they are tellable and are told and retold over the course of a long period of time. (p.21)

In marking out her territory, Linde has boldly established a much richer and more extensive way of looking at oral stories of personal experience than anyone else. It should constitute a launching pad for other studies based on very different informants. In spite of severe limitations to her data she offers a very wide sense of the function of life-stories, i.e. the ever-renewed attempt to achieve a coherent view of life.

> Just as the life-story as a social unit has some correspondence to an internal private life-story, so the coherence we produce for social consumption bears a relation to our own individual desires to understand our life as coherent, as making sense, as the history of a proper person. (p.17)

She says nothing of the way our continuous life-stories often reveal irreconcilable contradictions of which we may be intensely aware but may never resolve. Nevertheless it is probably true that we strive for coherence even if we never achieve it.

Let me return to Linde's definition for, innovative though it is, it raises some problems. Nowhere in it does she make explicit that life-stories are narratives about the speaker's past, a glaring and unexplained omission. Then there is the contrastive distinction between 'a point about the speaker' and 'a point about the way the world is'. Her own examples are (a) a hospital story that shows a speaker coping with difficult circumstances and (b) the same speaker relating the same experiences to show what is wrong with hospitals. But most stories do both sorts of things, though the balance shifts. When we listen to stories which tell us about the way the world is we always make judgements about the speaker. Thus the hospital story may lead us to judge the speaker as an incorrigible complainer or as a perceptive observer. At the other pole the story of my gall bladder operation might focus on my anxieties beforehand and delighted relief afterwards but at the same time it might be about the achievements of keyhole surgery.

Linde's enthusiasm for keeping her life-stories quite distinct from close relatives in the life-story universe leads her to ignore ways in which they might contribute to 'thicker' description of how we construct our life-stories. She might have considered letter-writing and diary-keeping and even the relationship between the written life-story and the cumulative one. However, she is not unaware of these possibilities even though she does not develop them.

> Of all written presentations of self, private journals and diaries bear the greatest resemblance to the life-story... A journal is a very private work; it may be written for the author alone, for a small audience selected by the writer or for an imagined audience. Unlike the writer of a publishable autobiography one need have no exceptional qualifications to write a journal. (p.42)

Having stepped across her own boundary, Linde hastily withdraws on the grounds that these forms are written and not universal. None of my criticisms should diminish this work as a ground-breaking venture in revealing a very basic way in which we both declare and discover who we are and assert our affinities through 'a coherent, acceptable and constantly revised life-story' (p.3). If 'acceptable' needs a more careful gloss then she is not prepared to give it (acceptable to whom?). We can overlook its conformist overtones by adding – acceptable to those by whom the speaker wishes to be accepted. Linde shows some awareness of this in her concluding chapter on Foucault's use of the term 'discourse'.

> If we were to talk about the discourse of resistance, we would certainly want to include examples of members of an oppressed group, telling stories of successful and unsuccessful acts of resistance, grumbling to one another, or composing and singing satirical songs about their oppressors. (p.223)

However, the opening sentence of the book tells us that an individual needs a life-story to show that he/she is 'a good, socially proper, and stable person' (p.3).

Contrast that proposition with the work of Barbara Meyerhoff (1979) who elicited the life-stories of elderly Jews in an old people's home in California. Amongst them is Shmuel Goldman who, she says, 'made everything ordinary something special' (p.29) and whose elicited life-story is recorded in the chapter 'Needle and Thread; the Life and Death of a Tailor'.

> He is in one sense an outsider to the community because his boldly-voiced atheism and political opposition to Israel provoke anger and rejection by other members of the centre. But he does not abandon the community ... The centre is the only place where he can continue to speak Yiddish. He also believes they need him to remind them of certain moral and political truths. This very outsider status, in addition to his erudition, and perceptiveness make him a powerful and eloquent voice to describe his shtetl childhood, his socialist and Jewish values and reflections on what his life has meant (Prell, 1989, p.245)

When he dies some of his fellows in the home deliberately absent themselves from his funeral, precisely because they do not regard him as 'a socially proper person'. The oppositional life-story deserves more than Linde's afterthought. the more so since there are many others now, not difficult to find.

I have through an inspection of some selected exemplar texts and practices sketched some developments in autobiographical and critical practice at this very moment. Others might easily have served. They are not all easily subsumed by the Protean term post-modernism. The vast assumptions about the self, the individual and the ego dissolve when they are perceived as being fractured and ever multiple and mutable. The notion of a carefully constructed identity expressed by the meaning-making coherent individual as the paradigm in autobiography is replaced by a view of autobiographies which sees them as internally contradictory narratives. I have stressed that, side by side with would-be or actual newnesses, long established forms continue to thrive not simply as tired old anachronisms (the 'residual' is Raymond Williams's term) but as evidence that there is life in the old dog yet. In Brooke-Rose's Remake we can soon perceive the post-modernist stance both in the flickering structure of the book and in the pyrotechnics of much of its prose. Nevertheless, the familiar voice of the storyteller can take over the text at any moment. The post-modernist and traditionalist rub shoulders.

* * * *

The historian Yerushalmi (1982), in a book of reflections on remembering and forgetting, registers a very sombre note.

> ... in the world in which we live it is no longer merely a question of the decay of collective memory and the declining consciousness of the past, but of the aggressive rape of whatever memory remains, the deliberate distortion of the historical records, the invention of mythological pasts in the service of the powers of darkness ... (p.116)

He goes on to say that against 'the agents of oblivion' 'the assassins of memory' and 'the conspirators of silence' -

> ... only the historian with austere passion for fact, proof , evidence which are central to his vocation can effectively stand guard. (p116)

Perhaps Yerushalmi's lament for an ignored or distorted past is a healthy corrective to indiscriminate celebratory gestures for any kind of treatment of the past, a sort of apotheosis of autobiographical acts and he does, after all, take his stand on the side of too much rather than too little 'for my terror of forgetting is greater than my terror of having too much to remember' (p.116/117). Nevertheless it is not the historian alone who hands to us the gifts from memory but all those who put before us their life-stories or parts of them, taking all from the unique alloy of memory and imagination.

Bibliography

Baddeley, A. (1989) 'The psychology of remembering and forgetting' in T. Butler ed. *Memory*. Basil Blackwell

Barthes, R. (1975) *S/Z*. Jonathan Cape

Barnett, F. (1932) *Remembering*. Cambridge University Press

Bashkirtseff, M. (1928) *Journal*. Dutton

Bauman, R. (1977) *Verbal Art as Performance*. Waveland Press

Bauman, R. (1986) *Story, Performance and Event*. Cambridge University Press

Bennett, A. (1994) *Writing Home*. Faber and Faber

Benstock, S. Ed. (1988) *The Private Self: Theory and Practice of Women's Autobiography*. Routledge

Bhabha, H. (1994) *The Location of Culture*. Routledge

Blythe, R. (1972) *Akenfield*. Penguin

Bornat, J. (1994) 'Is oral history auto/biography?' in Lives and Work, special double issue of *Auto/biography* 3.1 and 3.2

Bornat, J. (1995) *Reminiscence Reviewed*. Open University

Brée, G. (1980) 'Michael Leiris: Mazemaker' in J. Olney, ed, *Autobiography: Essays Theoretical and Critical*. Princeton University Press

Brés, J. (1992) 'De la production d'identité dans la mise en récit d'une action carnavalesque' in *Langage et Societé,* No 62 Dec

Brewer, W. (1986) 'What is autobiographical memory?' in D.C. Rubin, ed. *Autobiographical Memory*. Cambridge University Press

Brewer, W. (1988) 'Memory for randomly sampled autobiographical events' in N. Neisser and E. Winograd, eds. *Remembering Reconsidered: Ecological and Traditional Approaches to Memory*. Cambridge University Press

Brodski, B. and Shenk, C. eds. (1988) *Life-Lines: Theorising Women's Autobiography*. Cornell University Press

Brooke-Rose, C. (1996) *Remake*. Carcenet

Brown, R. and Kulik, J. (1977) 'Flashbulb memories' in *Cognition*. 5.

Bruner, J. (1983) *In Search of Mind: Essays in Autobiography*. Harper and Row

Bruner, J. (1990) *Acts of Meaning.* Harvard University Press

Bruner, J. (1990) *Actual Minds: Possible Worlds.* Harvard University Press

Bruner, J. (1993) 'The autobiographical process' in R. Folkenflik, ed. *The Culture of Autobiography.* Stanford University Press

Buchanan, K. and Middleton, D. (1993) 'Discursively formulating the significance of reminiscence in later life' in N. Coupland and J. Nussbaurn, eds. *Discourse and Lifespan Development*

Burnet, J. ed. (1974) *Useful Toil.* Allen Lane

Burnet, J. ed. (1982) *Destiny Obscure.* Penguin

Butler, T. (1989) *Memory.* Basil Blackwell

Carter, R. (1990) 'When is a report not a report? Observation from academic and non-academic settings' in W. Nash, ed. *The Writing Scholar: Studies in Academic Discourse.* Sage

Charke, C. (1989) *The Well-known Troublemaker: A life of Charlotte Charke.* Faber and Faber

Chodorow, N. (1978) *Psycho-analysis and the Sociology of Gender.* University of California Press

Clare, J. ed. E. Robinson (1983) *John Clare's Autobiographical Writings.* Oxford University Press

Clare, J. Eds. E. Robinson and D. Powell (1996) *John Clare by Himself.* Carcenet Press

Conway, M. (1990) *Autobiographical Memory.* Open University Press

Cullwick, H. (1984) *The Diaries of Hannah Cullwick.* Virago

Damasio, A. (1994) *Descartes's Error: Emotion, Reason and the Human Brain.* Brosset/Putnam

Darwin, C. (1845/1889) *Voyage of the Beagle. Darwin's Journal during the Voyage of HMS Beagle round the World.* Ward Lock

De Beauvoir, S. (1965) *The Prime of Life.* Penguin

Defoe, D. (1722/1966) *A Journal of the Plague Year.* Penguin

Derrida, J. (1978) *Writing and Difference.* Routledge and Kegan Paul

Douglas, M. (1980) *Evans-Pritchard.* Fontana

Eakin, P. (1985) *Fictions in Autobiography: Studies in the Art of Invention.* Princeton University Press

Eco, U. (1992) *Interpretation and Misinterpretation.* Cambridge University Press

Evans, W. and Evans, T. (1837-50) *The Friends' Library.* Philadelphia

Facey, A. (1981) *A Fortunate Life.* Penguin

Fentress, J. and Wickham, C. (1992) *Social Memory.* Basil Blackwell

Fischer, M. (1994) 'Autobiographical voices (1,2,3) and mosaic memory: experimental sondages in the (post) modern world' in K. Ashley et al. eds. *Autobiography and Post-modernism.* University of Massachusetts

Fleishman, A. (1983) *Figures of Autobiography: The Language of Self-Writing in Victorian and Modern England.* University of California Press

Folkenflik, R. ed. (1993) *The Culture of Autobiography.* Stanford University Press

Fortey, R. (1994) *The Hidden Landscape: A Journey into the Geological Past.* Pimlico

Friedan, B. (1963) *The Feminine Mystique.* Penguin

Friedman, S. (1988) 'Women's autobiographical selves: Theory and practice' in S. Benstock ed. *Theory and Practice of Women's Autobiography.* Routledge

Frisch, M. (1990) *A Shared Authority: Essays on the Craft and Meaning of Oral and Public History.* Suny

Frow, J. (1986) *Marxism and Literary History.* Basil Blackwell

Gaite, M. (1983) *The Back Room.* Columbia University Press

Gates, H. (1994) *Colored People.* Alfred Knopf

Genette, G. (1980) *Narrative Discourse.* Basil Blackwell

Gergen, K.J. (1982) *Toward Transformation in Human Knowledge.* Springer-Verlag

Goffman, E. (1959) *The Presentation of Self in Everyday Life.* Doubleday Anchor

Goffman, E. (1981) *Forms of Talk.* Basil Blackwell

Gorki, M. (1940) *Fragments from my Diary*, Penguin

Gorki, M. (trans. 1952) *1913 My Childhood. 1916. My Apprenticeship. 1923 My Universities.* Foreign Languages Publishing House Moscow

Gosse, E. (1907) *Father and Son.* Heinemann

Grandin, T. (1986) *Emergence: Labelled Autistic.* Costello

Green, H. (1940) *Pack my Bag.* Hogarth Press

Grumet, M. (1990) 'Retrospective autobiography and the analysis of educational experience' in *Cambridge Educ. Journal* Vol 20, No.3

Gusdorf, G. (1980) 'Conditions and limits of autobiography' in J. Olney, ed. *Autobiography: Essays Theoretical and Critical.* Princeton University Press

Haight, B. and Webster J. (1995) *The Art and Science of Reminiscing.* Taylor and Francis

Halbwachs, M. (1992) *Collective Memory.* University of Chicago Press

Harré, R. (1990) 'Some narrative conventions of scientific discourse' in Christopher Nash, ed. *Narrative and Culture.* Routledge

Harrison, J. (1925) *Reminiscences of Student Life.* Hogarth Press

Harrison, T. (1984) *Selected Poems.* Penguin

Harvey, W. (1628/1906) *Anatomical Disquisition on the Motion of the Heart and Blood in Animals.* Dent

Heath, S.B. (1983) *Ways with Words.* Cambridge University Press

Herzen, A. (1861-6, trans. 1968) *My Past and Thoughts: The Memoirs of Alexander Herzen.* Chatto and Windus

Heslop, H. (1994) *Out of the Old Earth.* Bloodaxe Books

Hudson, D. (1972) *Munby: Man of Two Worlds.* John Murray

Hunt and Clarke, eds. (1826-1833) *Autobiography: A Collection of the Most Instructive and Amusing lives Ever Published, Written by the Parties Themselves.* London

Hymes, D. (1971) 'Competence and performance in linguistic theory' in R. Huxley and E. Ingram, eds. *Language Acquisition: Models and Methods.* Academic Press

Hymes, D. (1981) *In Vain I Tried to Tell You.* University of Pennsylvania Press

Infeld, L. (1941) *Quest: The Evolution of a Scientist.* Gollancz

Infeld, L. (1978) *Sketches from the Past.* McGill, Queen's University

Jefferson, A. (1990) 'Autobiography as intertext: Barthes, Sarrante, Robbe-Grillet in M. Worton and J. Still eds. *Intertextuality: Theories and Practices.* Manchester University Press.

Jelinek, E. ed. (1980 *Women's Autobiography: Essays in Criticism.* Indiana University Press

Jones, L. (1935) *A Victorian Boyhood.* Macmillan

Joyce, J. (1992) *Portrait of the Artist as a Young Man.* Penguin

Kafka, F. (1976) 'The Diaries 1910-23' in *Franz Kafka*. Secker and Warburg

Kafka, F. (1976) 'Letter to his father' in *Franz Kafka*. Secker and Warburg

Kempe, M., Butler Bowden, W. (1936) *The Book of Margery Kempe: A Modern Version*. Jonathan Cape

Kingston, Maxine Hong (1975) *Woman Warrior: Memoirs of a Girlhood among Ghosts*. Random House

The Konin Memorial Book (1968) *Kehilat-Konin be-trehata u ve-Hurbana*, Tel Aviv

Kovalevsky, S. (1978) *A Russian Childhood*. Springer-Verlag

Labov, W. (1972) *Language in the Inner City*. University of Pennsylvania Press

Langer, S. (1953) *Feeling and Form*. Routledge and Kegan Paul

Leiris, M. (1946/1963) *L'Age d'Homme (Manhood)*. Gallimard

Leith, D. (unpublished. n.d.) Storytelling and a Scottish Traveller Folk Tale, 'The Green Man of Knowledge'

Lejeune, P. (1989) *On Autobiography*. University of Minnesota Press

Lessing, D. (1995) *Under my Skin*. Flamingo

Lewis, O. (1962) *The Children of Sanchez*. Secker and Warburg

Linde, C. (1993) *Life Stories: The Creation of Coherence*. Oxford University Press

Linton, M. (1986) 'Ways of searching and the contents of memory' in D. Rubin, ed. *Autobiographical Memory*. Cambridge University Press

Luria, A. (1967) *The Mind of a Mnemonist*. Havard University Press

McCarthy, M. (1957) *Memoirs of Catholic Girlhood*. Heinemann

Maclean, M. (1988) *Narrative Performance*. Routledge

McNeil, G. (1994) *Soul Providers*. Virago

Makarenko, A. (trans, 1951) *The Road to Life: A Poem of Education*. Progress

Mandel, B. (1980) 'Full of life now' in J. Olney, ed. *Autobiography: Essays Theoretical and Critical*. Princeton University Press

Marcus, J. (1988) 'Invisible mediocrity: the private selves of public women' in S. Benstock, ed. *The Private Self: Theory and Practice of Women's Autobiography*. Routledge

Marcus, L. (1994) *Autobiographical Discourses*. Manchester University Press

Mason, M. (1960) 'The other voice: autobiographies of women writers' in J. Olney, ed. *Autobiography: Essays Theoretical and Critical*. Princeton University Press

Meyerhoff, B. (1979) *Number Our Days*. Dutton

Matthews, W. (1955) *British Autobiographies. Bibliography of British Autobiographies Published or written before 1951*. University of California Press

Middleton, D. and Edwards, D. (1990) 'Conversational remembering' in D. Middleton and D. Edwards, eds. *Collective Remembering*. Sage

Miller, K. (1993) *Rebecca's Vest*. Hamish Hamilton

Miller, N. and Morgan, D. (1993) 'Called to account: the CV as an autobiographical practice' in *Sociology* (Vol.27 No.1)

Miller, P. (1988) 'Early talk about the past: the origins of conversational stories of personal experience' in *Journal of Child Language*, 15

Miller, P. (1990) 'Narrative practices and the social construction of the self in childhood' in *American Ethnologist* 17,2, May

Miller, P. (1994) 'Narrative practices: Their role in socialisation and self-construction' in U. Neisser and R. Fivush, eds. *The Remembering Self: Construction and Accuracy in the Self-narrative*. Cambridge University Press

Millet, K. (1974) *Flying*. Ballantyne Books

Millet, K. (1977) *Sita*. Virago

Misch, G. (1950) 2 vols, *A History of Autobiography in Antiquity*. Routledge and Kegan Paul

Morris, P.E. and Gruneberg, M. eds. (1994) *Theoretical Aspects of Memory*. Routledge

Neisser, U. ed. (1982) *Memory Observed: Remembering in Natural Contexts*. W.H. Freeman

Ochs, E. (1979) 'Transcription as theory 'in E. Ochs and B. Schieffelin, eds. *Developmental Pragmatics*. Academic Press

O'Hagan, A. (1996) *Peter Yorke's Eighties*. London Review of Books

Okazawa-Rey, M. et al. (1987) Teachers, Teaching and Teacher Education. *Harvard Educational Review*

Olney, J. ed. (1980) *Autobiography: Essays Theoretical and Critical*. Princeton University Press

Oxford Companion to the Mind (1987) Oxford University Press

Pascal, R. (1960) *Design and Truth in Autobiography*. Harvard University Press

Paulson, R. (1993) 'Hogarth's Self-representations' in R. Folkenflik, ed. *The Culture of Autobiography*. Stanford University Press

Peterson, L. (1993) 'Institutionalising women's autobiography: Nineteenth century editors and the shaping of autobiographical tradition' in R. Folkenflik, ed. *The Culture of Autobiography*. Stanford University Press

Phelps, L. (1993) 'Writing the new rhetoric of scholarship' in T. Enos and S. Brown, eds. *Defining the New Rhetorics*. Sage

Polkinghorne, D. (1988) *Narrative Knowing and Human Sciences*. Suny

Porter, R. (1993) 'In me the solitary sublimity. Posturing and the collapse of the romantic will in Benjamin Robert Haydon' in R. Folkenflik, ed. *The Culture of Autobiography*. Stanford University Press

Prell, R. (1989) 'The double frame of life history in the work of Barbara Meyerhoff' in The Personal Narratives Group, eds. *Interpreting Women's Lives: Feminist Theory and Personal Narratives*. Indiana University Press

Prince, G. (1982) *Narratology*. Mouton

Prince, M. (1831/1987) *The History of Mary Prince*. Pandora

Richmond, T. (1995) *Konin*. Jonathon Cape

Roberts, E. (1984) *A Woman's Place: Oral History of Working-Class Women 1890-1940*. Cambridge University Press

Roberts, E. (1995) *Women and Families: Oral History of Working Class Women 1898-1940*. Cambridge University Press

Robin, E. (1928) *Ibsen and the Actress*. Hogarth Press

Robinson, J. (1986) 'Autobiographical memory: a historical prologue' in D. Rubin, ed. *Autobiographical Memory*. Cambridge University Press

Robinson, Mrs. (1826) 'Memoirs of the Late Mrs Robinson, Written by Herself' in Hunt and Clarke

Rose, S. (1992) *The Making of Memory: from Molecules to Mind*. Banton Press

Rosen, H. (1972) *Language and Class: a Critical Look at Theories of Basil Bernstein*. Falling Wall Press

Rosen, H. (1975) 'Out there or where the masons went' in *English in Education* Vol.9 Spring

Rosen, H. (1982) *Stories and Meanings*. NATE

Rosen, H. (1988) 'The autobiographical impulse' in D. Tannen, ed, *Linguistics in Context*. Ablex

Rosen, H. (1993) *Troublesome Boy*. English and Media Centre

Rousseau J.J. (1781 trans) *The Confessions of Jean-Jacques Rousseau*. Penguin

Rowbotham, S. (1973) *Women's Consciousness: Man's World*. Penguin

Rubin, D. (1986) *Autobiographical Memory*. Cambridge University Press

Rybarczyk, B. (1995) 'Using reminiscence interviews for stress management in the medical setting' in B. Haight and J. Webster, eds. *The Art and Science of Reminiscing*. Taylor and Francis

Sacks, O. (1973) *Awakenings*. Duckworth

Sacks, O. (1995) *An Anthropologist on Mars*. Picador/Macmillan

Said, E. (1993) *Culture and Imperialism*. Chatto and Windus

Sakharov, A. (n.d) 'How I came to dissent' in *Anthology: Selected Essays from Thirty Years of the New York Review of Books*

Salaman, E. (1970) *A Collection of Moments: A Study of Involuntary Memories*. Longman

Samuel, R. and Thompson, P. eds. (1990) *The Myths We Live By*. Routledge

Sartre, J.P. (1964) *Words*. (Les Mots) Hamish Hamilton

Sassoon, S. (1928) *Memoirs of a Foxhunting Man*. Faber and Faber

Sassoon, S. (1930) *Memoirs of an Infantry Officer*. Faber and Faber

Schafer, R. (1976) *A New Language for Psychoanalysis*. Yale University Press

Shotter, J. and Gergen, K. eds. (1989) *Texts of identity*. Sage

Smith, S. (1987) *A Poetics of Women's Autobiography: Marginality and Fictions of Self-Representations*. Indiana University Press

Smollett, T. (1766/1981) *Travels through France and Italy*. Oxford University Press

Smyth, E. (1919/1981) *Impressions that Remained*. Da Capo

Stahl, S. (1977a) 'The oral personal narrative in its generic context' in *Fabula* 18 (1977b) 'The personal narrative as folklore' in *The Journal of the Folklore Institute* 14 (1983) 'Personal experience stories' in *Handbook of American Folklore*, Indiana University Press

Stanley, L. (1992) *The Auto/biographical I*. Manchester University Press

Stanton, D. (1984) *The Female Autograph*. University of Chicago Press

Steedman, C. (1986) *Landscape for a Good Woman*. Virago

Stein, G. (1933/1990) *The Autobiography of Alice B. Toklas*. Penguin

Sterne, L. (1768/1995) *A Sentimental Journey*. Wordsworth

Sturrock, J. (1993) *The Language of Autobiography: Studies in the First Person Singular*. Cambridge University Press

Terkel, S. (1966) *Division Street-America*. Allen Lane/Pergamon (1972) *Working*. Pantheon

Thatcher, M. (1993) *The Downing Street Years*. Harper Collins

Thompson, P. (1988) *Voices of the Past*. Oxford University Press

Thomson, A. (1990) 'The Anzac Legend' in R. Samuel and P. Thompson, eds. *The Myths We Live By*. Routledge

Tonkin, E. (1992) *Narrating Our Past: The Construction of Oval History*. Cambridge University Press

Tulving, E. (1983) *Elements of Episodic Memory.* Oxford University Press

Vincent, D. (1975) The Growth of Working-Class Consciousness in the First Half of the Nineteenth Century: A Study of the Autobiographies of Working Men, Ph.D. Thesis, Cambridge

Von Rezzori, G. (1991) *The Snows of Yesteryear: Portrait for an Autobiography.* Vintage

Waley, A. (1946) *Chinese Poems.* Unwin

Walker, N. (1988) 'Wider than the sky: public presence and private self' in Dickinson, James and Woolf' in S. Benstock, ed. *The Private Self: Theory and Practice in Women's Auto-biography.* Routledge

Warnock, M. (1987) *Memory.* Faber and Faber

Watson, J. (1993) 'Shadowed Presence: Modern Women's Autobiographies and the Other' in J. Olney, ed.

Watt, C. ed. David Frazer (1988) *The Christian Watt Papers.* Caledonian Books

Wesker, A. (1959) *Chicken Soup with Barley.* Penguin

Wesker, A. (1994) *As Much as I Dare.* Century

Winograd, E. (1994) 'Naturalistic approaches to the study of memory' in P. Morris and M. Gruneberg, eds. *Theoretical Aspects of Memory.* Routledge

Woolf, V. (1977-84) *The Diary of Virginia Woolf, 1977-84.* 5 vols. Harcourt Brace Jovanovich

Woolf, V. (1978) *Moments of Being.* Granada

Woolf, V. (1978) *A Sketch of the Past.* Granada

Yerushalmi, Y. (1982) *Zakhor.* University of Washington Press

Young, A. (1792/1977) *Travels in France.* Dent

Index

197